EDUCATION FOR THE NEW EUROPE

EDUCATION FOR THE NEW EUROPE

Edited by
Dietrich Benner and **Dieter Lenzen**

Berghahn Books
Providence • Oxford

First published in 1996 by
Berghahn Books

Editorial offices:
165 Taber Avenue, Providence, RI 02906, USA
Bush House, Merewood Avenue, Oxford, OX3 8EF, UK

Library of Congress Cataloging-in-Publication Data

Education for the new Europe / edited by Dietrich Benner and Dieter
Lenzen.
        p.   cm.
    Papers from a conference held in Dortmund in 1994.
    Includes bibliographical references (p.).
    ISBN 1-57181-074-9 (cloth : alk. paper)
    1. Education--Europe--Congresses. 2. European Union--Congresses.
I. Benner, Dietrich. II. Lenzen, Dieter.
LA622.E3812   1995
370'.94--dc20   95-31517
                                                             CIP

British Library Cataloguing in Publication Data
A catalogue record for this book
is available from the British Library.

Printed in the United States on acid-free paper.

Contents

Preface

Dietrich Benner and *Dieter Lenzen*

The Maastricht Treaties include hardly any decisions concerning the future of the European educational system. One reason for this is to be found in the fear that the different regions of Europe might lose their identity if the process of European unification standardised too many things in the sphere of education. Nevertheless, the Treaties contain, outside this sphere, innumerable clauses relating to mobility and liberalisation, especially in respect of labour markets, that will not remain without consequences for national systems of education. If a craftsman is supposed to be able to ply his trade just as much in Jutland as in Gibraltar, if a physician on the Shetland Islands is supposed to provide the same standard of medical services as in Greece, educational and training processes will inevitably also have to be co-ordinated. This applies to vocational training as much as to general education. If the Europeans are to achieve a better understanding among themselves, this presupposes agreements about language instruction as well as about the interpretation of European history and about the safeguarding of cultural traditions.

In this situation the German Association for Educational Research resolved to hold its 14th Congress under the theme of 'Education and Training in Europe' in Dortmund in 1994 and to invite experts from some thirty European countries. The aims of the Congress were to describe the new situation that had arisen after Maastricht, to take stock of the starting conditions in the individual countries and to develop perspectives for the future of the academic discipline of education. The extensive results of papers and discussions on many detailed problems relating to the process of European union have been presented in the German-language report on the Congress (Benner and Lenzen, 1994). The papers collected in this volume represent the public lectures that were given on the overarching questions. They provide an insight into the current state of play and the future tasks of the discipline of education in Europe.

The volume starts with the contributions of the recent Chair of the German Association for Educational Research and his newly elected successor. Both raise, *inter alia*, the question of the common theoretical and cultural roots of the European idea of *Bildung*. Two contributions, by Andrea Kárpáti (Hungary) and Hans Merkens (Germany), deal with the divergent empirical situations of young people in one country of Eastern Europe and one of Western Europe after the removal of the Iron Curtain. The volume continues with two historically oriented articles about pedagogics and politics, one by Gert Geißler (Germany) who writes about the first two years in the Soviet-occupied zone of Germany, and the other by Gabriela Ossenbach-Sauter (Spain) who reports on the challenges to the Spanish educational system since 1970. The contribution by Peter Mortimore (Britain) follows with an investigation of a question that is common to most European governments, i.e., that of the growing costs and declining standards of the school systems. This fact might be thought to promote a renaissance of private education in place of a public one. Thomas Rauschenbach (Germany) argues against this in his paper. From his point of view what must be written is a second chapter of professional education that includes the educational and socialising responsibilities of the public. New tasks will emerge for the discipline of education from these developments, among them that of the pedagogical control of social risks – a question that Frieda Heyting (Netherlands) focuses on. In this respect we must also reflect upon the consequences for education economics, as the contribution by François Orivel (France) demonstrates, who deals with the situation of research in this field in his country.

Works that describe and examine the educational situation in Europe after Maastricht are still rare today, and we are still far removed from a European research effort in the field of education. With this volume we seek to make a contribution which will open up a dialogue in this field.

Berlin, November 1994

References

Benner, D. and Lenzen, D. (1994), 'Bildung und Erziehung in Europa?', contributions to the 14th Congress of the German Association for Educational Research, 14-16 March at Dortmund University, 32. *Beiheft der Zeitschrift für Pädagogik*, Weinheim/Basel.

Chapter 1

Opening Address

on the Occasion of the 14th Annual Congress of the
German Association for Educational Research
(Deutsche Gesellschaft für Erziehungswissenschaft–
DGfE) on 14 March 1994

Dietrich Benner, Chair, DGfE

Ladies and Gentlemen,

In the name of the executive committee of the DGfE I welcome you
cordially to its 14th Congress, which will discuss the theme of 'Education and Training in Europe' and has been organised under the
patronage of Edzard Reuter as a member of the *Initiativkreis Ruhrgebiet*.

* * *

This Congress has not been prepared by just one national scientific
association, but has resulted from the co-operation of scholars in sis-
ter associations of many West and East European nations. This is
reflected in the keynote lectures as well as in the symposia, the panel
discussions and the workshops of this meeting. Experts contributing
come from Austria, the Baltic States, Belgium, the Czech Republic,
Denmark, Finland, France, Germany, Great Britain, Greece, Hungary, Italy, Luxembourg, the Netherlands, Norway, Poland, Ruma-
nia, Russia, the Slovak Republic, Spain, Sweden, Switzerland, and
the Ukraine.

We have not succeeded in getting a politician or administrator
from the European Union to participate in this opening session and
to sit on the panel. At this time economic and fiscal topics seem to
have a much greater weight in Strasbourg and Brussels than questions of pedagogics and education. Still, I would like to express the
hope that many important impulses and initiatives will emanate

from this Congress for the exchange of research results and for a greater understanding in the educational field in Europe.

The Congress is taking place in the middle of the Ruhr area – a region that is by no means shaped merely by German traditions, it is also shaped by the contributions and the culture of all those who migrated here during the course of history, in order to find work and a livelihood. For some time this region has undergone a major economic and social upheaval that has made high demands on individuals, the politicians that represent them, the system of labour, culture and social life. These have also involved the education and training of children and young people within the family, in public and vocational schools as well as in related fields and in institutions of pedagogical practice. The high rate of unemployment, which is still rising, and the new xenophobia toward foreigners must be taken as clear signs that we frequently fail to do justice to these demands in the sense of general human rights and of the principles of freedom, equality and solidarity.

Today we face the problem of developing our society further toward a 'civil society' that

– views the recognition and respect for every individual, irrespective of his or her gender, or cultural or national origin, as a highly valuable resource that state and society must protect and not violate.

– counters the reawakening and strengthening of old and new nationalisms and fundamentalisms.

– allows for a plurality of such cultures and lifestyles that reach a consensus among themselves over universal basic norms, rights and duties that are interpreted as culture-specific, yet at the same time culture-transcendent.

After the end of the Cold War and the competitive struggle between Capitalist and Socialist systems of society, the task is to make the Europe that is now emerging into a citizens' society of this kind. For this purpose it is necessary that we see Europe not merely as a common economic area, nor as a European mega-state, nor as another power that dominates the world together with the other world powers, but as a place where people of divergent cultures live together in a way marked by cosmopolitanism, freedom and solidarity.

One condition of this, which is certainly not all encompassing, but is nonetheless vital, would be that we become conscious of the advances that have been made, but also of the unresolved global problems, many of which originated in Europe. On the side of progress we may list the historic achievements of the ancient and modern Enlightenment. Modern science and technology, the modern humanities and social sciences and the reflexive arts occupy an outstanding position in this respect. Here, modern ethics that are directed by the principle of the unconditional recognition of the dignity of every individual is just as indispensable as the pedagogical norm of a universal capacity of human beings to learn, and thus to be educable and self-determining, and as are human rights and democracy as a principle of government to be codified in constitutions. As to the problems that emerged from this development, we are confronted with difficult questions of economics, ecology, ethics, society, politics and religion, existing within an emergent global society that is determined by a great plurality of traditions and cultures and by the concern about how the natural foundations of life can be secured and nurtured over the coming generations.

Both aspects – the achievements and the worrying consequences of modernity – should put us on our guard against placing our trust, all too quickly and naïvely, into an assumed universality of a uniform European image of human-kind and an educational ideal. They should also warn us against expecting from these ideals the constitution of a new European identity. Advances in self-reflection that originated in Europe were founded less in notions of unity than in the experiences of difference, and achievements of differentiation that constantly produced new problems of communication. Here I may merely refer to the separation of church and state, without which tolerance, democracy and the public space of citizens are impossible; or we might think of the differentiation of state and society and of legality and morality that is indispensable for the granting and claiming of individual freedom. Separations and differentiations like these were achieved in the struggles for the religious and civil wars and in the conflicts between the nations of Europe. They were later firmly defined by the Enlightenment in Europe and North America, though they were subsequently, time and again, called into question by ever new nationalisms and fundamentalisms. Among these latter challenges were also those that originated in Germany during the two World Wars.

At a time when, in the heart of Europe, in a civil war between the states that emerged from multi-ethnic Yugoslavia, lasting traditions that have grown over centuries and stem from extra-European cultures are being destroyed, we should be clarifying in our minds that no European educational ideal is capable of healing the wounds that people have, and continue, to inflict on each other in Europe. Instead of forgetting the victims of history and/or legitimising their deaths retrospectively, in the service of some notion of progress and with the aid of a kind of 'sleight of hand', the task is to sharpen our awareness of the fact that, as a matter of principle, no restitution is possible for the destruction of life in wars, in the Holocaust and in the genocide of minorities.

Warning of the dangers of a Eurocentric image of human-kind and an educational ideal also extends to the problematic consequences of the process of unification of the two postwar German states. These consequences cannot be solved by the notion that we are dealing here with no more than the combination of two divergent societal systems within a larger Europe. The global ruptures in the systems of politics, economics and science are much more radical in that they can be overcome and made more tolerable with the help of a 'march toward a united Europe'. In a global society, Europe can be no more than an exemplar.

After 'real existing socialism' as an alternative to the Western form of economic and societal organisation has reached the end of the road, we must counter the trend toward the emergence of so-called 'two-thirds societies' that can no longer be ignored. To this end it is necessary to conduct a social, educational and economic policy that does not turn the chance to participate as a learner in a self-enlightening societal practice, and the securing through one's own labour of the economic basis for the utilisation of freedom into the privilege of a majority vis-à-vis a new minority.

In this connection discourse and the promotion of understanding between the countries of Europe may be able to facilitate reciprocal access to the cultures of Europe, to augment the richness of cultures that are accessible to all and to impede the resurgence of traditional nationalisms. However, the precondition for this to succeed, is that the creation of a new European nationalism to replace the old ones is prevented.

Securing the humanitarian qualities of the modern state and preserving the multitude of national cultures will remain linked in the past, and also in future, to a differentiation between the generality of a state's legal norms, the specificity of cultural peculiarities, and the individuality of each human being, which in its turn will have to be set apart again from those other two conditions. Only then will it be possible to pursue that great goal, which individuals are able to develop under the conditions of a general constitutional order and against the background of a society that is not under the state's tutelage; the right of an individual to freely join other national cultures and participate in their transformation.

As can be seen from the programme of this Congress, the questions that have been broached here are of far-reaching significance for the shaping of Europe's system of education and training and for the discipline of education.

Education must not be restricted in Europe to transmitting the achievements of European civilisation, but must also introduce people to the world of labour and to the daily problems of living together. This is why the tasks of general education and vocational training are to be seen to be of equal weight.

The changed conditions under which children and young people grow up and the mechanisms that impact upon them from other social systems, demand that the training of teachers and work in the teaching profession from pre-school education to pedagogics, to special schooling, vocational and economic pedagogics and to social pedagogics, adult education and leisure organisation are adequately supported structurally as well as financially.

For this purpose it will be necessary that educational reform in Europe abandons the abstract and outdated assumption that there exists a balance, that is preordained or is to be created, between individual talent, educationally acquired claims and social position. Instead we should reopen the public discussion of the problem of how the balance between the partial systems might be achieved.

This requires, however, that educational policy once again brings to bear more clearly its relative autonomy in the context of the various ministries and regards itself as part of a dynamic social policy-making process. Such an educational policy will no longer make it possible for other parts of policy-making to ignore the issue of education, but will also subject the complex inter-dependencies between modern societal systems to a pedagogical analysis and critique.

With these references some of the actual topics of the public lectures, symposia, and workshops and of the concluding panel discussion have already been alluded to. That we are able to discuss these and other topics with the participation of scholars from almost all European countries, would not have been possible without the support of the *Initiativkreis Ruhrgebiet*. Since its founding in 1989, this Circle has gained extraordinary merits through its promotion of cultural, scientific and sports events in the Ruhr area. We thank this Circle that it has included our Congress in its support program and Edzard Reuter for assuming the patronage.

Herr Reuter is unfortunately prevented from being at this opening meeting in person. Frau Bennigsen-Foerder, who is also a member of the Circle, will be speaking to us.

We also wish to thank the *Deutsche Forschungsgemeinschaft*. Having refereed parts of our programme, it has contributed in order that educationalists from other European countries were able to travel to Dortmund to participate in this Congress.

Finally, I would like to thank the University of Dortmund and the local organising committee, in particular its chair, Herr Spies, most cordially for their work in the preparation and execution of this Congress.

It is my hope that we will succeed, with this volume, in analysing and reflecting upon aspects of the process of European unification that are significant from an educational and pedagogical point of view.

Chapter 2

Education and Training for Europe?

Dieter Lenzen

In his new book Jacques Delors states the view that the citizens of Europe must 'genuinely have the feeling that they are involved in this joint adventure (Europe).' (Delors 1993:241). There is no denying that the decision to pursue a top-down policy, developing paths for integration, by beginning at the top (p. 306), must be paid for. Now culture, including education and training, is expected to make good this neglect *ex post*, through a bottom-up policy, although Delors only devotes two of his 350 pages to these themes, and somewhat surprisingly, refers primarily to 'high-definition television' (p. 120). We are asked. Are we? Had we been asked, we would have advised involving the relevant members of the public at a rather earlier stage. Some forty-two years have passed since the European Coal and Steel Agreement, and thirty-six years since the Treaty of Rome, and during that time those in positions of responsibility in Strasbourg and Brussels have given little thought to ways of generating an awareness of our European-ness among us all in the states of Europe. There can be no doubt that the education and training system would have played a vital role in this process. The concern in most of the countries of Europe that the homogenisation of the educational system would inevitably imply a loss of national identity has had a serious impact. It has not only been responsible for a hesitancy in making the necessary adjustments in specific areas of education. In fact, it has also led to an unwillingness to reflect on the question of Europe on the part of those with a responsibility for the training and education sector. They include the representatives of what is sometimes referred to as the 'German syndrome', i.e., the educational sciences, pedagogy.

Notes for this Chapter begin on page 26.

However, such self-criticism would be missing the point, if one were to oversimplify the explanation for this lack of enthusiasm for Europe within our discipline by focusing solely on the concern in the conference halls of the European Union about specific aspects of education. After all, other sciences have been equally reticent about matters European, at least in Germany. On closer inspection it seems that this lack of interest in the pragmatic issues of everyday European life is more evident among the humanities and social sciences than among the economists, or in the fields of jurisprudence and technology. I believe that the causes of this phenomenon can be found in the history of the pan-European idea, and all that this implies. And it seems to me that certain historical reasons exist to explain the critical hesitancy to embrace pan-European notions, motivated not by a fear of being oppressed, but rather by a desire to avoid being seen as the one doing the oppressing. Those whose work in the educational and training sector involves regular co-operation with colleagues in other European countries [know that our particular discipline is acknowledged for its strengths, in a country] in which close links previously existed between the state, which financed and controlled the educational system, and the relevant specialist field. However, we are not simply experts in this area, but also intellectuals, and members of a public with a reasonable fund of historical experiences, and therefore we should allow room for both scepticism and emphasis. I shall begin with scepticism.

Scepticism 1

The uniqueness of the current process of European unification. Leafing through their reference books, some optimists have pointed to a number of occasions when union has featured largely in the history of Europe. Examples exist in the Mediterranean region under Roman domination, in ancient Greece, in the Carolingian empire, the union of the Low Countries in 1588, and the consolidation of a number of smaller states to form a unified Germany in the nineteenth century. However, none of these processes involved independent states with equal rights (see Meier 1991:41). More importantly, an event such as the establishment of the German Reich followed on from a long drawn-out intellectual process, and was aided by the existence of a common language. However, firstly an awareness of the situation had to be fostered in the small, and the very small, states. Goethe's project, a Book of the German People, referred to this need. Goethe sought to enlist Niethammer's services for this book, which was to be a major work, bestowing an identity, encompassing the entire race in a representative and monumental way, and also serving to educate.

Among its many tasks, education was expected to endow a sense of national identity, a view held by others as well as Goethe. Another name that should be mentioned in this connection is that of Wilhelm Flitner, who described the fourth aspect of the 'Volksschul' concept as the 'national policy motivation of popular education (Volksbildung)' (Flitner 1949:80ff.). Wander's establishment of the General German Teachers' Association was also motivated by national considerations (see Günther et al. 1958:279). There are some cogent reasons why, following the completion of the national unification process, education degenerated and became a means of stratifying those sections of the bourgeoisie with educational aspirations. A functional equivalent of education in this nineteenth-century sense is not immediately apparent today. For Ernst Robert Curtius this role is fulfilled by the literary tradition in the twentieth century, and T.S. Eliot adopts a similar approach, stating: 'We need not remind ourselves that, as Europe is a whole (and still, in its progressive mutilation and disfigurement), the organism out of which any greater world harmony must develop), so European literature is a whole, the several members of which cannot flourish, if the same blood stream does not circulate throughout the whole body' (Eliot, quoted by Assmann 1993:98). However, this comparison does not lend itself to our purposes, because the reference to a shared tradition suggests a tradition that has always existed,[1] and not an intellectual effort undertaken solely for the purposes of the unification process. I shall return to the matter of tradition when discussing emphasis. To this extent one can concur with Hornstein and Mutz, who write: 'In contrast to the Weimar period, there is virtually no public discussion today by literary figures, writers and intellectuals, provoking a public response, in which "visions" of a Europe of the future are developed' (Hornstein and Mutz 1993:19).

Scepticism 2

The mental differences between the European nations, especially between East and West, are not insurmountable, but are nevertheless deeply rooted.

Since 1989 any discussion about Europe that ends at the banks of the Oder, at the Bavarian Forest or in Trieste is outmoded, and this has intensified the problems associated with such differences. The fundamental distinction between East and West is not a result of the events of 1945 but has its origins in the collapse of the Roman Empire. In this context a schism has occurred, the implications of which have outlasted any secularisation since 1917. Riedmiller, for example, points to the relative historical randomness of the spread of Christianity in Russia in 987 AD: 'The scouts [serving Prince Vladimir] returning from Germany felt that church services there lacked beauty ... whereas the rituals of the Eastern Church, such as those in Constantinople, satisfied the Slav tribes' need for ceremony, pomp, colour and fervour' (Riedmiller 1985:906). Despite all the apparent signs of a greater receptiveness to the West, Riedmiller claims that no actual mental process of Westernisation has ever been observed in the sense of an adaptation of Western standards of democracy and human rights. The story of a popular Czar acting as a carpenter, as the plot of an operetta, had its parallels in Peter I, who was known to participate in the execution of political opponents. And although Catherine I did import Western technology, she ruled a strictly centralist and authoritarian state. Even Zinovieff pointed out that Moscow was an imperialist rather than a cosmopolitan city (see Riedmiller 1985:914). These views were formulated in 1985, and now the Berlin Wall is history. The same applies *mutatis mutandis* to the description by Pomian, claiming that two instances of European unification had taken place. In both cases the description centres around a kind of cultural automatism, and not an activity selectively uniting Europe too (see Pomian 1990); but does this necessarily mean that such attitudes have vanished with it? Taking only a few items from the Study of European Values of 1991/92, we find some far-reaching differences between the attitudes of West and East Europeans. For example, in Eastern Europe 71 per cent of those questioned were prepared to fight a war on behalf of their country, while the corresponding figure in the West was 46 per cent. In the East 82 per cent want to see a more widespread use of technology to achieve progress, compared with 56 per cent in the West, while 76 per cent of East Europeans and only 34 per cent in the West believe that it is essential for a woman to have children in order to be fulfilled (see Gönner 1993:65).

However, let us not be mistaken: significant differences can be found in the established nations of the European Union too. These include a north-south discrepancy in attitudes to the law. Thus the respect for the law that is so evident in Germany is probably due not so much to a desire to 'be a good citizen' as to the existence of 'intermediate authorities', acting as agencies between the state and its people. In contrast, France is a highly centralised country, where the individual deals directly with the state, and feels perhaps that he or she is also at the mercy of the state. This engenders behaviour in which compliance with the law is not always the dominant feature, because the state, in its efforts to safeguard for itself the loyalty of the masses, is far less able to risk interfering with citizens' rights, even though these may not be enshrined in law. In a situation that has particular relevance to the EC such as the licence exemption for hunting weapons in France, this produces some almost insurmountable problems (see Münch 1993:160ff.). Major differences also exist in cultural areas that have a far greater relevance to education. For example, the freedom of art and science is guaranteed by the constitutions of only Germany, Greece, Italy, Portugal and Spain, and in only five European countries does the constitution insist on compulsory school attendance. Legal stipulations on the rights of parents with regard to such obligations also differ widely, reflecting fundamentally different attitudes about the role of the state in training and education, with inevitable implications for the process of European integration.

Scepticism 3

The concept of a united Europe is established and burdened by history. Nation Europa was the title of a propaganda magazine published by the Nazis during the Second World War and aimed at intellectuals in the subjugated countries. Its purpose was to ensure their productive inclusion in the ideological growth of a new, German-dominated Europe after the war. There can be no doubt that Hitler too, subscribed to the idea of a united Europe, although under a different set of conditions to those of today. The notion of one Europe was not confined to the Führer alone, but nevertheless he was closely identified with it, a fact that non-German Europeans have still not forgotten. One example is that of Cees Nooteboom, recipient of the German Publishing Trade's 1993 Peace Prize (see Nooteboom 1993:11), who sees more merit in cosmopolitanism than in Europeanism. Another is Spain's avowed anti-European, Heleno Sana, recalling from his viewpoint on the northern rim of Africa the words of Frantz Fanon: 'Europe's prosperity and progress have been created with the sweat and the corpses of the blacks, the Arabs, the Indians and the yellow races' (Fanon, quoted by Sana 1993:25). One could also include Milan Kundera, with his statement that Central Europe no longer had any rights to its own history. Instead it declines into a 'non-historicism' that produces nothing more than a 'taste for the diverse pathologies of daily life' (quoted by Nooteboom 1993:44f.)

In the light of recent German history, no one should be surprised at the suspicion aroused by the apparent urgency of the German chancellor in matters European, especially in those countries to Germany's east. One might think that the inhabitants of these countries are even more familiar than the Germans with the writings of Bis-

marck, who once stated: 'I always find the word "Europe" on the lips
of those who want other powers to do what they themselves are not
prepared to attempt' (quoted by Bohrer 1991:1060). References to
the second major proponent of the European idea, France, are of little assistance. The fact that the Paris-Bonn axis exists and thrives is
not a matter of chance, but follows a rediscovery of shared values
after the collapse of Hitler's fascism. Hitler himself embraced a concept of Europe based on a German-Prussian version of European
superiority, an approach that resisted any attempts at revival after
1945. If Germany was at least to retain an important role in decisions
about the European process, Adenauer was an ideal figure, being
both anti-Prussian and Catholic, attributes that made him a more
acceptable German figure to the French. It was Adenauer who maintained that the Asian steppes begin at Brunswick, and that, during the
rail journey to Berlin, he would draw the curtain at Magdeburg and
spit out of the window when crossing the River Elbe (see Faber
1979:173). Probably without realising it, Adenauer was able to make
use of a two thousand year old foundation for his European policy,
referred to by Curtius as Latinitas, and implying more than simply
shared religious convictions. He wrote that: 'One is a European
when one has become a "civis romanus"' (Curtius 1969:22). 'Latinitas means more than a shared language, such as that which linked the
Roman peoples. Latinitas is the most concise expression of civilisation, which has been seeking for more than 2,000 years to implement
the European ideal, despite various setbacks' (Eberle 1966:230).

Curtius would have found it hard to accept the almost total absence
of educational policy in the process of European unification, a fact that
we are better placed to comprehend when we realise the importance
of Prussian Protestantism for German educational thought and, consequently, for pedagogy too. We are also aware that, by favouring a
suitable level of representation for the educational sciences in current,
and also in non-European, educational policy, we are also bound to be
seen as opposing something, although this is certainly not our intention. There is a historically induced trap, whereby it is suggested that
we are seeking to make common cause against a Catholicism with its
roots in the Middle Rhine region, and that, as far as its social ethics are
concerned, a different approach in dealings with the coming generation is evident, compared with that of the Königsberg line.

Scepticism 4

*The nationalism of the Europeans is a paradoxical attitude with deep his-
torical roots.* A nation is a 'social organisation, which claims to possess

a transcendental character, which is treated as an (imaginary) community by the majority of its members, and which relates to a common apparatus of state' (Elwert 1989:446). The imaginary aspects of an organisation of this kind consist of the fact that the properties of such a community are based on assertions whose empirical content is actually irrelevant, and that such characteristics may serve both for collective self-interpretation as well as for the construction of an individual concept of the self. In other words, the nation is a historical invention. It had its origins at the time of the European Enlightenment, culminating in the French Revolution, and this in turn gives rise to a major paradox. Norbert Elias has described this two-hundred year process as follows:

> Among the European middle classes in most European countries there was a tendency between the eighteenth and twentieth centuries for a shift in priorities, away from humanist, moralistic ideals and values, which are generally applicable to mankind as a whole, and towards (the confirmation of) more nationalistic values, elevating the idealistic image of one's own country and nation above the ideals associated with humanity in general and with morality ... (Elias 1989:174)

This development appears to have been accompanied by a 'shift in attitudes, from a belief in change for the better to a belief in the immutable values of national identity and tradition' (Elias 1989:176). According to Elias, 'All in all, one's identification with one's own compatriots became stronger, while the identification with people of one's own class and social standing in other countries declined' (Elias 1989:187). In fact the predictions by Marx and Engels of a century of class struggle failed to materialise. The wars of the nineteenth and twentieth centuries have been national and ethnic in nature, and this situation continues even into the present day. The war currently raging in the Balkans is just the latest example, and is also notable for the fact that it represents a European conflict in which clear lines are being drawn. After all, the ethnic groups confronting one another are not just any European peoples: what we have is basically a conflict between eastern Christendom and Islam, to define the boundaries of Europe. The paradox referred to earlier is therefore not only one of the history of ideas, inasmuch as the basic values of the French Revolution contradict the emergence of French nationalism, or that protagonists of the concept of a shared German culture, men such as Herder, Goethe or Schiller can barely be equated with a violent narrow-minded nationalism. Instead, the values of each individual were imbued by this paradox:

> Each individual assumes within his own personal manifestation the preservation, the integrity, the interests of his own, independent collective, and what it stands for, and this is the guideline for his actions, which,

in certain situations, can and must give the lead to others. At the same time this individual continues to grow, with a humanistic and egalitarian moral code, the supreme and determining values of which are those of the individual person as such. (Elias 1989:204)

It is unclear whether this nationalistic paradox, which relates both to the history of ideas and to an individual level, is one that ought to be resolved at all. The creation of such paradoxes is symptomatic of the modern age, and there is also an increasing tendency to leave them unresolved. This is particularly evident in the notion of multiple identity, which has been the subject of discussion over the past twenty years. However, implicit in this notion is the possibility for a disconcerting tendency to destabilise the process of European unity. The conditions by which internalised orientations are activated by European individuals, or kept latent, are, after all, a matter of coincidence, or else simply unknown. The European idea has always been characterised by this ambivalence, partly because this same European idea also claims to incorporate universal values, and yet confines itself to a small geographical area of the west Asian peninsular. One could also say that it refers to a collective relation, located between a rejection of nationalism and a sacrifice of universal ideals as one extreme, and suspicions about Eurocentrism as the other. Fear of the latter has, according to Agnes Heller, caused Europe to 'relativise its own culture, to the extent that it is now a veritable cultural masochism' (Heller 1988:34).

Although nationalism certainly still exists today, according to an investigation by ZUMA it has been suppressed with greater vigour in Germany than anywhere (see Wiegand 1993:330). Its abiding problem, however, is not the existence of active nationalists, but the fact that we simply do not know under what conditions people in Europe release their latent nationalism, which they certainly possess, along with their universal and pan-European sentiments. There are two possibilities if one wishes to ensure that the citizens of a particular country retain a stable European bias. One is to investigate the conditions under which nationalist and, I would add, ethnic interpretations and actions can be stimulated, and to prevent the emergence of these conditions. These could consist of social hardship, inequalities within Europe, violent attacks by members of specific ethnic groups, and by other groups that are only partially politically motivated. Alternatively, the mental contradiction between Europeanism and nationalism can be eliminated by ensuring that a European bias is made to appear a national one. In considering these alternatives we are concerned with a European nationalism, which appears at first glance to incorporate all the negative implications of any other kind of nationalism. If we are to learn anything from Carl Schmitt it is this: that a state distinguishes itself by defining its opponents and waging war against them. He believes that the desire for peace and an awareness of mankind as a complete entity will eventually eliminate the concept of the state (see Schmitt 1963:102ff.). In the same way the chairman of Poland's Solidarnosc, Geremek, believes that, following the fall of Constantinople and the siege of Vienna, fear of a Turkish invasion was one of the main factors in the formation of a European, Christian and Western identity (see Dahrendorf et al. 1993:12f.).

However, there is at least one logical exception to this rule, and that is when the idea of humanity itself forms part of the concept of the state, and when the required external definition of Europe's boundaries become not geographical but moral. Several factors favour this idea: in the traditionalist re-orientation of nationalism in various European countries one sees evidence of an attempt to implement the postulates of the Enlightenment, aided by a powerful state, which owes its strength to the loyal support of its citizens (see Im Hof 1993:243). It is possible that the concept of a European patriotism is better suited to such a European bias in which a section of mankind, i.e., the Europeans, define themselves by their ability to think and act as human beings. However, there are also substantial reasons for rejecting such a ploy, and these are linked with the question of whether a teleological concept of mankind can still be effectively applied today. In the context under consideration here it is necessary to ask whether Europe's common interests are sufficient to justify such hopes. And this brings me from the sceptical to the emphatic, or, to be more accurate, the constructive section of my observations.

Construction 1

Romanticism is the lost root of Europe. The spread of nationalism in Europe was not the only movement on this continent. Of course, by seeking to produce a cosmopolitan Europe, the French Revolution destroyed the very idea itself, and a fairly accurate description of the reasons for this can be found. This idea was, as we know, linked with the notions of radical democratisation, or more accurately, with a focus on the people as the source of all power. This in turn led to a need to be able to identify what actually constitutes the 'people', and at the same time to distinguish them from the cosmopolitan manifestations of the nobility, which had become well established as setting the patterns for lifestyles and thought from Paris all the way to St Petersburg. These lifestyles and mental attitudes differed widely.

They were replaced by simplicity, fraternity, puritanism and, strangely enough, by a celebration of the principle of totalitarian leadership, certainly by the time of Napoleon, which put a stop to any form of cosmopolitanism. This attitude was clearly shown by the banning of the well-known book *de l'Allemagne* by Mme de Staël, in which she wrote: 'Il faut, dans ces temps modernes, avoir l'esprit européen' (quoted by Curtius 1925:292). The reaction to this was not only an unequivocal nationalism on the part of other peoples, who had lost their own cosmopolitanism as a result of the revised mental attitudes of the French nobility. Of equal importance was the powerful romantic movement, which was more intellectual than political. Amid the tumult of the Revolution and the Napoleonic Wars, within a period of just twenty-five years, this movement had increasingly become the custodian of the pan-European idea. It was characterised by anti-rationalism, a sense of history, and an appreciation of the true value of art and aesthetics. It offered evolution and individuality in place of revolution and collectivism: in short, it was a cultural and sometimes a religious movement, but to a much lesser extent a political one.

However, it was only a short-lived phenomenon. The national catastrophe that was the 1848 revolution extinguished all hope of a lasting, culturally dominated change, not only in Germany. From all these interwoven, historical strands arose a new, latent contradiction at the end of the twentieth century: on the one hand, although unaware of this fact, the pan-European idea effectively had its origins in the Romantic movement. This is clearly evident in both the Treaty of Rome and that of Maastricht, which largely ignored the cultural sector. On the other hand the common European cultural heritage that was invoked was at least more rationalist in nature, and thus had the same origins as the nationalism of the French Revolution and the other forms of nationalism that followed it. Karl Jaspers summarised these rationalist features as follows: Capitalism, universal science, ethos, calculability and foresight as the vital underlying principle of all work (see Jaspers 1947:9).

To these assets we can also add the common legal system, drawing on Roman law, and the comments on it by the Bologna School in the eleventh century. Moreover Wilhelm Flitner also saw two other foundations of European civilisation: Christian belief and Greek education. It is fairly obvious that such efforts to comprehend the European identity, efforts that have had a certain part to play following the second major war of this century, should systematically exclude any actual pan-European, Romantic tradition. We find no reference there to André Gide or Marcel Proust, Blake, Browning or Dostoyevsky. Neither is there room for those German Romanticists who have expressed their views about a European concept. The same is true of Novalis, who, in 'Die Christenheit oder Europa', proposed a restoration of the religious as a unifying, European element, implying a rejection which is fully understandable in a secularised Germany. It also applies to Ernst Moritz Arndt who, though not in the mainstream of thought, argued in 1803 against the ghostly aspects of the rational spirit: 'His talk and plotting had removed art and energy from the world; since then it had to maintain a standpoint of lesser artificiality and expression of strength, always consisting of individual bursts and explosions in certain directions, but never at an even pace' (Arndt 1940:124f.). We can also include August Wilhelm Schlegel, whose lectures on aesthetics were an attempt to bridge the gulf between rationality and aesthetics, with reference to the Greek language, and who wrote: 'After all that has taken place, one should not assume that the beauty of the Greek language is that of a cold, dead evenness; it expresses the very character of Greek education' (Schlegel 1989:548). He saw in this European nation a harmonious fusion of individual aspects with more general ones. One is inclined to agree with Milan Kundera when he says: 'In speaking about Europe today, one must speak of the things of which Europe has been robbed' (quoted by Nooteboom 1993:45). There is no hope for the idea of a union if it is not aware of its own cultural Europeanism.

However, this does mean accepting the romantic tradition, but not exclusively, because, after all, the polarity that exists between a rationalist, scientific approach and the romantic, artistic option is not an irremediable one. As far as the other rationalist tradition, which has been long lost in nationalism, is concerned, Hans-Georg Gadamer reminds us that a close relationship exists between the German humanities with their roots in Protestant tradition, following on from the ideas of Dilthey, and the moral sciences that are based on the concepts of the humanities of the Roman Republic and those of French literature (see Gadamer 1990:45f.). To this extent the humanities are not only 'unavoidable' (see Marquardt 1986), but are in fact vital for European cultural integration. It is therefore important to study the part played in pedagogy by those approaches that have been not entirely dismissed from the tradition of the humanities. An open-minded attitude to our discipline is needed on the part of the cultural sciences. This discipline is, after all, one of the factors that commands respect outside Europe in particular. To quote Susan Sontag: 'If asked to describe what Europe means to me as an American, I would begin with liberation. Liberation from those things that pass for culture in America. The diversity, seriousness, the claims, the density of European culture all form an Archimedean point from which I can, intellectually, set the world in motion' (Sontag 1988:131f.).

Construction 2

Aesthetics are one of the historical assets of European culture. However, this rational and moral bias exists not only when one attempts to sum up common European assets, in an effort to define the reasons for European unification. Future needs for an inner European harmonisation can be consistently traced through rationality and morality. The need for action will be more apparent in the legal field, for health legislation, consumer protection, environmental protection, safety at work and the protection of national monuments. And, quite justifiably, it will be seen to exist in the social sector, because the social discrepancies that exist from Sicily to Jutland are substantial.

Hornstein and Mutz have identified three main problem areas, firstly the area of work, not working and unemployment, secondly that of children and youth, and thirdly issues concerning work within the family and gainful employment. In all of these areas, and including the requirements for greater harmonisation of the legal system, we are faced with a need to solve the serious problems of inequality and injustice arising from these social and legal differences. This is immediately evident if we consider, for example, the issues surrounding the abortion law. Such issues only appear to be culturally neutral. According to Hornstein and Mutz, 'the question of when and in what form a social occurrence becomes a social problem is largely determined in a cultural context' (Hornstein and Mutz 1993:61). Cultural affiliation determines the pattern of interpretation that the members of a particular culture employ in order to understand a social occurrence. But I believe that its significance is more far-reaching: the forms of perception that precede such interpretation are also determined, and this places us fairly and squarely in the field of aesthetics. The point at which a social occurrence becomes a problem for which people require a solution, in the sense of greater equality, depends on the cultural context in which they perceive this occurrence, and from which they draw their interpretations of it. Researchers into feminist issues are familiar with this complex, for example, when women activists encounter a situation in which those women from a particular culture who are most affected by the question of abortion, appear to have no difficulty in accepting its strict prohibition, despite the fact that their quality of life is affected, at least when viewed from a northwest-European standpoint. If women are continuously bearing children they will be unable to earn a living, and thus cannot improve their economic situation. This is obviously a specifically educational problem. One other consequence of this situation is the tendency for their children to suffer as well. Therefore a discipline such as pedagogy must also concern itself with the problem of aesthetic perception, if it is to avoid being seen as a science that applies social engineering in order to improve social and educational conditions, contrary to the material experience of its subjects. This applies especially when these conditions are not even seen by these subjects as being in need of improvement, for the simple reason that they (the subjects) perceive these conditions in a different way from the scientists conducting such research.

The development of such perceptive capabilities refers, however, not only to the fostering of an awareness of their suffering among those affected, but, even more, to the process of making the uninvolved aware that their status may differ from that of the others, possibly for historically random reasons, and that they may be totally unaware of this, or interpret it as being right and proper. Enabling such qualities of perception is, I emphasise, not a matter of legal provisions or simply one of more perceptive insights. In other words it is not a question of common sense and morality, but of aesthetics, in the sense of the concept of *aisthesis*. If there is no awareness of social suffering at an emotional level, not only on the part of those affected, but also on the part of those helping them, any intervention that occurs at all will remain cold and superficial. For pedagogy, the avoidance of such a rationalistic and moralistic bias is more than just a question of effectiveness, but one of survival, because, as has already been shown, this bias has been linked with anti-European sentiments and with nationalism. The nationalism of the French Revolution and the modernisation produced by scientific advances are nourished from the same source. Pedagogy is the offspring of both, and puts all its assets at risk when the counterpart to its parents, romanticism and aesthetics, become indispensable upon the implementation of the pan-European idea, as a means of binding people more closely together. Pedagogues have always been conversant with the aesthetic quality of their work. When the educational sciences became a genuine profession, suspicions were aroused that the identification by the helpers with the suffering of others was mere rhetoric. This reflects a major dissonance within this discipline, which used to be discussed as a conflict of theory and practice, although now it is seen more along the continuum of professional/layman. I believe that this is quite mistaken. After all, professional pedagogic activity without a human emphasis is probably just as inappropriate as an emphatic compulsion to assist, if this is not supported by professional knowledge.

Some interim questions about education with a European identity

If we seek to define more accurately the tasks confronting the education and training sector as a result of the inseparability of culture itself from the legal and economic aspects of European unification, we in the field of education would be wrong to conclude that we must immediately force our way into the next available round of political consultations. Instead we should consider for a moment the implications for the educational sector arising from the processes of cultural harmonisation. At this present time anyone seeking to contribute to European harmonisation must, I believe, adopt an unequivocal position with regard to four main questions.

1. In what way will Europe define its external boundaries?

If the question of defining Europe's external boundaries for the purposes of promoting an internal identity is one that cannot be avoided, one should not assume that these boundaries are geographical in nature. Talk of a 'fortress Europe' has, quite correctly, been dismissed, although this should not imply that a kind of internal 'fortress' can be dispensed with. With the exception of the business world and a European police force, any European union would be meaningless if it did not include at least a minimum consensus about the extreme limits of what is morally acceptable for anyone claiming to be a European. Gadamer has quite rightly said that it is 'a widely held misconception that tolerance is a virtue that rejects looking after one's own interests, and which treats the interests of others as being equally valid'. What is implied here is not 'self-surrender and self-effacement in favour of a general acknowledgement, but instead ... the application of the self in order to recognise others, and in order to obtain recognition by the other person' (Gadamer 1989:59f.). It follows that, in a multicultural Europe, no part of any one culture can claim to determine what should be applicable to all. While I realise that this position leads to serious logical problems as regards a final authority, I also see a far greater risk in efforts to meet the need to define Europe's external boundaries by military rather than by moral means.

2. How are we to deal with the problem of internal alienation in Europe?

A definition of Europe's external boundaries in accordance with legal theory does nothing to solve the problem of internal alienation. It should be remembered that, historically, Europe is a continent of migrants, a fact that is all too often overlooked these days. Following the October Revolution some 2.5 million Russians fled to the West. Between the First and Second World Wars 450,000 Poles and 60,000 Czechs emigrated in the same direction, and after the Second World War 16 million Germans escaped to the West, 200,000 Poles to France and Britain, 415,000 Karelians to Finland, and 500,000 people quit the Balkans. In the 1950s 1.5 million Italians and 1 million Yugoslavs moved to western central Europe. The problems have been solved in less than a generation, but nevertheless fear of the alienness of others is greater today than it ever was. It does not require any fundamental knowledge of psychoanalysis to support the hypothesis this fear is also a fear of the alien, the darkness within ourselves. In such a situation the prospect of creating a multicultural society simply does not offer a sufficient incentive. Instead I would like to suggest that we strive to accept the multicultural dimension within ourselves, and renounce the fiction that the people of Europe have monocultural personalities.

Acceptance of this fact could pave the way for the formation of multicultural attitudes, which started to become established some time ago in everyday life. The pressure of expectations about unity, and with it the calculability of the individual, is still considerable in Western Europe, for various historical reasons. Bearing these factors in mind, we should therefore not be surprised that, in psychological terms, an identification arises with imaginary (leader) figures. If a lasting, multicultural manifestation is to become established, then, as Bandura has shown, using a model learning process (see Bandura 1976), membership of the cultural group indicated in each case is bound to appear attractive. In other words: it must appear, and become visible. It is against this background that we should consider the third question.

3. In what way should we consider the relationship between regionalism and supraregionalism in the future?

The attitude referred to above can be seen in the following context: from the very beginning the various treaties and agreements intended to create a European union tended to assign a secondary role to culture, and we must therefore assume that the regional cultures could consider their solipsism as being thereby confirmed. In my view the option open to regional cultures, for which the German system of cultural federalism provides an excellent example, represents a thoughtless conservatism. If one can assume that nothing has changed in the region where one has settled, then the entire European process can be regarded with indifference. Such an attitude contradicts the concept of a multicultural manifestation, because it assumes a mixing of the cultural dimension with that of the areas occupied by particular ethnic groups. The prospects for Europe as a moral idea can exist only if membership of geographical and ethnic units, in the sense of one's origins, cannot be denied, but this also requires that people derive their strength from such an origin, not for their own interests, and without wanting to monopolise it, but when they adopt a way of life that allows for adaptation of another cultural attitude. Confronted continuously as one is by the impact in the media of other regional cultures, the European, equipped with the cultural capital of their homeland, will either have a multicultural identity or none at all.

From the viewpoint of a pedagogy that draws on the traditions of European thought, there could hardly be any alternative. One cannot conceive of a specific form of pedagogy for the Allgau any more than one could imagine a special form for the descendants of French Huguenots. Only superficially does this viewpoint conflict with the option for individuality, with the second, neglected historical dimension. After all, the multicultural identity demonstrates its individuality by the specific form that it adopts and integrates with its particular cultural setting. Perhaps this is another way of expressing education as self-improvement, in a form that has been adapted for the new Europe. At least in Western Europe the conditions for such a development at the end of the present century are better than ever. If there is one feature that epitomises the past two decades, it is surely the obvious trend towards greater individuality and personal freedom.

A European multicultural attitude is produced by a rejection of cultural hegemony, accompanied by a renunciation of cultural separatism.

4. Is the set of legal and contractual European regulations, in place in 1992, and referring specifically to education and training, actually aimed at developments in this field?

This question cannot be answered by a simple yes or no. On the one hand, an attempt has been made in the overall EC process to respect the importance of cultural independence. In the educational and training sector, Article 128 of the EEC Treaty of Rome included certain much-quoted provisions regarding vocational training: 'In response to a proposal by the Commission, and following hearings by the Economic and Social Committees, the Council has drawn up general guidelines for implementing a common policy, with regard to vocational training, which can contribute to the harmonious development not only of individual national economies but of the Common Market too' (quoted by Richter 1993:33).

The new Articles, Nos. 3b and 127, that were agreed at Maastricht are a consequence of the principle of subsidiarity, and do not include any mention of harmonisation or a common policy, even in the vocational-training sector. We may therefore conclude that the new version of the agreement that was signed at Maastricht does not represent a breakthrough in terms of a common European educational policy, implying instead that this should be left to economic forces and cultural consumption, and that, furthermore, this approach in particular will produce a specifically European dimension in both culture and education (Richter 1993:42). In other words, the formal decision to exclude educational policy has resulted in the creation of an area that, although devoid of facts, is not outside the scope of the law, and that will no doubt be filled, but not as a result of any direct control mechanism. Consequently any efforts to apply a pan-European education policy cannot fall back on any European legal provisions. Although it need not necessarily give cause for complaint, the development of a new European educational concept will be determined by what is to some extent a natural cultural process. For this very reason it is necessary that those in the field of pedagogy must reconsider the entire situation. After all, if the cultural integration of Europe is very obviously a matter for individual regulation by the various member states, it is incumbent upon those responsible for education policy in each of these countries to decide how the implementation of a European-wide dimension is to be encouraged, taking as a basis the individual perception in each country or region of what constitutes culture. The actual tasks and obligations of pedagogic research should include the various aspects under consideration in this context, together with the ensuing planning measures.

Construction 3:

The multicultural attitude. It seems that, for the time being, the EC process has acquired its final form through the Maastricht Agreement. Although this does not provide the conditions for implementing the three minimum requirements referred to previously, culminating in the notion of a multicultural attitude, some thought must be given to the implications of such minimum requirements for a new 'Europeanised' educational concept, always assuming that a suitable consensus can be found. We have to accept that the current situation is a difficult one. It was the fate of pedagogy in Germany generally to avoid politics from the 1920s until the 1940s, but it made up for this shortcoming both theoretically and practically, in the 1960s and 1970s. However, the politicisation of pedagogy does not substantially further the European process because, in their agreements and treaties, at least at a European level, the Europeans themselves have taken it out of the political sphere and instead made it part of the cultural process. Even a pedagogy that sees itself as a political science is forced to act at a solely national or even regional level. If it seeks to expand its scope, and still be productive, it must endeavour to find a role for itself in the European cultural discourse, of which the educational discourse is a part. Moreover, in other European countries such a process does not always form part of the brief of a pedagogic discipline that is set up and maintained for this purpose, but emanates instead from the pens of writers, journalists and media figures, none of them professional academics or researchers. Pedagogy in Germany has not been fully prepared for this. It has rarely had any dealings with members of professions outside the realm of pedagogy, who would have had something to contribute to the subject of education. On the other hand, without implying any false national bias, with its empirical and analytical bent, German pedagogy has demonstrated exemplary professionalism. If it shows a willingness to reopen the educational debate with other cultural sectors, which do not come within the scope of pedagogy, this offers an opportunity for making a valuable contribution, by introducing a cultural element to the whole educational concept, without neglecting its rationalist and political potential. In fact, it can significantly assist the process of integration.

However, any consideration of the multicultural attitude that I have proposed should also involve certain political decisions, which would at least require a change of outlook in current German educational policy (if indeed such a thing can be said to exist at all). I believe that this should involve the following:

> – A long overdue political recognition of the fact that educational processes have become separated from economic needs, and that this is indeed a necessary development. Given the current life expectancy of between seventy and eighty years, no one should be expected to have to make decisions about education and other vital matters at the age of eighteen, simply on the basis of changing economic data. Let us have no more criticism that our students are individually spending too much time in obtaining what they need from their education, and which they could not obtain from a highly specialised secondary education.
>
> – More flexible curricula in public-sector education, not only at universities with a school-like structure, but also in those other educational establishments in particular that are subject to strict guidelines. In this way young people, their objectives reinforced by their parents, can develop an individualised educational profile. 'Is all well with German curricula?' asked Heinrich Roth (1968). We should reiterate this question, launching a new wave of criticism of curricula and textbooks, even though some painful insights may emerge.

I believe we must reconsider the role of the state, and its public education system, in its efforts to produce a new generation of people to fulfil vital roles in society. Does the state provide the guarantee of an education that is both individual and capable of meeting specific social requirements, or has its power been eroded to such an extent through the introduction of even more rules and regulations, under the pretence of legally imposed equality, that the exact opposite of the objectives of the reforms of the 1970s has been achieved? The question now is not whether children and their parents are allowed a sufficient voice in the education process, but how much state involvement the members of society are prepared to allow in education. I support the development of a concept of intercultural learning. This implies more than just a pedagogy dealing with the subject of foreigners. The development of a multicultural attitude does not presuppose an educational process among foreigners, but among the local population: an educational process in which, recalling learning models, the foreign cultural element is depicted as something that is lacking, generating feelings of one's own alienation. A concept of this kind should assume a concrete form, extending even to the more strenuous realms of language teaching. A European incapable of speaking at least two foreign languages remains a foreigner, even within their own continent, and a teacher who does not master at least three, even if his subject is biology, may still be able to teach well in German, but he will not be a good European teacher.

I believe that this should also include involvement, in a deconstructive sense, with public information media. A polemic against the creeping 'McDonaldsisation' of Europe is futile if we cannot raise the energy to make our refusal visible. An educational and training system that makes so little use of new information technology and confines itself to simply chiding the media has become obsolete, without even noticing that the social impact on the next generation is not the result of its activity but of its inactivity. With the last two recommendations I am endeavouring to show that I am reluctant to leave the various aspects of the impending reforms to party politicians. We are the ones who must state what is to be done. We, and in European educational matters I do not mean only German pedagogy, could easily be accused by our European neighbours of wanting to establish a hegemony, for two reasons. Firstly, no other European country can claim such a widespread science of education, and, secondly, accusations of nationalisation will continue to be made as long as it continues to identify with its intellectual father, Franco-German rationalism, and not with its mother, European Romanticism, which, although of equal standing, has for the past two hundred years occupied a different area, being identified instead with art. Such a pedagogy will be truly European. It can be an interested observer of the impending process of European integration, a rational critic of the risks involved in education planning, a historical reminder of European ideas on education, and a free-thinking ironist. A European pedagogy of this kind would not succumb to the temptation of seeking to 'make' European citizens.[2] It will favour a bottom-up educational policy, implemented and supported not by states but by their citizens, and it will not hesitate to express its astonishment that pedagogy is not one of the disciplines at the only European university, the European University in Florence, which is amply funded by the EC.

Perhaps the Deutsche Gesellschaft für Erziehungswissenschaft (German Association for Educational Research) should seize the initiative and join with other, expert European representatives to produce a European Declaration on Education, to fill the educational policy vacuum in the EU, and to formulate minimum European requirements for the benefit of national and regional decision-makers. In contrast to such activities one could, of course, maintain that it is only right and proper to leave everything in the hands of the regions and, under the pretence of respecting regional autonomy, remain indifferent as to whether Europeans are to remain strangers to one another, while the Community concerns itself with matters such as the limits imposed on the number of infected pigs that are slaughtered. However, such an attitude will do little to combat xenophobia either here or elsewhere, without simultaneously losing credibility.

In closing, I should like to refer once again to Cees Nooteboom, and his re-reading of Ovid's 'Abduction of Europa', recalling how easy it was for Europa, in this myth.

> As white as untouched snow is the skin of this adored bull, his horns are perfectly formed, as if by an artist. The maiden, Europa, was almost unafraid, as she held flowers to his snow-white lips, mox adit et flores ad candid porrigit ora, the transformed, divine admirer is delighted, and kisses her hands. She sits upon his back and then it happens: he rises and walks towards the sea, and vanishes with her to the invisible island, tremulae sinuantur vestes, and her garments sway behind her in the wind ... That was long ago. Now we are Europe and must arrange our own abduction ... (Nooteboom 1993:13).

Notes

1. The same applies *mutatis mutatis* to the description by Pomian, claiming that two instances of European unification had taken place. In both cases the description centres around a kind of cultural automatism, and not an activity selectively uniting Europe (see Pomian 1990).
2. Regrettably, examples of such attempts already exist, e.g. Mickel (1991), who submitted a 'Didactics of European Education', in which educational objectives such as 'The European citizen comes of age', or the formation of a 'European awareness' up to school textbook level for the various disciplines of the social sciences were worked out in minute detail.

References

Arndt, E. M. (1940), *Germanien und Europa*, reprint of 1803 (Altona) edn, Stuttgart/Berlin.

Assman, A. (1993), *Arbeit am nationalen Gedächtnis*. *Eine kurze Geschichte der deutschen Bildungsidee*, Frankfurt/New York.

Bandura, A. (1976), *Lernen am Modell*. *Ansätze zu einer sozial-kognitiven Lerntheorie*, Stuttgart.

Bohrer, K. H. (1991), 'Europrovinzialismus', in *Merkur* 45, 11, pp. 1059-68.

Curtius, E. R. (1925), *Französischer Geist im neuen Europa*, Stuttgart/Berlin/Leipzig.

— (1969), *Europäische Literatur und lateinisches Mittelalter*, Berne.

Dahrendorf, R., Furet, F. and Geremek, B. (1993), *Wohin steuert Europa? Ein Streitgespräch*, Frankfurt/New York/Paris.

Delors, J. (1993), *Das neue Europa*, Munich/Vienna.

Eberle, J. (1966), *Lateinische Nächte*. *Essays über die lateinische Welt*, Stuttgart.

Elias, N. (1989), *Studien über die Deutschen*. *Machtkämpfe und Habitusentwicklung im 19. und 20. Jahrhundert*, Frankfurt.

Elwert, G. (1989), 'Nationalismus und Ethnizität. Über die Bildung von Wir-Gruppen', in *Kölner Zeitschrift für Soziologie und Sozialpsychologie* 41, pp. 440-64.

Faber, R. (1979), *Abendland*. *Ein politischer Kampfbegriff*, Hildesheim.

Flitner, W. (1949), *Die vier Quellen des Volksschulgedankens*, Hamburg-Wandsbek

— (1967), *Die Geschichte der abendländischen Lebensformen*, Munich.

Gadamer, H.-G. (1990), *Das Erbe Europas*, Frankfurt.

Gönner, J. (1993), 'Religiöse Überzeugungen und gesellschaftliche Wertvorstellungen. Ein Ost-West-Vergleich anhand der europäischen Wertestudie 1991/92', in *Kirchliche Zeitgeschichte* 6, 1, pp. 61-9.

Günther, K.-H. et al. (1958), *Geschichte der Erziehung*, Berlin (DDR).

Heller, A. (1988), 'Europa - ein Epilog?', in *Literaturmagazin 22. Sonderband. Ein Traum von Europa*, Reinbek/Hamburg, pp. 25-39.

Hornstein, W. and Mutz, G. (1993), *Die europäische Einigung als gesellschaftlicher Prozeß*, Baden-Baden.

Im Hof, U. (1993), *Das Europa der Aufklärung*, Munich.

Jaspers, K. (1947), *Vom Europäischen Geist*, Munich.

Marquard, O. (1986), 'Über die Unvermeidlichkeit der Geisteswissenschaften', in *Apologie des Zufälligen*. *Philosophische Studien*, Stuttgart, pp. 98-117.

Meier, Ch. (1991), 'Europa - ein paradoxer Befund', in *Neue Rundschau* 102, 1, pp. 36-48.

Münch, R. (1993), *Das Projekt Europa*. *Zwischen Nationalstaat, regionaler Autonomie und Weltgesellschaft*, Frankfurt.

Mickel, W. W. (1991), *Lernfeld Europa*. *Didaktik zur europäischen Erziehung*, Opladen.

Nooteboom, C. (1993), *Wie wird man Europäer?*, Frankfurt.

Novalis (1924), 'Die Christenheit oder Europa', in *Sämtliche Werke*, edited by E. Kamnitzer, vol. 3, Munich, pp. 7-27.

Pomian, K. (1990), *Europa und seine Nationen*, Berlin.

Richter, I. (1993), 'Grundzüge eines europäischen Bildungsrechts', in K. Schleicher (ed.), *Zukunft der Bildung in Europa*, Darmstadt, pp. 27-44.

Riedmiller, J. (1985), 'Sind die Russen Europäer?', in *Merkur* 35, 9/10, pp. 905-14.

Roth, H. (1968), 'Stimmen die deutschen Lehrpläne noch?', in *Die Deutsche Schule* 60, pp. 69-76.

Sana, H. (1993), *Die Lüge Europa*, Hamburg.

Schlegel, A. W. (1989), *Vorlesungen über Ästhetik* I, edited by E. Behler, Paderborn et al.

Schmitt, C. (1963), *Der Begriff des Politischen*, reprint of 1932 edn, Munich.

—– (1984), *Römischer Katholizismus und politische Form*, Stuttgart.

Sontag, S. (1988), 'Noch eine Elegie', in *Literaturmagazin 22. Sonderband. Ein Traum von Europa*, Reinbek by Hamburg, pp. 131-6.

Wiegand, E. (1993), 'Einstellungen zu Fremden in Deutschland und Europa' in H. Meulemann and A. Elting-Camus (eds), *26. Deutscher Soziologentag. Lebensverhältnisse und soziale Konflikte im neuen Europa*, Opladen, pp. 328-31.

Chapter 3

Hungarian Adolescents of the 1990s
Ideals, Beliefs, Expectations

Andrea Kárpáti

The milieux in which the attainment of political emancipation can take place, i.e., communities dealing with politics, have never been established in Hungary. Generations have grown up without experiencing a political community. Socialising institutions, such as school, the mass media and youth organisations, took the social class or group, and not the individual as the subject of social processes. At the same time, institutional socialisation was characterised by aspirations for standardisation, the imposition of uniformity, depersonalisation and adjustment to one single norm. Thus, socialisation led to the creation of a new feudal consciousness. The content of what was transmitted in institutionalised forms intensified the individual's feeling of helplessness, against which there was no communal defence.

Empirical studies show that, for children, social circumstances appear in socialisation as natural endowments, i.e., as unchangeable things. These studies aimed to assess the age at which children start to consider the political sphere to be influenceable and controllable, and at which they regard themselves as political factors. In Central and Eastern European societies many generations have grown up, in my view, without becoming adults in the political sense of the term. (Szabó 1993)[1]

Introduction

In the last few decades, the socialisation process of Hungarian adolescents may rather be called *dissocialisation*. In her study quoted above, the sociologist Ildikó Szabó tries to find explanations as to

---

Notes for this chapter begin on page 40.

why the 'mind-shaping institutions' responsible for the political education of the young have largely proved unsuccessful and contributed to the crisis of values of several generations. Through the
analysis of the media, schoolbooks, public rituals and other forms of
verbal and visual communication, the author concludes that the *truth
declared and the truth experienced were totally different* and thus dealing
with politics at school or during the free-time activities that were
offered became both a repulsive and a senseless activity for youngsters even in their early teenage years. The typical life strategy of
Hungary in the 1970s and 1980s was to:

> compensate collective frustrations in the domain of individual successes
> (such as consumption, a moderate accumulation and the opportunity to
> travel abroad). The opportunity to make bargains was one of the special
> 'achievements' of the 1956 revolution. The Kádár era failed to offer the
> people new behavioural patterns as values, but it provided them with the
> possibility of a pragmatic success. However, from the early 1980s, the
> increase in the number of signs indicating a crisis in all areas of social life
> showed more and more clearly, not only that the continuous renewal of
> the system was an illusion, but that the mere perpetuation of the existing
> circumstances was also illusory. The only possibility that remained was
> the individual way of counteracting the socialisation system. (Szabó 1993)

Lack of interest in 'politics', total disbelief in their ability to shape the
future of their land, distrust in success in any sphere of human life –
Hungarian adults, who proved to constitute one of the most pessimistic nations in Europe according to polls both before and after
the change of regime, inculcated a generation of young people with
these moral attitudes.[2] After the first free elections of 1990, profound
changes also occurred in educational policy-making. The humanistic
approach of alternative school models, new subjects focusing on
moral issues, textbooks about the history of Hungary after the Second World War and the proliferation of church-based youth organisations were all meant to counteract the loss of social identity of the
young. It seems worthwhile for educators to face the process of
change in mentality and lifestyle of students, in the way that best
monitors the success of our efforts to educate liberated citizens, who
will be able to further the democratisation of their country.

The study quoted here replicates part of a larger German research
project carried out by a group of sociologists attached to Potsdam
University. Dietmar Sturzbecher and his team utilised a questionnaire to reveal the structure and contents of the value system of East
German adolescents in 1991, as a part of a survey of political socialisation of youth in the German state of Brandenburg. As most of the
questions included in his questionnaire were relevant to the situation
in Hungary we translated and adapted it, and are now using it as a
measure for values and attitudes in a survey of the *visual environment*

of youth subcultures in Hungary.[3] This survey provides data on the quality and personal significance of living and working environments, hair, make-up and dress styles, personal objects and other forms of visual expression of Hungarian young people between fifteen and twenty-three years of age. Its major aim is to modernise their aesthetic education through establishing meaningful contents in art, design, crafts and art criticism/art history studies. As the contemporary Hungarian art world experiences a period of 'classicist avant garde', a new paradigm for arts education reflecting on changes both in art and life is urgently needed.[4]

Our sample involved sixteen- to seventeen-year-old second-graders attending secondary grammar schools and vocational schools in Budapest and Szolnok – a county seat about a hundred kilometres from the capital. Our sample of 427 persons, although not representative for the areas concerned, is large enough to allow assumptions concerning the validity of the data collected. It breaks down almost evenly into boys and girls (213 and 214 respectively, with an average age of 16.9 years for boys and 17.3 years for girls), young people living in the capital and in the country (230/197), grammar-school students and vocational-school students (187/240). Five vocational schools were selected so as to include a variety of trades. The six grammar schools in our sample represent a variety in geographical location (city versus suburb) and educational level (university internship schools and new schools serving working-class families on a housing estate were equally included). Questionnaires were administered without names – only sex, age, school name, type and grade were registered. Teachers, almost without exception, welcomed the questionnaire as an opportunity to discuss the issues raised with their students.

Hungarian and German adolescents were also compared in terms of their lifestyles, professional and private aspirations and future expectations (optimism/pessimism) in a study by Zinnecker and Gábor in 1989 and 1990 – providing data about youth in Hungary at the very beginning of the change of regime.[5] The study is based on the paradigm of Bourdieu concerning 'youth-centrism'.

> In youth-centrism the conflicts young people experience regarding the culture and authority of the adult world find an expression. Adults can serve as a positive reference for youth, providing guidance, direction and mobility into adult roles for the oncoming generations. But adults can also serve as a negative reference group – representing control, supervision, compromised morals and questionable political ethics … Research on youth-centrism … has shown an adult-oriented variant connected with positive attitudes towards adults … Conversely, the negative variant can serve as a specific kind of 'ethnocentrism', in which the culture and politics of the youth are opposed to the world of adults. (Gábor 1991)

This paper will focus on the aspects of political socialisation as reflected in the lifestyle, family relationships and beliefs of adolescents. The comparison of East German and Hungarian adolescents based on the results of the questionnaire study are to be published elsewhere (Kárpáti and Kovács [forthcoming]). We will show how traditionally compromising, adult-oriented youth culture gains a new direction and develops original, 'youth-centrist' variants of socialisation patterns and subcultures.

Role Models at Home and at School

Basic manners of behaviour as well as values and tastes are best transmitted by immediate family members – parents, siblings and other relatives.

> Young people remain attached to their families during both phases of development. Only a part of them appears in the political, cultural and consumption fields of society as an independent factor. ...

> In the West European model youth as a life phase develops outside the family. Due to the limits of the space that has been left for them outside the area of professional status, East European young people start families and raise children. ... The process of the erosion of class positions is taking place simultaneously with the development of a new kind of mass culture and mass consumption, which are due partly to the appearance of the mass media. Thus, new ideas and lifestyles, which are independent of former social status are more and more out of reach. Ideologies involved in 'mass media packages' are available to help young people form their own individual lifestyles by adapting new interpretations of identity. (Gábor 1991)

The other basic value transmitter group is composed of teachers, classmates and other members of the school community. In a series of questions we enquired about relationships with family members, peers and teachers. First, the family as transmitter of social and cultural values will be examined. The success of family-based transmission of values depends largely on the intensity and positive character of the relationship of family members. Our results show that both girls and boys trust their fathers more than their mothers; however they find mothers more understanding and both parents equally fair and reliable. There is a significant difference between their attitudes to their mothers: girls find their most immediate female role model more trustworthy and less strict, and quarrel with them less than boys do. However, the dominance of the – mostly absent – father is unquestionable and the emotional support for both sexes remains the mother. It is she who stimulates the adolescent. In agreement with our expectations, adolescents do not experience parental oppression. In fact, parents do not seem to control their children's free-time activities – they also rarely take part in them. Adolescents find there are frequent arguments with their families and help very little with household chores.

The adolescents spend little time with their families – boys significantly less than girls. Due to economic instability, growing inflation and joblessness, and the necessity of second and third incomes, from the 1970s we have constantly been in a situation in which people ruin themselves physically in order to survive economically. The Hungarian family as a transmitter of values serves as a negative or neutral model for most adolescents, who turn elsewhere for patterns of socialisation. Education may affect changes in many ways – through the acquisition of more marketable skills, but also through the development of new structures of values and attitudes. The prerequisite for an effectively functioning school environment is, however, the network of positive, nurturing and emotionally satisfying relationships. Most Hungarian teenagers have friends whom they find trusting and caring, but they do not feel they are fully accepted by classmates. Neither boys nor girls manifest any fear of rejection – boys even less than girls – but they do not find their classmates caring or inclined to recognise their merits. They seem to have much more positive experiences with the spirit of their gang than with their class, which is natural, if we remember how negatively they assess their life at school.

Young people in our sample find education rather unpleasant and the pressure at school quite intense. They often feel restricted and hardly ever experience personal recognition. Neither girls nor boys believe that teachers care about them – boys considerably less than girls. Almost none of them finds among teachers an adequate role model ('idol') and many of them are convinced that teachers quite often lie.[6] School, the respondents felt, was obliged to monitor politically acceptable and desirable facts and values secretly opposed at home – a dual education that necessarily resulted in the discrediting of both parental and educational value systems.

The socialisation process is greatly hindered by the negative attitudes of students towards their schools; this is caused mainly by the impersonal manner of teaching, characterised by *Frontalunterricht,* observable in most Hungarian classrooms in spite of increasing reform efforts (Pataki 1991; Kozma 1985:351, quotation; on the groups playing a part in the shaping of educational policy and the process of policy-making, see Hálász 1986). It seems that the most important influences on young people will be those encountered by them in their free time, spent away from home and school.

Free-time Activities as means of Socialisation

Most students in our survey wished they had much more free time
and found that school duties influenced to an excessive degree their
choice of how to spend it.[7]

> The school itself is not able to develop new cultural habits and demands,
> yet it does not leave enough time for the students to orientate their needs
> of this kind towards other institutions. ... Students have no opportunity
> for realising their preferences and pursuing their own interests. It seems
> that, due to the fact that their desires and needs are constantly hindered
> or come to nothing, they do not experience their spare time as spare time
> ... (Laki-Fazekas 1992)

Most Hungarian adolescents in our sample spend their free time, as
expected, with friends and classmates, although the number of those
who are often alone in their free time or spend hours on the streets
is surprisingly high.

Characteristic of Hungary seems to be the insignificant role of
family and relatives in free-time activities of young people. Adults
do not set patterns of activities and rarely try to pass on personal
hobbies and interests – they simply never have the time. Families
have lost their feeling for traditional feasts and get-togethers.
Although most Hungarians do not move more than twice in their
lifetimes, and the size of the country does not prevent frequent
encounters, most Hungarian teenagers see their extended families
only at Christmas, Easter and funerals. Grandparents are regularly
visited in vacation time when children are small and totally forgotten once 'baby-sitting' is no longer needed. The role of the family
in the life of the Hungarian youth is that of the provider: adolescents, college students and even young workers or professionals
depend almost entirely on their families for all their financial needs.
Finding temporary jobs is increasingly hard in a country where
almost thirty per cent of the adult population is jobless, but in any
case this practice had never been traditionally established.[8] Lack of
financial means restricts free time possibilities and may be partly
responsible for the numbers of those who seem to have nothing to
do, nowhere to go.

Less than half of the boys and girls spend much of their free time
with their parents – grammar-school students doing so considerably
more than future skilled workers. The percentage participating in
sports is alarmingly low: only a quarter of the girls and a little more
than a third of the boys engage in any sporting activity. In this
respect, grammar and vocational-school students seem to be very
similar. 'Cultural events' (theatre, concerts, exhibitions, etc.) are
equally unattractive – only a little more than every tenth girl and

boy visits them often, and every fifth never. Here, too, the results of grammar- and vocational-school students are quite similar. In his survey quoted above, K. Gábor has similar findings: grammar-school students of the early 1990s tend to 'lower' the level of their free-time activities and, in their choices, resemble skilled-worker students more than university students. In an upcoming research study on the interests of adolescents we shall probably be able to analyse in detail the patterns of interest lying behind the fact that young people seem to be much less interested in the forums of the acquisition of 'high culture' than were the preceding generations. Aesthetic education focusing on the academic interpretation of historic styles seems to be responsible for the lack of interest – and even information – about places where art experiences may be gained (for a brief history of Hungarian art education, written in English, see Karpáti [in press]).

Ideas, Beliefs and Prejudices – Adolescents Interpret 'Hot Issues' in Politics

An interesting section of the survey, to be discussed in a separate paper, lists pairs of opposing characteristic features and asks which of them best suits members of a given nation. This set of scaled questions reveals the national prejudices that constitute one of the major problems of contemporary Hungary.[9]

'Fear of foreigners' (*Ausländerangst*), described by Sturzbecher as a feeling characteristic of the majority of East German adolescents, is attributed by him to the shortage of jobs and flats and the general belief that immigrants – a cheap labour force – actually occupy jobs and dwellings that could and should be given to native citizens. In Hungary, immigration is a fairly recent phenomenon but similar feelings are beginning to manifest themselves. There is a striking similarity between the attitudes of East German adolescents in the Sturzbecher study and those in our sample. Although percentages are lower for the acceptance of slogans such as 'Foreigners go home!' and 'Most criminals are foreigners', a good third of Hungarian boys still share these views. (It is consoling, though, that far fewer girls are in favour of these highly prejudiced expressions.) As with the German sample, vocational-school students are more intolerant than grammar-school students. We fully agree with Sturzbecher: fear of immigrants is closely linked to the fear of not finding a job in the future. As most of those foreigners who seek asylum in Hungary are skilled workers but not degree-holders, future academics have no reason to be anxious about competition from them. It is interesting to see how members of different nations are characterised in relation to their concurrent potentials.[10]

Fears and Hopes about the Future

In 1990, a group of sociologists headed by Ildikó Szabó carried out research among fourteen-year-old schoolchildren in Budapest using the method of the index of words (Pecheron 1974). Our study aimed at assessing the children's attitude towards politics. 'The equality of people' was one of the most appealing ideals for them. But as soon as we asked them about concrete ethnic groups, such as the Gypsy, the Arab, the Russian, the Czech and the Jew (the enumeration could be continued with the Slovak, the Serb, etc.), the ideal accepted on the level of generalisations turned out not to work any longer.

It is worth considering the actual fears of children as they appear in the gradation made by them. The following notions and groups can be seen at the top of the gradation, which was based on the proportion of those giving the answer 'I am afraid of ...':

1.	the Gypsy	44 %
2.	revolution	41 %
3.	nuclear power-stations	36 %
4.	strikes	35 %
5.	socialism	25 %
6.	the army	23 %
7-8.	the future	21 %
7-8.	communists	21 %
9-10.	the Arab	18 %
9-10.	the Romanian	18 %
10.	the Russian	15 %

The answers show that certain groups (such as the Gypsy and the Arabian) that are the objects of prejudices are also the objects of fears.

Sturzbecher finds that there is a 'striving for normality' (*Normalitätssehnsucht*) observable among East German adolescents – their major aspiration is a secure workplace and living with a family in a decent home and possessing a car. Young Hungarians seem to prefer the same values and have expectations very similar to those of their adult compatriots. According to a recent poll by the Gallup Institute, value preferences in Hungary have remained basically stable over the last fifteen years. According to the Gallup poll, adults find financial wellbeing increasingly important, but equality – a concept that lost its attraction on the eve of the new regime – is gradually regaining its status. People favouring government parties prefer Christian values such as obedience, opposition supporters are in turn more in favour of common sense, logical thinking and tolerance. The median of dominant values changes only slightly between 1979 and 1992: the first six on all preference lists includes peace, family life, financial wellbeing, happiness and satisfaction and national security.

Naturally, these dominant values will define major fears and anxieties that are actually manifest in the results of our questionnaire.

About one-third of both boys and girls are unsure about their abilities, almost every second boy and girl has doubts about getting a job – although only one-third of them are unable to define their professional aspirations. These figures are higher than those reported by Sturzbecher – data reflect the different economic positions of the East German territories – relying on their 'Western brothers' – and Hungary, crisis-ridden and completely left to its own resources. Although life in our country does not seem very promising, only seventeen boys and ten girls, out of 412 respondents, are definite in their desire to seek a better future in the West. (In an epoch of bilateral brain drain – Western countries attracting Hungarian intellectuals whose salaries are ridiculously low in comparison to those in the West, while Hungary becomes the target country of Eastern European and one-time Soviet specialists for very similar reasons – this result is more than reassuring – although the intentions of youngsters may change once they actually enter the labour market.)

In several surveys Hungarians were found to be one of the most pessimistic nations during the early 1990s. A survey called 'Eurobarometer', commissioned by the European Community at the end of 1992, is a good example. Involving representative samples from eighteen countries, it aimed to obtain data about political and economic attitudes. From among the nations represented, Albanians were most optimistic about the direction of changes in their country and Hungarians shared the last place with Armenia. In Hungary only eighteen per cent of the people found the present political system to be better than that of the past. Seventy-one per cent of Hungarians declared that they were worse off than before. Here the lowest percentage was that of Romania: fifty-five per cent. It is noteworthy that fifty-six per cent of the Czechs, whose situation is often judged to be similar or equal to that of Hungary, considered that their life was better since the change of regime. Peculiarly enough, although more than half of Hungarians (fifty-seven per cent) had no positive expectations about the development of the national economy in 1993, fifty-six per cent still consider the market economy a good model to follow.

Hungarian teenagers in our survey are quite negative about the benefits produced by the social market economy but are by no means in favour of the former system. They unanimously reject slogans often heard from their parents' generation against entrepreneurs and capitalism. The subcultures characteristic of the 1990s actually include young entrepreneurs and yuppies as two new groups that manifest themselves in taste, style and values.

> The first characteristic representatives of youth subcultures were the so-called *csöves* vagrants appearing in the late 1970s. Punks made their debut at the beginning of the decade, followed soon after by the skinheads. Punk spread among students and youths in the outer city and on housing estates. Another subcultural trend, first called new wave, then 'underground', became popular mostly among educated youth. Though the founders have already left the 'underground', a similar tendency has been emerging recently.

> From the late 1980s hard rock music has returned ... Its devotees identify themselves as rockers and heavy-metallists.

> The death- and other-world-oriented 'occult' subcultures appeared about the turn of the decade including Satanists, grufties (after the German *Gruft* =grave) and various illusionist groups.

> In 1991 several skinhead groups and others identifying themselves as Fascists are also present among the Hungarian youth subcultures. They take a militant stand against foreign students and Gypsies.

> At the beginning of the 1980s the subcultures articulated the social crisis by exposing issues of poverty and deviancy (e.g. drug addiction). They were a reminder of the fact that these problems could not be discussed in public; indeed, not even the words themselves were allowed in the mass media.

> Contemporary subcultures also have a 'message': the occult subcultures and the consequent moral indignation expose issues of religious influence/secularisation; the violent, Fascistic groups stress the problems of an exclusive and intolerant nationalism/ethnocentrism (Rácz 1992).

It is interesting to compare results with those of Sturzbecher: while young East Germans clearly reject the market economy, Hungarian adolescents have a positive attitude towards it. It is quite astonishing for the Hungarian reader that so many East Germans want to get rid of 'capitalism' – right after decades of living in a practically non-functioning socialism. The events which, according to the author, explain these attitudes – loss of financial security, the closing down of public institutions that made life easier for women, etc. – are all happening in Hungary as well. Young Hungarians are pessimistic but do not consider themselves losers as a result of the change of regime – a feeling seemingly characteristic of their East German contemporaries. Perhaps this is the basic difference in attitudes and values between the two groups. As surveys indicate, it is their parents' generation that seems to have lost hope and prospects. In the 'Eurobarometer' survey quoted above, seventy-one per cent of Hungarians declared their dissatisfaction with the way their country is managed – a figure that ranks among the highest in the poll of eighteen Eastern Central European nations. The hope of the adult generation – if they have any hope left – clearly lies with youth. Surveys about party preferences showed, until recently, a growing sympathy for the Young Democrats – Hungary's unique political phenomenon, a liberal democratic party established in March 1988 in the then still-strong Communist regime. This party of the young that only recently abolished an upper age limit of thirty-five years for members, won nine per cent of parliamentary seats in 1990, has successfully established itself in political life with a strong professional image and soon became the front-runner in party preference lists. Although its popularity has decreased recently because of a split between its liberal and conservative wings, this party is very likely to form part of the next Hungarian government. Quite obviously, this will change the attitudes of the generation of the young politicians about politics and their role in political life. For the first time in Hungarian history, young people see positive role models from their own generation successfully establishing themselves in a democratic, multi-party system. The consequences will hopefully be seen in the return of the young to the forums of social action.[11]

It is interesting to note that, while more than a half of the adolescents asked consider democracy the best from of government, a good third of them have no opinion on this issue – a clear sign of the loss of illusions in a 'post-revolutionary' era. Most girls, but only half of the boys, are worried about the growth of Fascism in Germany – grammar-school students are more concerned than those attending vocational schools. Significantly more boys than girls are worried about the growing popularity of István Csurka, the extremist politician of the largest governing party. (Girls are generally much less interested in 'politics' and choose the 'no opinion' alternative more often than boys.) The number of those who agree with terrorism (13 out of 427) is small enough to be considered insignificant – probably a joke to ease the boredom of a lengthy questionnaire.

Ildikó Szabó (1985:80) concludes:

> If for a longer period (or, possibly, for generations) they have the experience that they have little influence on the formation of their own life, their feeling of defencelessness will necessarily increase. A possible consequence of this is that they will give up planning their future, 'life strategies' will not even take shape and their lives will be based on the principle (and morality) of *carpe diem* and 'survival'. If incalculability is considered only as a negative phenomenon, people will adjust their ethic of success to what currently seems to be certain and not to what is profitable on the long term. An empirical study in 1982 showed that, for the young, the notion of succeeding was not a definitely positive one. A considerable part of them wished only to get by and not to succeed, and many were of the opinion that those who are successful do not merit it.

Notes

1. A further interesting finding from the same research group about the lack of political interest and detachment of youth: in 1982, children aged ten to fourteen living in Budapest were asked to mention words in connection with politics. One third of them only mentioned words that were connected with foreign politics and another third mentioned words at least half of which referred to foreign politics (Szabó and Csepeli 1983).
2. For details of the survey entitled 'Eurobarometer', commissioned by the European Community at the end of 1992, see below.
3. For a description of the research project aimed at establishing new teaching contents and educational/art theoretical approaches for curricula for art and design education see Kárpáti and Kovács (forthcoming).
4. For a description of art education in Hungary in the 1980s, see Kárpáti (1987).
5. This research was founded on the evaluation involving 1,500 West German and 1,500 Hungarian young people involving workers, training-school and secondary grammar-school students as well as university students. The German sample was taken in 1984, the Hungarian in 1985, to determine basic characteristics and differences of youth living in Eastern and Western Europe. Another, smaller sample was taken in Hungary in 1989 and in the Hungarian-populated area of Timisoara, Romania in 1990 involving 504 young people attending the above types of educational institutions. The results quoted in this paper will refer to this latter sample. The study is reported in detail in Gábor (1991).
6. Teachers' lack of credibility is due partly to the official requirements regarding moral issues and even facts taught in history, literature or philosophy classes. The 'rewriting of history' began in the second half of the 1940s: all major reform endeavours of the past were reinterpreted according to the Communist mentality. Thus, the middle classes, including the intelligentsia, lost their roots in tradition, tradition that represented a certain continuity of values and a basis of identification for dealing with politics. Revaluation involved not only a huge area of historical traditions and religion, but also civil values such as the relative autonomy of privacy, or the concept of national identity, the sanctity of private property, and to some extent civil rights, etc.
7. According to recent surveys, grammar-school students generally have seven hours of obligatory study daily and spend most of their weekday evenings preparing for the next day's lessons – without a chance to refresh themselves, thus with little efficiency. Their spare time is also dominated by school. No time-consuming free time activities are favoured: watching television dominates (197 minutes daily), while 'conversation' with family members lags far behind with only twenty-five per cent of the tv-watching time.
8. A set of questions in our questionnaire enquired about the amount of free time spent earning money. Only a fraction of the youth group we questioned has to work regularly to contribute to the family budget but 11.4 per cent of the boys and 9 per cent of the girls often work while 46.7 per cent and 39.6 per cent sometimes work voluntarily to realise personal aims.
9. Thus far, our task of matching response categories employed by Sturzbecher had not caused any serious problems. But with the selection of nationalities to be involved in the matching task, it would have been impossible to find the valid Hungarian alternatives for the Vietnamese or the Poles – both representing large immigrant groups, cheap labour supply and one of them being an ethnic group that racists consider inferior. Our selection was the Gypsy nationality – a minority that has always been the target of Hungarian racism – and Romanian immigrants – mostly of Hungarian origin, mostly skilled, satisfied with half the wage a Hun-

garian skilled worker or even unskilled help would require. Much to our satisfaction, a considerable number of students (nearly ten per cent) actually refused to answer this question. On their questionnaires they called the procedure of assigning characteristic features – half of them negative ones – to a nation as a whole 'a Fascist practice' or 'a sure sign of chauvinism'. Still, the majority replied and their attitudes clearly reflect prejudices characteristic of adults.

10. Here are some typical findings from the analysis of the items that required the characterisation of nations. In the eyes of Hungarian adolescents, Gypsies are humble, disorderly, dirty, intolerant, stupid, stingy, shifty and undisciplined. Romanian immigrants receive an almost equally negative description. Germans – traditional models in Hungary for sobriety, efficacy and diligence – are found orderly, clean, brave, self-assured, disciplined and intelligent, but also oppressive, intolerant, conceited and only slightly co-operative. It is peculiar to note that while only a few significant differences were found in the assessment of the former two nationalities, Germans are judged in a very different way by grammar-school students and vocational-school students, by whom Germans are seen less positively. Girls tend to give more neutral judgments than boys. When judging their fellow Hungarians, boys also resorted to giving neutral judgments. Evidently, the more you know of a nation the less it is possible to assign a single feature to it as a whole. (Methodologically, this item raises many questions. Using stories to illustrate a character trait and asking about the possible nationality of those involved or asking respondents to judge the validity of jokes about members of a nation would perhaps have been a better way of eliciting national prejudices.)

11. At present, the largest Hungarian organisation involved in political socialisation is the Alliance of Pioneers (67,000 members), followed by the Scout Association (20,000), Left-wing Youth Association (BIT, 14,000), Youth Democratic Forum (the youth wing of the largest coalition party, 4,000), Young Democrats (the youth organisation of Free Democrats, the biggest opposition party, 1,500), the Young Christians' Association (1,100), and Young Socialists (500). Apparently, they attract only a very small minority of their age groups and thus their effects in the political socialisation process is rather insignificant.

References

Gábor, K. (1991), 'Youth Culture and Political Culture in Eastern Europe', *Proceedings, Conference on Theory and Methods in International Youth Research*, Utrecht.

Hálász, G. (1986), 'The Structure of Educational Policy-making in Hungary in the 1960s and 1970s', *Comparative Education*, 22, no. 2, pp. 123-32.

Kárpáti, A. (1987), 'Based on the Disciplines: Research and Practice in Contemporary Hungarian Art Education', *Canadian Review of Art Education*, 15, 1, pp. 35-41.

— (in press), 'The History of Art Education in Hungary', in M. F. Chavanne, (ed.), *International Tendencies in Art Education*, Paris.

Kárpáti, A. and Kovács, Z. (forthcoming), 'Youth Subcultures in Hungary: Emerging new Models for Hungarian Art and Design Education', paper submitted for consideration to the *European Journal of Art and Design Education* in March 1993.

Kozma, T. (1985), 'Conflicts of Interest in Educational Planning', *Prospects*, XV, no. 3, pp. 347-60.

Laki-Fazekas, Cs. (1992), 'Life Style of Students Today', in F. Gazsó, and I. Stumpf (eds) (1992), *Youth and the Change of Regime*, Budapest, pp. 159-74.

Pataki, J. (1991), 'Political Changes Necessitate Educational Reform', *Report on Eastern Europe*, 2, no. 18, pp. 20-4.

Pecheron, A. (1974), *L'univers politique des enfants*, Fondation National des Sciences Politiques, Paris.

Rácz, J. (1992), 'Subcultures of Hungarian Youth', in F. Gazsó, and I. Stumpf (eds) (1992), *Youth and the Change of Regime*, Budapest, pp. 109-20.

Szabó, Ildikó (1985), 'Az érvényesülés konfliktusai' ('The conflicts of succeeding'), *Medvetánc*, 1985/2-3.

— (1993), 'After the changing of the system and before the changing of the values', in J. Wichmann and P. Knoost (eds) (in print), *Education, Youth and Reform in Eastern Europe*, Peter Lang 'Comparative Education' series, Frankfurt am Main/Berne/New York/Paris.

Szabó, I. and Csepeli, G. (1983), *Nemzet és politika a 10-14 éves gyerekek gondolkozásában (Nation and politics in the mind of children aged 10-14)*, Budapest.

Chapter 4

Youth at Risk

Attitudes and Value Concepts among Young People
in Europe at a Time of Social Change

Hans Merkens

Introduction

There are several reasons for my use of the metaphor 'Youth at Risk'
in the title of this paper:

Firstly, youth is subject to danger in terms of individual development; young people can in addition be endangered by their social
environment. In the latter instance, the phrasing suggests that the
optimism that is, in everyday life, associated with the life stage
'youth' – youthfulness as a social value – also often contains a dangerous component, that of failure (see Engel 1992:201f.). In this
respect, it is especially appropriate for pedagogical reflections which,
in considering youth, must bear in mind this element of possible
failure. Another concept, frequently used in German research on
youth, that of the moratorium (see for example, *Jugendwerk der
Deutschen Shell*, vol. 1, 1992), proceeds from the notion of a period of
grace (see Schefold and Hornstein, 1993: 919).

Secondly, at present, a wide-ranging investigation that can be sub-
sumed under the topic outlined above is being undertaken in a variety
of selected settings in the United States. The project unites development psychologists, educational psychologists, sociologists and crimi-
nologists. The intention is to detect individual and social risk factors
for development in young people. A similiar project is planned for
parts of Canada. This risk metaphor thus allows the present author's
research to be examined in the light of these projects, both in theoretical terms and in a comparison of the empirical research. Interest in

the topic is also growing from another standpoint, as the current course of processes of change in Europe are understood to offer opportunities for the testing of theories and a challenge to the research accompanying it. Research of this kind must be designed to form longitudinally oriented projects, if it is to be successful (see Engel 1992).

In addition, a final reason can be perceived in the metaphor's enabling the reintroduction to research on youth of one of the basic pedagogical assumptions: if youth as a life stage is an adventurous one, one strategy in dealing with youth could be a reduction of the risks, by narrowing down the fields of freedom in which young people can act. One can however also interpret the idea of hazardousness by observing that youth is expected to make choices requisite for entering adult life. This is true, both with regard to goals, for instance, as in reference to future occupation or to life in general, and to ways and means. Young people must experiment with the means available or those that they can make available to themselves, in order to achieve the goals they hold desirable. In the process, they confront both individual limitations and the boundaries set by society.

Seen against the background of this approach, it is not surprising that young people more often display deviant forms of behaviour, if compared with individuals at other stages of life. Any venture incorporates, either temporarily or permanently, a risk of failure (see Hagan 1991). Thus, the argument concerning the first of the three variants can be concluded. Taking risks consists of testing one's capabilities during the process of finally becoming responsible for one's own development. Being brought up by others can then come to an end. The individual makes the transition into self-education. From a pedagogical standpoint, this can be regarded as the goal of development during the life stage 'youth'. From this viewpoint, self-education means assuming responsibility for oneself with regard to goals and the ways and means of achieving them.

At this point a flaw, for which educational science as a discipline must bear the responsibility, becomes apparent: the life stage 'youth' has never been systematically defined. At best, it has been defined in terms of certain forms of its articulations: historically, for example, the *Jugendbewegung,* in terms of social services, for instance, delinquency; or, in terms of school pedagogy, students of secondary education, stages I and II, have been, and are, treated.

Youth itself retains a distant image. If one tries to define the topic in terms of the entire discipline, it is therefore, that phase of life in which being raised by others comes to an end. Educational science has to date, however, been more concerned with the conditions of achieving and maintaining pedagogical relations rather than with reflecting on the question of how they are brought to an end.

On the Problems of Comparative Research

A second *a priori* problem to be resolved, results from the desire to present results drawn from differing cultures in comparison to one another. At the dawn of larger investigations of this kind stands the work of Hofstede (1980) with his IBM study entitled 'Culture's Consequences', in which he researched similarities and differences in the scales of values of IBM employees from forty countries. He categorised his results under four headings:

- power gradients
- striving for security
- individualism
- masculinity

Hofstede was able to demonstrate that for his samples from the various countries, a network could be discerned among the data categorised under these headings, which consisted, with one single exception, of the two best rankings from countries under one heading being coupled with middle or lower rankings under the other headings. However, we must concur with Smith and Bond (1993:42), who put forward the objection that it was not the members of differing cultures that were examined, but rather IBM staff from different countries. The question remains unanswered as to whether IBM attracts a specific type of person.

Of greater consequence is the objection that all the means of measurement employed by Hofstede were developed from within the traditions of Western nations. As a result, a group of investigators, who call themselves Chinese Culture Connection (1987), have developed instruments from within a Chinese context. According to a model utilising four factors, they delineated only three factors displaying similarities to those of Hofstede:

Chinese Factors	Hofstede's Factors
integration	collectivism
human cordiality	masculinity
moral discipline	power gradients

No equivalent for 'concern for security' was discovered. Instead, another factor whose connotation can be paraphrased as 'Confucianist work dynamics' was discerned.

Schwartz (1992) has, in comparative research, elicited twelve different dimensions of values, which Smith and Bond (1993) assume can be regarded simply as refinements of Hofstede's classification, for they contradict in no way the originals.

As a consequence of such investigations, a central question of whether there are such things as cultural universals is raised. It is an assumption that is, for instance, with respect to the organisation of scales of values in particular cultures, basic to approaches such as that of Piaget (1973) and Kohlberg (1981, 1984). In such an approach, there can only be differences in emphasis in the value scales in different cultures, but no differences in the configuration of the attitudes itself. The larger part of all investigations in cultural comparison has been carried out under such a general premise.

Utilising such a premise, a series of comparative studies on youth have been undertaken since German reunification. A trend has emerged, according to which the differences between young people in the two parts of the country appear to be smaller than had been suspected when research began. Four variants offer themselves as possible interpretations:

1. The position of young people in industrial society is independent of differences in primary socialisation. The tasks of development individuals need to complete are so similar that the effects of differences between different systems are not apparent (convergence hypothesis);

2. Young people in East Germany have, during the process of reunification, adopted Western patterns of thought so quickly that previously existing differences have been rapidly eliminated (assimilation hypothesis);

3. Internal erosion in the former GDR and other former Comecon states was so advanced that, particularly in the instance of youth, important processes of adaptation to the West had already been set in motion (see Behnken, I., et al. 1991 for the former GDR; acculturation hypothesis);

4. The results are really to be regarded as artefacts that have, in fact, been generated by the nature of the instruments of measurement as well as by the statistical methods employed in data evaluation (see Schefold and Hornstein 1993; Boehnke and Merkens 1994).

It is evident that variants 1 to 3 can be discussed only after variant 4 has been clarified.

Problems of method are discussed in cross-cultural psychology in terms of:

• emic/etic
• indigenous versus universalistic constructs
• various approaches to equivalence.

Unfortunately, all these means of discrimination are less clear-cut than they appear to be (see Malpass and Poortinga 1986). It is equally disastrous that the choice of statistical model in the evaluation of data can influence the results considerably with respect to differences or similarities (see Boehnke and Merkens 1994). Thus the question of the correct choice of model or approach can, objectively, only be made with great difficulty. The appropriateness of the results can be verified in each case only if the original data record is again made available.

In the following, therefore, a strategy of analysis based on compromise is adopted. In this manner, varying facets of the same data record can be brought into the foreground. Furthermore, a procedure that is oriented towards the emic/etic differentiation as well as the model of differing equivalences will be selected. Three different stages can be discerned in the later case:

- functional
- conceptual
- metrical equivalence.

Functional equivalence allows us, with respect to youth, to ask whether the same or very similar functions are attributed to it in the various societies included in the comparison. This question can hardly be answered during the preparatory stage, for it is always a component in the empirical analysis of the data. In the research presented here, this question loses some of its potency, because it is, in all instances, a matter of youth still attending school, that is, young people in a phase of life that is most suited for a comparison including individuals from different societies.

To what extent conceptual equivalence can be said to exist is one of the points that I shall discuss when presenting the empirical results. Metrical equivalence is situated at the level of the analytical instruments. Only in the case of sufficiently good translations, can it be said to be given. Beginning the examination at the level of checking equivalence means adopting a radical change of perspective with respect to the research discussed at the outset of this section, for the question is approached at the level of culturally specific constructs.

Values and Attitudes

Both concepts are, in the following, employed synonymously, for no advantage of a system differentiation can, in the case of the object of our analysis, be discerned. Moreover, the combination of the two offers the advantage that during the operationalisation of the value concept it can be extended to include attitudes. This means, in connection with the theme of this chapter, restricting ourselves to the question of goals.

For educational science, values form one of the central categories in determining both the praxis and research to be investigated. With regard to praxis, this dictum is applicable because the value relationship forms one of the categories by means of which the educational act may be differentiated from all other everyday actions. Thus it is essential that this value relationship is considered carefully, in order to differentiate education from other processes. Because education raises the question of 'what for', such a correlation comes into being naturally, so to speak, and is regarded in this manner by, for instance, advocates of an empirical educational science (cf. Brezinka 1969). As evident as such a relationship may appear, it cannot suffice as long as that which creates values is not demonstrated.

Because human beings always behave interactively, the relationship of value to behaviour can only provide information on the reason why the assertion regarding its relevance for educational science just discussed is true. In the distinction drawn by Schütz (1974), behaviour assumes an act to be based on a previously extant plan, that is, it represents a selective decision mediated by action. In many approaches, values are regarded as one of the criteria instrumental in the planning of action. Value aspects are suited 'for establishing limitations in the choice of means and purposes' (Luhmann 1985:279). Values are stylised expectations 'to which one can generally commit oneself, even if corresponding effects arise neither at this moment or ever' (Luhmann 1973:36). From such a point of view, values can be interpreted in general terms as preferences for situations or events in instances of action alternatives. This does not mean that values affect actions in the sense of comprising a causal model. Attention is drawn only to a connection that consists in values influencing actions, when two or more alternatives can be chosen (see Jaufmann and Kistler 1992).

On the Selection of the Value Concepts and Attitudes to be Analysed

In comparing the value concepts in Central and Eastern European countries, an obvious choice is to select such values and attitudes among which one suspects a maximal difference. This could be the case with work. Regarding work, there have been, in Western industrial countries and, in particular, in West Germany, a series of inquiries into, and a sustained debate on, the evaluation of work. In this area there has been a tendency for the interpretations to surmise a growing scepticism among the young regarding work (see Brock and Otto-Brock 1992). Brock and Otto-Brock (1992) have opposed this prevailing view with a thesis, according to which there has been a shift within modern orientations toward work. This is an implicit criticism of the discussion's lack of consideration of the evaluation of work. On the contrary, work has been regarded as something necessary to life (see Merkens 1990). Correspondingly, a theory of educational formation that takes work as its point of departure has never been developed within the Western tradition, although numerous proposals have been made. At the most, it would suffice to assert that work, or, more frequently, vocational training, is the equivalent of general education. In contrast, education and educational formation in the countries formerly belonging to Comecon were geared to polytechnic education and formation. The goal was to situate work as the concrete expression at the centre of education and formation. While in Western considerations of education, this was relegated to a marginal position, in the theoretical reflections and in attempts to put these into practice in Eastern European countries, it was allocated a central position. It can therefore be assumed that in both West and East Europe differing conceptualisations of work have developed. This thesis is to be examined in the following.

Eight statements are raised that relate especially to the evaluation of, or to the attitude towards, work respectively. These statements have been posed in the same form in research by the department of Educational Sociology of the former Academy of Pedagogical Sciences of the GDR, from the end of the 1970s onwards. They were initially adopted in the Berlin study and, later, in the international comparative research relating to the young in Central and Eastern Europe. Following is the wording of these statements:

1. Without work, life would certainly be meaningless.
2. Without work, one can hardly obtain money, one would not be able to afford very much.
3. One should try to be able to live contentedly even without work.
4. One simply needs work to lead an orderly life.
5. The main thing is that besides work, there is enough time and leisure for oneself and one's hobbies.
6. The main thing is having work which pays very well.
7. The main thing is having an interesting occupation which corresponds with one's own inclinations.
8. The main thing is to succeed in one's occupation. That brings the respect of others, lets one get on in life.

Results

The data for this research were collected at two separate junctures. The first extended from October 1991 to April 1992, and the second from October 1992 to April 1993. During the first period, interviews were undertaken in East and West Berlin, Frankfurt-on-Oder, Slubice, Prague, Warsaw and Ioannina. During the second period, samples from Bratislava, Budapest, Sofia and Corfu were added to those of the first set. During both periods, samples of about six hundred students from classes seven to ten, that is, of young people between the ages of thirteen and sixteen, were taken in all localities. The samples included more or less equal numbers of male and female students. They also always included a slightly larger number of younger, and a slightly smaller number of older, young people. In order to test the validity of the assumption that in the various countries differences in attitudes towards or in the evaluation of work have developed, the mean values of each item for the country samples were established (see Table 1):

Table 1

Results of interviewing young people in various Eastern and Central European countries on the value of work – 1992 (mean values)

Item	Total	Ioan	Corfu	Mosc	E.Berl	W.Berl	Prag	Frank	Slub	Wars	Sofi	Bratis	Buda
1. W'out wk, life meangl.	2.0	1.9	1.9	1.9	2.2	2.3	2.2	2.1	1.8	2.1	1.9	1.8	2.4
2. W'out wk, no money	1.9	2.1	2.1	2.0	1.7	1.8	2.2	1.6	1.8	1.9	1.9	2.0	2.1
3. W'out wk, no happyn.	3.1	2.4	2.6	3.9	2.9	2.7	3.2	2.8	3.1	3.3	3.0	3.4	3.5
4. Wk/ord. life	2.1	2.1	2.1	2.0	2.2	2.2	2.3	1.9	1.9	2.1	2.0	2.0	3.0
5. Leisure	1.5	1.7	1.6	1.6	1.6	1.5	1.4	1.4	1.4	1.3	1.4	1.3	1.6
6. Good income	2.3	2.6	2.5	2.1	2.5	2.5	3.1	2.1	1.8	1.7	1.9	2.7	2.8
7. Inter.occ.	1.6	1.8	1.7	1.6	1.8	1.9	1.5	1.8	1.5	1.3	1.5	1.5	1.6
8. Success	1.9	1.7	1.7	1.9	2.3	2.4	1.9	1.9	1.9	1.8	1.7	1.8	2.1

The differences among the mean values are not particularly large with regard to single items. Nevertheless, the system differences among the samples are all of the significance of a per cent level or even higher. At the level of single items, a highly significant difference in the attitude to work among the countries included in the interviews can be assumed to be discernible. For a number of the cities, the same questions had already been posed in 1991. The results of these interviews are listed in Table 2.

Table 2

Results of interviewing young people in various Eastern and Central European countries on the value of work – 1991 (mean values)

Item	Total	Ioan	Mosc	E.Berl	W.Berl	Prague	Frank	Slub	Wars
1. W'out wk, life meangl.	2.0	1.9	1.9	2.2	2.4	2.0	2.1	1.8	2.0
2. W'out wk., no money	1.8	2.1	1.8	1.7	1.7	1.7	1.7	1.8	2.0
3. W'out wk, no happyn.	3.0	2.4	3.7	3.0	2.6	2.9	3.0	3.3	3.3
4. Wk/ord. life	2.0	2.0	1.8	2.1	2.2	2.0	2.1	1.9	1.9
5. Leisure	1.5	1.7	1.6	1.5	1.5	1.3	1.5	1.4	1.3
6. Good income	2.3	2.6	2.1	2.5	2.5	2.8	1.7	1.7	2.8
7. Inter.occ.	1.6	1.8	1.6	1.7	1.9	1.4	1.7	1.5	1.3

Comparison of Tables 1 and 2 reveals an astonishing result: although the interviews from 1992 include four extra samples, the mean values for the entire sample are almost identical during both periods. This can be regarded as an indicator of very similar evaluations of the attitudes included by us in questions in all Eastern and Central European countries or, if the samples in the same countries at differing times are examined, of a relatively stable attitude among the interviewees. This second assumption is also confirmed by demonstrating that in differentiating between the first and second investigation periods, with each young person taking part in both enquiries, in something less than fifty per cent of all items no difference whatsoever could be established. Greater shifts in the form of a more negative evaluation of work were present only in the sample from Prague. Most cross-sectional differences in the other samples lie close to zero. Thus there is a concordance between the correlations of survey periods one and two, as the coefficients demonstrate, being all highly significant. The coefficients vary between 0.20 for the following statements:

- without work, one can hardly obtain money, one would not be able to afford very much.
- the main thing is that besides work, there is enough time and leisure for oneself and one's hobbies.

and 0.48 for

- the main thing is having work that pays very well.

With such a background, it is worth casting a glance at the emphasis of single attitudes in the samples, in which the question is posed as to whether anything like a ranking series of the samples exists, with regard to the emphasis of attitudes (see Table 3).

Table 3

Ranking series of samples for the attitudes to work.

	W'out work, life meangl.	W'out wk, no money	W'out wk, no happyn.	Wk/ord. life	Leisure	Good income	Inter.occ	Success
Sofia	3	5	6	5	5	3	2	2
Slubice	1	4	7	1	6	2	3	7
Warsaw	7	6	9	6.5	1	1	1	4
Frankfurt	8	1	4	2	3	5	10	9
Bratislawa	2	9	10	4	2	10	4	5
Corfu	4	10.5	2	6.5	9	8	8	1
Moscow	5	7	12	3	10	4	6	6
Ioannina	6	8	1	8	12	9	11	3
E. Berlin	9	2	5	9	11	7	9	11
W. Berlin	11	3	3	10	7	6	12	12
Prague	10	12	8	11	4	12	5	8
Budapest	12	10.5	11	12	8	11	7	10

The sequence of the samples in Table 3 was assigned on the basis of cross-sectional ranking. In this manner, interesting correlations not obvious in the previous presentations can be discerned. It can be expected that the values of samples drawn from the same countries lie close together in this presentation. This is true of Warsaw and Slubice, of Corfu and Ioannina, somewhat surprisingly for East and West Berlin but not for Frankfurt-on-Oder and East Berlin. In Berlin in particular, it seems that there is something like a 'metropolitan effect' that overrides all others. In this consideration, the case of Berlin is not a persuasive example for testing system differences. Furthermore, it becomes apparent that the supposition set up at the beginning, according to which something like a system effect regarding the value of work might be proved, does not appear to be valid. Between East and West Berlin, there does seem to be a conceptual equivalence. The ranking of the samples from Corfu, Ioannina and West Berlin lie between those of the former socialist countries. Samples made in the former Comecon countries achieve a ranking that either signals the highest degree of assent to an attitude to work incorporated in the items (Sofia, Slubice, Warsaw), or demonstrates the highest degree of scepticism (Budapest, Prague). It is interesting that there is a considerable difference between Prague and Bratislava. As with all other results, this can be interpreted in line with the assumption that cultural differences between the various samples are highly effective. This, at least, seems to have a greater effect than is the case in the differences in systems. The difference between Prague and Bratislava in particular seems to confirm this supposition. Problems are presented, however, if results of this kind are discussed with relation to their contents. As all that is asked is whether there are differences and furthermore whether these differences are statistically significant, these results can only be confirmed, they cannot be interpreted. The 'etic' perspective, which has directed evaluation up until now, cannot, in principle, allow more. If one wants to know more of the configuration of attitudes, another approach must be suggested.

In a subsequent step, explorative factor analyses have been carried out for both periods of inquiry. The goal of this test was to discover whether the different samples display a similar dimensionalisation of the items relating to work for which the students in schools provided answers.

Tables 4 and 5 provide an overview of the results:

Table 4

Attitudes to work among young people of Central and Eastern Europe (Results of explorative factor analysis) First Enquiry

Item	Total		Moscow		E. Berlin			W. Berlin		Prague			Warsaw	
	Fak1	Fak2	Fak1	Fak2	Fak1	Fak2	Fak3	Fak1	Fak2	Fak1	Fak2	Fak3	Fak1	Fak2
1. W'out wk, life meangl.	.73		.75		.68		.69	.73			.77			
2. W'out wk, no money	.60		.58		.54			.61						.71
3. W'out wk, no happyn.	-.58		-.64		-.64				.55	-.53			-.55	
4. Wk/ord. life	.60		.80		.57			.63			.69		.68	
5. Leisure		.62		.5			.69		.62			.72		.58
6. Good income		.54		.71		.81			.68		.84			.64
7. Inter.occ.		.67					.75		.74			.78		.70
8. Success		.62		.68		.81		.67			.70			.69

The data in Table 4 reveal an interesting perspective. All the samples from former Comecon countries display the same results with regard to the first factor. (In Prague, the weighting of this second item comes out as lower than .50. It amounts to .45. For this reason, the city is not included in Table 4.) The four items mirror an opinion of work that can be summarised as the belief that life without work is meaningless, that work is necessary in order to be able to lead an orderly life, that without work one can never be happy and without work one cannot obtain money. West Berlin proffers another image. The item according to which one can never be happy without work is eliminated and replaced by two items, according to which one must earn a lot of money and achieve success in one's occupation. Thus, while in the former Comecon countries a work concept in which personal happiness is linked to work prevails, in West Berlin a largely instrumental attitude to work dominates. This corresponds closely with other studies of the attitude to work of young people in the Federal Republic of Germany (Brock and Otto-Brock 1992:360). The result demonstrates that, contrary to the assumption of conceptual equivalence between East and West Berlin just formulated, it cannot be proven. It does however appear to be present quite clearly among the successor states to the former Comecon. To this extent, the mean-values comparison should not have been made. The conception of work does appear to differ at the level of system between the Eastern and Western samples.

An examination of the other four items offers no such homogeneous picture. Therefore, in this instance, we shall dispense with an interpretation. It is typical that, with regard to the former Comecon countries, solutions involving more than two factors result only in the remaining four items being divided between two factors.

By the time of the second period of inquiry, some changes had taken place (see Table 5). With two exceptions (Moscow and Warsaw: two-factor solution), the other samples result in three-factor solutions. However, more samples were included from now on in the analysis, either because the data record was complete (Ioannina) or because information on the cities was available for the first time. Changes in the factoral structure of the entire sample might result from such alterations. In principle, this is also true of the partial samples, for these, too, were partly newly formed. However, should there be repetitions, these might be particularly interesting because they would be the result of samples taken in two years, the one following on the other. Both in Moscow and Warsaw, the two-factor solution is confirmed. However, only in East Berlin and Warsaw does the make-up of the first factor remain consistent. Below the level of similar mean values, a grave change in the meaning attributed to work has occurred in many samples. It is possible to characterise them roughly by noting that increasingly a view more easily described as instrumental is replacing a view of work better formulated as humanistic. Together with Brock and Otto-Brock (1992:361), we can interpret the change as demonstrating that a growing number of young people in Eastern European countries are also becoming sceptical as to whether it is even possible to redeem the desire for self-realisation in work. The growth of such scepticism is especially apparent among male youths. In the former Comecon countries, a degree of disenchantment regarding the value of work is spreading among young people. What we have called 'risk' in the title of our paper is apparently related, in the formulation of the question pursued here, to a change in the conditions of the societal environment, to which youth begins to adapt itself. They discover that their view of work is no longer apt.

Table 5

Attitudes to work among young people from Central and Eastern European countries (Results of explorative factor analysis)

Item	Gesamt			Ioannina			Moscow		E. Berlin			W. Berlin		
	Fak1	Fak2	Fak3	Fak1	Fak2	Fak3	Fak1	Fak2	Fak1	Fak2	Fak3	Fak1	Fak2	Fak3
1. W'out wk, life meangl.	.72			.62			.63		.76			.82		
2. W'out wk, no money	.70			.80			.54		.55			.66		
3. W'out wk, no happyn.			.86			.78		.63	-.69					-.52
4. Wk/ord. life	.66				.56		.69	.61			.78			
5. Leisure		.72			.60					.79			.82	
6. Good income				.58				.69			.82			.70
7. Inter.occ.		.80		.81			.56			.84			.82	
8. Success						.63		.54			.74			.73

Item	Prague			Warsaw		Corfu			Sofia			Budapest		
	Fak1	Fak2	Fak3	Fak1	Fak2	Fak1	Fak2	Fak3	Fak1	Fak2	Fak3	Fak1	Fak2	Fak3
1. W'out wk, life meangl.	.77				.78	.68			.71				.75	
2. W'out wk, no money	.62				.63	.74			.71				.63	
3. W'out wk, no happyn.			.76	-.50				.81		.78			.66	
4. Wk/ord. life	.71					.63	.53			.71				
5. Leisure		.63		.63						.73			.71	
6. Good income			.74	.66		.63				.73		.77		
7. Inter.occ.		.80		.67			.85				.79			.79
8. Success		.61		.61			.77		.74					

The factor analyses reveal an astonishing similarity among the solutions in the various samples: with the exception of Ioannina, the following three items are unified in a single factor:

- that life without work is meaningless,
- that without work, one can never obtain money,
- that one needs work, in order to be able to lead an orderly life.

In the case of Ioannina, only the first two items are present. Furthermore, the Greek samples from Corfu and Ioannina display another peculiarity. In these cases, the key item is the second one. The most important aspect is therefore that without work one cannot obtain money. That is evident in the items joined in this factor, in which the connection between a good income and work is made. In all other samples, this item does not belong to the factor. In East Berlin and Warsaw, the item, according to which without work one can never be happy, also belongs to this factor.

If one considers the results of the factor analysis, an interpretation with regard to the content of the value of work, some results are at one extreme; characterised in East Berlin and Warsaw, according to which the value of work is derived from the idea of polytechnic edu-

cation and formation, and another extreme stems from Corfu and
Ioannina, with an instrumental view of work, in which is regarded as
necessary, in order to be able to earn money. This evaluation
demonstrates that attributions such as those described by Schreiber
(1992:166) to the effect that people from the former Eastern bloc
tend to conform to general values, which is expressed in a less critical attitude towards cars and to technology, cannot be maintained.
There is another attitude of differing dimensions to work and – it
may be added – to technology, which cannot be delineated along the
parameter 'more/less'. A further correspondence can be discerned
in most samples. The items which assert that

- the occupation must be interesting,
- one needs in addition to work, time for one's hobbies,

can be loaded onto a single factor. Beyond these common features, there
are a series of differences, which however will not be discussed here.

The explorative factor analysis has provided indications for similarities and differences among the various samples in the configuration of the attitudes relating to the value of work. It points to a
currently observable change in this point of view in Eastern and
Central European countries, as a year previously, results which were
divergent in some respects from these had been obtained. Explorative factor analysis provides a method for determining such differences and similarities. Moreover, one is positioned in the tradition of
the emic approach, or that of the indigenous constructs respectively.
At least as far as the conception of work is concerned, there appears
to be common ground among the samples from the Comecon successor states, which in some samples appears to be extended by
means of a cultural dimension, as the other results from Prague and
East Berlin suggest.

The disadvantage of the items employed can be perceived in the
fact that they all contain not a single question, but rather at least two.
Therefore, in the following an index construction will be developed
which is based more on inspection and decision, and does depart
from the classical procedure for index construction. For the items
employed above regarding the attitude towards work as well as for
eight further items, in which questions relating to everyday values –
which range from 'work' to 'assessments of the family' or 'friends' –
are contained, a correlation matrix was first developed, in which the
inter-correlations between the two interview periods were included.
For the entire sample of those who participated in both the first and
the second set of interviews, all the correlation coefficients were
shown to be particularly significant. In all, the attitudes toward work,
as demonstrated by the items, could be regarded as satisfactorily sta-

ble over both periods of interviews. As a result, the intercorrelation coefficients for all items on the value of work and everyday values were subsequently calculated.

From this matrix, two differing indices were formed. The following statement was used as a starting point for the first:

• the main thing is to get work which pays very well.

All other items whose correlation with this item was higher than 0.15 were included in the index. They were the items:

• In everyday life, good contacts are very important ... (0.20)
• Without work, one obtains no money ... (0.20)
• In everyday life, everything depends on money ... (0.27)
• In everyday life, everything depends on one's being able to learn to subordinate oneself ... (0.21)
• The main thing is to suceed in one's occupation ... (0.35)

Following the same pattern, the second index took as its starting point the statement:

• In everyday life, the important thing is work that satisfies.

The following items correlated to the requisite degree:

• In everyday life, the main thing is a harmonious family life (0.25)
• In everyday life, the main thing is to achieve something of societally useful (0.22)
• In everyday life, the main thing is to know a lot and be able to do a lot ... (0.22)
• Without work, life would certainly be meaningless. (0.18)
• One needs work, in order to be able to lead an orderly life (0.16)
• The main thing is to have an interesting occupation (0.15)

One of the conditions of the index construction was that no one item should be included in both indices. The initial items had therefore to be chosen in order that these conditions were fulfilled. The first of the indices so obtained was named INSAR (instrumental conception of work), because it gathered together all items in which money, success and work were viewed as means to other goals. The second index was named INTAR (integrated conception of work), because it gathered together all items in which work was viewed as an integral part of life and the everyday world. This index construction was designed on the basis of an etic approach. An evaluation in this tradition begins with a comparison of the samples (see Table 6).

Table 6

Attitudes to work of young people from Eastern and Central Europe
(Second period of interviews)

Index	Total	Ioan	Corfu	Mosc	E.Berl	W.Berl	Frank	Slubi	Wars	Prag	Bratis	Buda	Sofi
INSAR	13.6	14.4	14.3	13.2	13.9	14.2	12.1	12.3	12.3	15.3	13.3	13.3	15.1
INTAR	12.8	13.0	12.9	11.8	13.8	14.5	12.8	11.5	11.6	12.8	13.8	15.0	12.6

As the index INTAR contains an additional item, the values for this
index would be thought to have always turned out at least one point
higher in the case of registration of an identical intensity of approval
or rejection. In fact, the opposite is true. This indicates that the
approval of INTAR is greater than that of INSAR. Only in West
Berlin and in Bratislava does the difference in approval turn out to
be smaller than in the other cases. The mean values of the samples
from Ioannina and Corfu as well as from Slubice and Warsaw lie
close together; similarly this is true of East and West Berlin. Between
East Berlin and Frankfurt-on-Oder a greater discrepancy can be registered. The possibility of a 'metropolitan effect', already mentioned
above, appears once again. With regard to the two concepts of work,
the reply behaviour in the Polish sample is most consistent. The
rankings 2 and 3 are for INSAR and for INTAR, the rankings 2 and
1. In contrast, the ranking in Prague varies from 12 to 5. The comparison of the samples allows the perception of differences in behaviour cross-sectionally. Variations in the mean values of the samples
allow the assumption of a high significance for differences between
the samples. However, both here and at the level of individual items,
the qualification that reflections within the context of an etic
approach permit, only with difficulty, the delineation of reasons for
reply behaviour can be applied. This is especially true of the case of
mean value comparisons, as has been made up until now.

The perspective of the evaluation should therefore be altered once
again. In order to do so, the samples for which – in addition to the
cross-sectional investigations of two periods of interviews – longitudinal data can be obtained, are employed. As the research in Slubice
and in Frankfurt-on-Oder was carried out on the basis of another set
of questions, these two samples are also eliminated, although they
were quite adequate for the analytical criteria previously employed.

Table 7

Reliability coefficients for the indices INSAR and INTAR

Index	1991	Panel	1992	Panel	E.Berlin	W.Berlin	Warsaw	Prague
INSAR	.56	.62	.52	.58	.57	.61	.58	.48
INTAR	.59	.62	.56	.59	.50	.63	.63	.55

These reliability coefficients (see Table 7) are not particularly high, but they do achieve at least a satisfactory level. Subsequently, sets of multiple regression analyses were carried out, distinguished according to the two periods of interviews and also according to the panel samples at the level of single samples, in order to determine the size of influence on the goal variables INSAR and INTAR. Value concepts, personal qualities, school and family variables as well as biographical variables were fed in as independent variables. The results are presented in Figures 1 to 8. In each case, only beta values greater than 0.15 have been included in the presentations, in order to retain clarity.

Figure 1

Size of influence on INSAR (entire sample)

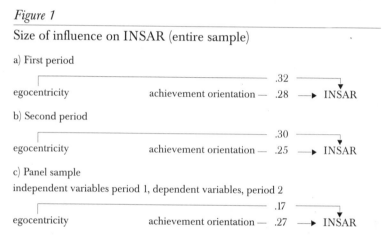

a) First period

egocentricity ——————————————————— .32 ——————┐
achievement orientation — .28 ——→ INSAR

b) Second period

egocentricity ——————————————————— .30 ——————┐
achievement orientation — .25 ——→ INSAR

c) Panel sample
independent variables period 1, dependent variables, period 2

egocentricity ——————————————————— .17 ——————┐
achievement orientation — .27 ——→ INSAR

In all three instances, there is an homogeneous picture. The value concept 'achievement orientation' and the personality characteristic 'egocentricity' influence the degree of an instrumental attitude to work. While in the two cross-sections, the personality characteristic always displays the greater influence, in the case of the panel samples, the reverse is true.

Figure 2

The size of influence on INTAR (entire sample)

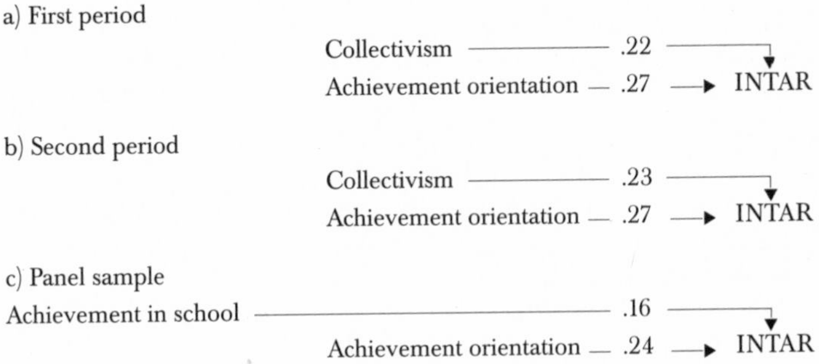

a) First period

Collectivism ——————— .22 ————⌐
Achievement orientation — .27 ——▶ INTAR

b) Second period

Collectivism ——————— .23 ————⌐
Achievement orientation — .27 ——▶ INTAR

c) Panel sample

Achievement in school ————————————————— .16 ————⌐
Achievement orientation — .24 ——▶ INTAR

In this instance, too, a similar result is obtained for the two periods of interviewing. Only the results of the panel sample deviate. Exactly as in the case of INSAR, there is, in all three calculations an achievement orientation influence. Also in each instance, it is the strongest. In addition, there is a strong attitude to collectivism influence in both the cross-section samples. As this is a case of occasional samples, that differ in the country samples, the second result can be regarded as a replication investigation. It appears to be a matter of a stable relationship, that should, in the majority of samples, produce replication. In the panel sample, it also becomes apparent that schooling has an influence as far as the degree of integration of the attitude to work is concerned.

Up to now, the analysis has always remained within the framework of an etic approach. Only when the level of the individual samples is adopted, can the change to the emic approach previously announced be made. In the following, we present three examples.

Figure 3

Size of influence on INSAR (East Berlin)

a) First period

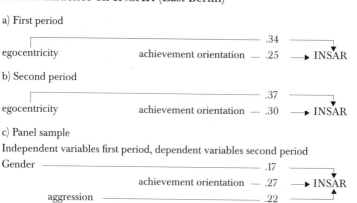

b) Second period

c) Panel sample

Independent variables first period, dependent variables second period

For the first and second periods of interviewing the result of the entire sample is replicated in the East Berlin samples. However, there is a change from the panel sample with a clear gender effect and a visible influence of aggressive behaviour at the first period to the instrumental attitude to work at the second period. This last result demonstrates particularly clearly that an instrumental attitude to work also displays undesirable features. But despite the increasing degree of change in East Berlin, the influence of the attitude to work remains stable.

Figure 4

Size of influence on INSAR (West Berlin)

a) First period

collectivism ——— .22 ———┐
achievement orientation — .27 ——→ INTAR

b) Second period

collectivism ——— .20 ———┐
achievement orientation — .40 ——→ INTAR
age ————————————————— -.16 ——┘

c) Panel sample

Independent variables period 1, dependent variables period 2

Family climate ——— .26 ———┐
collectivism ——— .16 ———┤
achievement orientation — .18 ——→ INSAR
anxiety for the future ——— .15 ———┤
age ————————————————— -.21 ——┘

While the results for periods one and two in East Berlin for the index INTAR are congruent with the results attained with the entire sample, at period two, in the case of the panel sample, the picture changes fundamentally, as an age effect becomes evident, to the effect that older young people approve sooner. Family climate now has the strongest influence. In second place is age, and achievement orientation is to be found only in third position. A further addition is 'anxiety for the future'. The network of relationships clearly increases in complexity and the influence of a variable which stands for one of the agencies of socialisation, namely the family, appears.

Figure 5

Size of influence on INSAR (West Berlin)

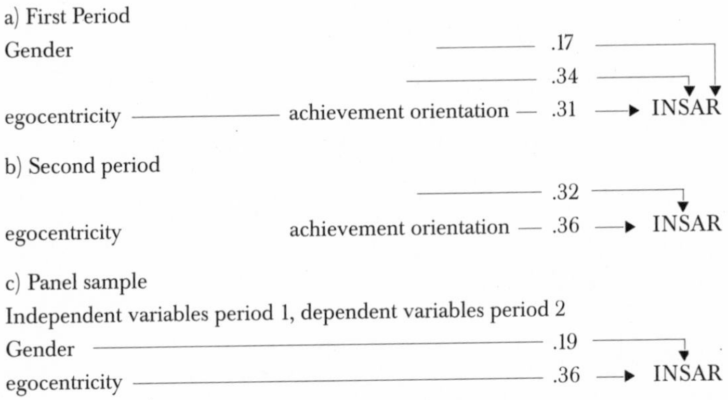

a) First Period

Gender ———————————————— .17 ————————————¬
       ———————————————— .34 ————————————¬
egocentricity ———————— achievement orientation — .31 ——▶ INSAR

b) Second period

       ———————————————— .32 ————————————¬
egocentricity   achievement orientation — .36 ——▶ INSAR

c) Panel sample

Independent variables period 1, dependent variables period 2

Gender ———————————————————————————— .19 ————————¬
egocentricity ————————————————————————— .36 ——▶ INSAR

In West Berlin, the influence of egocentricity is evidently the decisive factor in the case of an instrumental attitude to work. It is particularly clear in the case of the panel sample. Furthermore, a clear gender-based effect is demonstrable in that male youths hold this attitude to work particularly strongly.

Figure 6

Size of Influence on INTAR (West Berlin)

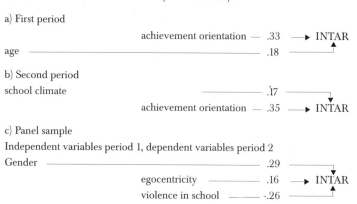

a) First period

achievement orientation — .33 ⟶ INTAR

age ——————————————— .18 ——

b) Second period

school climate ———————— .17 ———

achievement orientation — .35 ⟶ INTAR

c) Panel sample

Independent variables period 1, dependent variables period 2

Gender ——————————————— .29 ———

egocentricity ——— .16 ⟶ INTAR

violence in school ——— -.26 ——

In contrast with all other results presented up until now, at no point in West Berlin is there any indication of an influence of collectivism on the integrated perception of work. The difference INSAR/INTAR is lowest in this case, which is the result of an influence of 'egocentricity' in the panel sample. This could also have demonstrated when, in period two, not only beta values greater than 0.15, but that all signifi-cant beta values were included. It appears as if, quite independently of its form, work in West Berlin is not rated particularly positively.

Figure 7

Size of influence on INSAR (Prague)

a) Period 1

——————————————— .36 ———

egocentricity   achievement orientation — .15 ⟶ INSAR

individualism ———— .18 ——

b) Period 2

——————————————— .24 ———

egocentricity   achievement orientation — .19 ⟶ INSAR

individualism ———— .21 ——

c) Panel sample

Independent variables period 1, dependent variables period 2

——————————————— .20 ———

egocentricity   achievement orientation — .15 ⟶ INSAR

school achievement ——————————— -.18 ——

In Prague the previously established combination 'egocentricity' – 'achievement orientation' is expanded by means of the component 'individualism'. Together with the negative influence of school achievement becoming apparent in the panel sample, the negative attitude to this type of work in the Comecon successor states thus becomes more visible. Perhaps one could paraphrase it most easily with the conception of work that is associated with those countries in which upward mobility is often achieved by employing one's elbows.

Figure 8

Size of influences on INTAR (Prague)

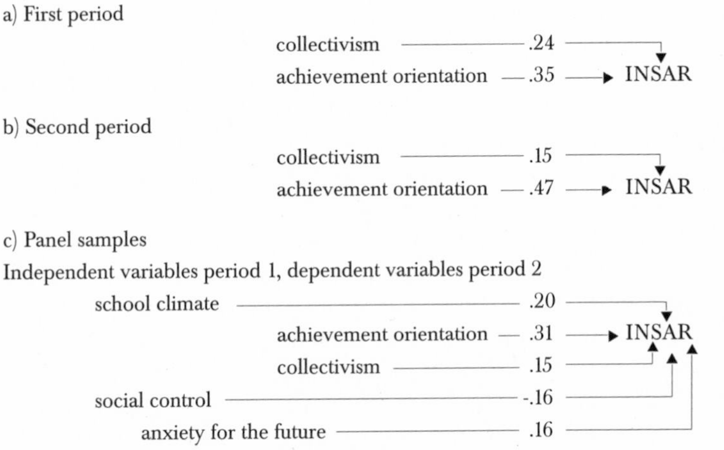

a) First period

collectivism ——————— .24 ———┐
achievement orientation — .35 ——→ INSAR

b) Second period

collectivism ——————— .15 ———┐
achievement orientation — .47 ——→ INSAR

c) Panel samples

Independent variables period 1, dependent variables period 2

school climate ————————————— .20 ——┐
achievement orientation — .31 ——→ INSAR
collectivism ————— .15 ——┘
social control ————————————— -.16 ——┘
anxiety for the future ——————— .16 ——┘

For Prague, once again a picture appears which is to be expected for the second index in the Comecon successor states. At both periods one and two, in the cross-sectional data there is the influence of 'achievement orientation' and 'collectivism'. In the panel samples additional influences become apparent. These demonstrate that 'school' and 'family' participate in the development of this conception of work among youth. At the same time, it becomes clear that 'anxiety for the future' also has an effect in this direction.

Should one try to make a resumé of this last evaluation, it is primarily apparent that the similarity of the values between West and East Berlin, which was noted above, can be traced to various causes. A somewhat positive attitude in East Berlin to the type of work comprised in the second index, is contrasted with a rather more negative conception of this type of work in West Berlin. Furthermore, it can be shown that there is a clear system effect for this second type, which points to similarities within Eastern European countries. This could also be demonstrated, if further samples from Eastern Europe were included for period two. In contrast, a negative attitude to work reveals itself in West Berlin. In the index INSAR, differences of this kind are not visible; they are demonstrable only in INTAR. It appears that the polytechnic education and formation in the former countries of Comecon have achieved success at the level of system, with regard to the value of work.

Summary

In a period of change, such as is currently taking place in Eastern Europe, the basis for attitudes towards work has remained largely stable, as we have been able to demonstrate with selected samples. Differences in the degree of emphasis of the attitudes are not generated by differences in the configuration of attitudes. In comparison with a Western European sample, the importance of this differentiation becomes clear, for the reverse is true in this instance, according to which similarities in the degree of emphasis of attitudes are not generated by similarities in their configuration.

Thus it becomes clear that, as we have already noted, what is meant by the term 'risk' in the title of the paper is to be found in changes in the social environment. Young people in the Comecon successor states look for a type of work and must learn that work is a very rare good, that is, they are threatened by unemployment, although, to a greater degree than youth in the West, they regard work as a condition for life being worth living.

The result is of particular interest for educational science for yet another reason. It can be shown that the value attitudes acquired during primary or early socialisation display a high degree of stability even in times of radical social change, which reflects on the effects of the agencies involved in socialisation. In contrast, adaptation at the level of the degree of emphasis of attitudes occurs at a much faster rate. It would undoubtedly be an error to regard the latter as the only interesting element. Many of the comparative studies based in East and West Europe need to be reanalysed in the light of the result presented here.

References

Behnken, I. et al. (1991), *Schülerstudie '90. Jugendliche im Prozeß der Vereinigung*, Weinheim.

Boehnke, K. and Merkens, H. (1994), "Methodologische Probleme des Ost-West-Vergleichs am Beispiel der Wertforschung zu Kollektivisums und Individualismus', in *ZSE*.

Brezinka, W. (1969), 'Über Absicht und Erfolg in der Erziehung', in *Zeitschrift für Pädagogik* 15, 245-72.

Brock, D. and Otto-Brock, E.-M. (1992), 'Krise der Arbeitsgesellschaft oder Entmythologisierung der Arbeit? Wandlungstendenzen in den Arbeitsorientierungen Jugendlicher im 20- bzw. 30-Jahres-Vergleich', in H. Klages, H. J. Hippler and W. Herbert (eds), *Werte und Wandel. Ergebnisse und Methoden einer Forschungstradition*, Frankfurt, 352-72.

Chinese Culture Connection (1987), 'Chinese Values and the Search for Culture-Free Dimensions of Culture', in *Journal of Cross-Cultural Psychology*, vol. 18, 143-64.

Engel, U. (1992), 'Risk Analysis in Longitudinal Youth Research', in W. Meus, M. de Goede, W. Knox and K. Hurrelmann (eds), *Adolescence, Careers, and Cultures*, Berlin, 201-15.

Hagan, J. (1991), 'Destiny and Drift: Subcultural Preferences, Status Attainments and the Risks and Rewards of Youth', in *American Sociological Review*, vol. 56, 567-82.

Hofstede, G. (1980), *Culture's Consequences: International Differences in Work-Related Values*, Beverly Hills.

Jaufmann, D. and Kistler, E. (1992), 'Sekundäranalyse zum internationalen Vergleich von Technikakzeptanz, Technik als Wert – Technik und Werte', in H. Klages, H. J. Hippler and W. Herbert (eds), *Werte und Wandel. Ergebnisse und Methoden einer Forschungstradition*, Frankfurt, 310-32.

Jugendwerk der Deutschen Shell (edited) (1992), *Jugend '92. Lebenslagen, Orientierungen und Entwicklungsperspektiven im vereinigten Deutschland*, 4 vols, Hamburg.

Kohlberg, L. (1981, 1984), *Essays on Moral Development*, vols 1 and 2, San Francisco.

Luhmann, N. (1973), *Zweckbegriff und Systemrationalität*, vol. 12, Frankfurt.
— (1985) *Soziale Systeme*, 2nd edn, Frankfurt.

Malpass, R. S. and Poortinga, R. (1986), 'Strategies for Design and Analysis', in W. J. Lonner and J. W. Berry (eds), *Field Methods in Cross Cultural Research*, Beverly Hills, 47-83.

Merkens, H. (1990), 'Vorüberlegungen zu einem Konzept der Arbeit', in H. Geissler (ed.), *Neue Aspekte der Betriebspädagogik*, Frankfurt, 33-51.

Piaget, J.(1973), *Das moralische Urteil beim Kinde*, Frankfurt.

Schefold, W. and Hornstein, W. (1993), 'Pädagogische Jugendforschung nach der deutsch-deutschen Einigung', in *Zeitschrift für Pädagogik* 30, 909-30.

Schreiber, K. (1992), 'Sind die Bundesdeutschen, die jüngeren Altersgruppen zumal, "Technikfeinde"?' in H. Klages, H. J. Hippler and

W. Herbert (eds), *Werte und Wandel. Ergebnisse und Methoden einer Forschungstradition*, Frankfurt, 147-67.

Schütz, A. (1971), *Das Problem der Relevanz*, Frankfurt.

–– (1974), *Der sinnhafte Aufbau der sozialen Welt*, Frankfurt.

Schwartz, S. H. (1992), 'The Universal Content and Structure of Values: Theoretical Advances and Empirical Test in Twenty Countries', in M. Zanna (ed.), *Advances in Experimental Social Psychology* 25, 1-65.

Smith, P. B. and Bond, M. H. (1993), *Social Psychology Across Cultures. Analysis and Perspectives*, New York.

Chapter 5

School Reform between the Dictatorships?

Pedagogics and Politics during the Early Years in the Soviet Occupation Zone of Germany

Gert Geißler

Reflecting the increased importance now being attached to various patterns of interpretation and to research interests, school reform in the Soviet Occupation Zone (SBZ) can be seen as forming a link between two periods of dictatorship, and between two totalitarian systems. This contrasts with the representation from the German Democratic Republic (GDR), by now historical, whereby school reforms were seen as one aspect of the 'antifascist-democratic upheaval'. Conditions in the SBZ can perhaps be more accurately understood if we assume the existence of a tension between the democratic and the dictatorial approaches, a tension that, as a relationship between reforming changes and the adverse reaction of power politics, left its imprint on pedagogics too. In the following text I shall endeavour to identify suitable points of reference to support this assumption, which resulted primarily not in a history of dictatorship or of heroic revolution, but in a social history, and a history of conflict between pedagogues.

Democratic of Dictatorial Socialism?

To a certain extent the theoretical and political tensions that were encountered in the immediate postwar years regarding the constitution of the future political system, can also be identified in the controlling bodies of the SED (Socialist Unity Party of Germany). A remarkable debate took place on 24 and 25 October 1946 at the 6th Conference of the Executive Committee of the SED. Although this party had, in April 1946, stated its objective to be 'the seizure of political power by the working class',[1] no agreement had yet been reached on how this power should be defined. Anton Ackermann,[2] the party's leading cultural policymaker, stated his view that dictatorship was a particularly Soviet phenomenon. In the USSR the working class 'acquired power under a special set of circumstances' and consequently its exercise of power assumed 'special forms too'. In contrast with the USSR, in Germany the working class forms the majority of the population, and its party has an opportunity of 'achieving power by democratic means' and of 'also continuing to exercise power by democratic means'.[3] Efforts to continue the development of Marxism, which must be regarded as an international science, one must 'refer to Marx and Engels, Liebknecht and Bebel, Plechanov, Kautsky, Hilferding, Lenin and Stalin'.[4] One of the greatest errors perpetrated by the KPD (Communist Party of Germany) was its attempt to mechanically adapt Soviet experiences to a completely different set of circumstances in Germany. This error was not rectified for many years and was partly responsible for the 'defeat of the working class in 1933'.[5] It would be 'the start of something extremely dangerous' if discussions were to take place here and there within the party about any deviation from the basis provided by the new political approach of 1945.[6] With these remarks, although made within the framework of Communist political theory, Ackermann clearly disassociated himself from the forms in which power was being exercised in the USSR, proposing instead the theoretical and political independence of his party and reacting to signs that were already apparent of a Stalinist tendency within the SED.

Otto Grotewohl, a former social democrat who had previously served as minister of education in Brunswick, and had by now become one of the two party chairmen of the SED, described Ackermann's remarks as 'excellent'.[7] He too regarded the 'very bloody and brutal dictatorship in Russia' as a product of a particular set of historical conditions, as a historically unique, transitional act.[8] Richard Weimann,[9] a former cultural policymaker with the Social Democrats and now one of the two heads of the Department for Schools and Education in the Cultural Department of the Central Secretariat of the SED, described these ideas about dictatorship as 'calamitous', and stressed that the party's policy should be based on 'the general theses of humanity, human rights, democracy'.[10] Among the speakers, Paul Wandel,[11] formerly a member of the leadership cadre of the KPD and by this time President of the German Central Administration for Education (DZfV) that was set up in August 1945, was the only speaker whose views differed significantly, although he too admitted that many of the aspects that had been inevitably intro-duced by military force[12] could not simply be adopted as they were.

However, 'whether the people like it or not', the supremacy of the working class would nevertheless be a dictatorship.[13] In establishing this supremacy 'there would be a very bitter struggle', even though it had majority backing.[14] Why was it that Wandel's views became established, rather than those of Ackermann? What explanation can be found for the fact that educationalists who had sustained democ-ratic ideas even under the conditions imposed by the National Social-ist state would subsequently associate themselves with a system which, from 1946 onwards, bore the stigma of 'Nazism painted red'?[15] Did the presence of pedagogues with political origins that were not communist but mainly social democratic, and who occupied posi-tions of some responsibility, figures such as Hans Ahrbeck,[16] Heinrich Deiters,[17] Robert Alt,[18] Ernst Marquardt,[19] Ernst Hadermann,[20] Fritz Rücker,[21] Max Kreuziger,[22] Hans Schallock[23] and Ernst Wildange,[24] provide a guarantee that the rule of force to which schools were also subjected after 1945 could be ruled out, or that dominance, were it to emerge, could be avoided? What explanation can be found for the fact that a small group of KPD functionaries in the Soviet Occupation Zone, primarily consisting of Paul Wandel, Hans Siebert,[25] Walter Wolf[26] and Wilhelm Schneller,[27] were able to succeed in imposing their views on educational policy in the early days of the SBZ? How could a reform of the school system in the SBZ take place which, despite its clearly defined programme, implying in real terms a process of democratisation, nevertheless failed to produce political freedom?

Initial Motives and Hopes

Society in twentieth-century Germany has been marked by a war, National Socialism and another war, and it was not only Communist educational and social reformers who saw an urgent need for radical changes in the structure of that society. With the best of intentions, but in some cases with reservations too, they sought to achieve a fun-damental reorganisation of society and to produce a school system that would reflect this development, under the popular slogan 'Never again war and fascism'. Radical democratic structural reforms[28] met with a response among the workers, the rural population and some sections of the middle classes. There was a widespread acceptance of the concepts of a command economy and socialist ideas, especially among the working classes. Communists and Social Democrats, and even Christian Democrats, felt that the capitalist economic system

was incompatible with the vital national and social interests of the
German people, and that 'capitalist efforts to safeguard profits and
hold on to power' should not be the objective nor the subject of a
new social and economic order.[29] For some, the immediate postwar
period was not one of collapse but of liberation, and in this general
mood of a new era, socialist hopes were intensified, resulting in a
kind of revolutionary romanticism, although the machinations of
power politics were also evident. At that stage in the SBZ no one
could be certain whether demilitarisation, denazification, decarteli-
sation and democratisation would lead to a revival of the evolutionary objectives of 1918 or to a Soviet-style society.[30]

Traditional Communists had, of course, every reason to expect to
be able to monopolise the new social order under the Soviet occupation, although these expectations were somewhat cautious and
within a timescale as yet undefined. However, many of the Social
Democrats who had merged with the Communists in April 1946 to
form the SED had taken the promises of democracy made by the
former KPD to imply that their ideas would also be incorporated in
the establishment of this new social order, and that social revolution
and reform would take place in consultation with the people as a
whole. Motivated by their Christian and liberal beliefs, leading
figures in the other authorised parties, in the teachers' trade union
that was dominated by former Social Democrats, in the *Kulturbund*
(cultural association)[31] and in other organisations in the SBZ, also
believed that they would be able to assert their own ideas.

At that time no one knew which side would gain the upper hand,
or whether a synthesis was possible between the different social
camps regarding the structure of society, the political system and
education in Germany and in the Soviet Occupation Zone. Answers
to this question basically depended upon the policy to be adopted
towards Germany by the victorious powers and upon the continued
co-operation between these countries. Political circles in the SBZ
and in the SED leadership could not be sure of the strategic political
intentions of the Western powers or those of the USSR.[32] No one
knew whether the Soviet occupying forces would support German
Communists at any price in the years to come, and under what circumstances a united but neutralised Germany might be established
in the interests of Soviet security. More recently, developments in
Soviet foreign policy and within the Comintern had shown that
Communist parties could indeed be sacrificed to the overriding
interests of the USSR. Under such conditions, for Communists and
Social Democrats alike, the establishment of the Socialist Unity
Party, the SED, was an experiment whose outcome depended on
developments on the global political stage. By 1946 it was already

clear that this new political system contained the potential to impose its dominance by force, and this became evident with the introduction of this experiment and the actions of the occupying force when dealing with anti-Soviet opposition to the fusion of the two parties.

The Pedagogic Consensus

The political views of those educationalists from the social democratic side who had joined the SED but who were less committed to party politics, were largely determined by the possibilities that would be open to them for implementing planned reforms as a result of making a common cause with, and eventually joining forces with the Communists. By the late summer of 1945 it was already apparent that preliminary decisions on educational policy had been made in the SBZ, favouring educational reform, for which a considerable consensus existed among Communists and Social Democrats and which also had the support of the occupying power. Several left-wing social democratic pedagogues such as Robert Alt and Max-Gustav Lange[33] had already joined the KPD in 1945 for this reason. Among the education policy objectives that linked Social Democrats and Communists were the desire to denazify schools, both in terms of personnel and on an intellectual level, the abolition of educational privileges, the establishment of a standard national school system, the separation of school from church, and the provision of guarantees of equal opportunities for education, not only in a social and political sense but also encompassing the structure of the school system. All this was to take place under an egalitarian social order and in accordance with socialist principles. The political problems of the unification process notwithstanding, Communist and Social Democratic educationalists alike sought to adopt a new, common political direction, united by such factors as their shared concepts of pedagogic reform and the educational policy coalitions emanating mainly from the early days of the Weimar Republic, and their subsequent, common experiences under the National Socialist dictatorship.

For social democrat educationalists it seemed initially that unrestricted possibilities existed for structuring their theories and their programmes, and at first there were hardly any signs of change even after the merger between the KPD and SPD. A draft of educational policy programmes,[34] prepared in the autumn of 1945 by leading representatives of the SPD such as Heinrich Deiters, Max Kreuziger and Ernst Marquardt, proposed an educational reform with objectives such as 'education to encourage independent thought and judgement', 'respect for others' opinions', 'social solidarity with one's own people', 'friendship with other peoples', the 'idea of humanity as a whole'.[35] These pedagogues envisaged a form of education that, as formulated by Deiters, would enable its recipients to 'live in a democratic community, as free people in a free society, based on work, a sense of community and a love of peace.'[36] According to the SPD in December 1945, in its 'Guidelines to Educational Reform', a 'comprehensive, uniform school system, from kindergarten to university, would be appropriate' for such an education, satisfying not only social requirements but also meeting the needs of those with varying talents. The schools should be a 'cultural focus in place of social welfare'. They should also stimulate a 'desire for culture', should 'educate to promote a joyful creativeness' and should be imbued with cheerfulness and not by a barrack-room atmosphere.[37] These sentiments were similar to those expressed by Communist pedagogues. In a draft educational reform, Karl Sothmann[38] described the aim of such education as 'the formation of a human being who would be liberal-minded in thought and deed, and who would assume full responsibility for his acts and omissions'.[39]

Such definitions of the objectives of education formed the basis not only for public debate about reform, but also for the discussions that took place among academics and administrators.[40] They assumed a concrete form in October 1945 in the 'Call by the Central Committee of the KPD and the Central Committee of the SPD for democratic educational reform',[41] in April 1946 in the 'Principles and objectives of the Social Unity Party of Germany'[42] and in May/June of the same year in the largely identical laws by the Länder (states) on the 'democratisation of German school'.[43]

The School Commission of the SED[44] had submitted a draft education programme[45] as early as January 1947, revealing distinctly reformist aspects, with its basis in the efforts encapsulated by the 1946 education law to achieve a synthesis between those schools teaching by activity methods and those in which the emphasis was on learning by rote.[46] [47] In accordance with this draft programme children were to be encouraged to 'develop into independent personalities, capable of thinking for themselves and acting responsibly'. Children at such schools would be required to undertake serious work, but the teaching would be lively, arousing 'the creative independence of the pupils' and making the school a 'place that was full of the joy of living'. The involvement of teachers, parents and social organisations should enable the school to assume the structure of a community of companionship, serving as 'a focal point for urban and rural culture. The draft plan specifies autonomy for the pupils and the right of religious communities to provide religious instruction for young people of school age. All pupils should be given access to mankind's cultural assets, and in this respect, 'due attention should be given to religious culture in accordance with its significance'. For the final years at primary school the draft plan provided not only for obligatory, joint instruction in the core subjects but also for 'special group instruction for different aptitude groups', so that the 'differentiation in aptitude that has already begun' could be continued at secondary schools.[48]

Interrelations between Education Policy and Pedagogy

Up until the late summer of 1947 there was a remarkable interrelation between education policy and pedagogy in the SBZ. Provided that they were not suspected of having collaborated with the National Socialist system, anyone in the educational sciences that were established during the Weimar period was initially tolerated, although some at the universities were already in conflict with the new ruling powers, or were in dispute within their particular disciplines as a result of the structural re-evaluation of the educational sciences. As yet such educationalists were not being subjected to political pressures, and neither had the proponents of socialist and Marxist educational ideas, as the protégés of the occupying power and the SED, yet gained the upper hand.[49] This exceptional interim period was certainly not a result of the efforts of orthodox SED party functionaries, and during this time the occupants of teaching posts in German educational sciences were able to meet and debate a remarkably extensive educational programme.[50] They ranged from Theodor Litt,[51] Peter Persen, Hans Ahrbeck, Karl Trinks, Heinrich Deiters, Max Gustav Lange and Robert Alt, and also included the recently appointed university lecturers Albert Reble, Hans Herbert Becker, Hans Mieskes,[52] Hans Rössger and Karl Schrader and leading pedagogues such as Erika Hoffmann, Otto Karstadt, Paul Oestreich and Otto Tacke. An 'open discussion about educational legislation and the educational programme' was conducted until the autumn of 1947, 'involving specialists from every pedagogic direction, along with practical experts from different quarters'.[53] Although perhaps no more fertile, the discussions that took place about education during this interim period in the early days of the SBZ were perhaps as important in some respects as those that took place in the Weimar Republic. At least during this period of transition, intellectual dominance had not been gained by any particular scientific school or tradition, as was the case in the Western occupation zones, despite the breadth of discussion about school reform there, for example in the Wallenburg Commission.[54] Different pedagogic tendencies coexisted, united in their rejection of Nazi ideas about education: traditional supporters of the Herbartian elementary school, various reformist pedagogic tendencies that gave pre-eminence to the idea of school teaching by activity methods, proponents of the 'gymnasium' system with its extensive subject matter[55] and largely devoid of any pedagogic or psychological ambitions, social pedagogics determined by the church and charitable organisations, humanities-based pedagogics, sociological approaches to education, as well as fragmentary German Marxist pedagogics, and the Soviet view of pedagogics that was first sanctioned in 1948. Such diversity also produced variety in teacher training and the schools themselves. However, pedagogics linked specifically to various Christian denominations, and educational concepts based on private schools, were excluded from the discussions. The state system still provided conditions that favoured such relative pluralism. In 1946 the educational sciences were still receiving unprecedented support at an institutional level, at least in formal and structural terms,[56] with the introduction of pedagogic faculties at all universities in the SBZ. Although central administration of school policy had been strengthened, the Länder and provisional governments were still able to apply their own individual emphasis.[57] Teaching staff enjoyed rights of codetermination[58] that in practice were also utilised in the sense of a school management system based on collective responsibility. The teachers' union 'Lehrer und Erzieher' gave pedagogues an organisation that represented their interests,[59] and although it was a standardised body it did grant them codetermination. Although the teachers' associations of the Weimar Republic no longer survived, expert discussions were stimulated in the 'socialist teachers' working groups.[60] The groups known as the friends of the 'new school'[61] comprised parents from different backgrounds. The FDJ (Free German Youth movement) continued to act as a homogeneous, non-partisan youth organisation, whose children's associations incorporated various ideas about educational reform. All these various aspects were not just a democratic façade in the sense of the pseudo-public system that was subsequently set up, but formed an area in which heterogeneous forces were allowed to act, that were linked together organisationally in their efforts to achieve political and social reforms, on a basis of shared historical experience.

Initially the non-communists carried considerable weight among the various forces involved in educational policy; this was even true of the SED itself. The diversity of opinions about school policy and education extended to the SED, which by this time counted most leading pedagogues among its members. Although many of this party's members held positions in school administrations, in the teaching profession and in the trade unions, this failed to stifle complaints about the lack of political stability among their members and some officials, about the willingness to embrace anti-Soviet views and about bourgeois tendencies, especially among those administrative employees who were members of the party. Even in July 1948 Walter Ulbricht confirmed that 'our party is not yet the leading party of the working class', and that it demonstrated 'the same fluctuations' as those that existed 'within the working class and working people'.[62]

As far as educational policy was concerned, the cause of such possible 'fluctuations' could be found not least of all in the fact that, when it joined the SED, only a few members of the KPD had any professional background in education. Although the forces of occupation had been able to fill some of the most important positions in the education policy field, drawing on this small group of persons or on professional officials from the central party apparatus of the KPD, such personnel policy had its limitations. Unlike the SPD, with its established reputation in the areas of cultural and communal policy, the KPD, founded at the end of 1918, had been unable to develop a significant core of experts in the school system or in education as a whole in the years up to 1933. By 1945, for various reasons, the few leading figures that it could claim in the field of education policy, former deputies in the national and regional governments such as Clara Zetkin,[63] Edwin Hoernle,[64] Fritz Ausländer,[65] Theodor Neubauer,[66] and Ernst Schneller,[67] were no longer available. Instead there had been an influx of a much larger group into the SED and thus also in schools, school administrations, in teacher training and in the educational sciences, whose concepts of democracy and education had been moulded during the Weimar period by social democracy or through socialist political groups positioned somewhere between the KPD and SPD. Especially among pedagogues, this group accounted for a disproportionately large block within the new party. In the months leading up to the party conference that had resulted in the fusion forming the SED, the increase in SPD membership among teachers was far greater than that attained by the KPD.[68] Pedagogues such as Deiters and Petersen entered into the SED as SPD members. Moreover the SED benefited from the fact that it was represented in the pedagogic faculties primarily by academics with non-communist political backgrounds, and furthermore by members with the same sort of background who had confidence in the probity of politics. However, political strategy and tactics in the central party apparatus and in most of the ministries in the various state governments were largely dominated by experienced cultural officials of the KPD. Such officials, for who Siebert in particular served as prototype and ideologue from the autumn of 1947, derived their understanding of the school system, education and children primarily from their politics and from the principles of Leninist revolutionary theory. They accordingly regarded the school as an instrument of class domination, and the aim was to take it out of the hands of the former ruling class. In contrast, the majority of those responsible for educational matters in the SED had come from the SPD, and tended to the view that schools were above party politics, social class and strata, and should instead act as a counterbalance and should be structured accordingly.

Whereas the leading communists among the cultural officials of the SED regarded education and training as a means of producing 'protagonists in the class struggle', the numerous party members whose political origins went back many years and had their roots in socialist democracy, and were particularly well represented in school administrations, in teacher training and at the universities, considered their guiding principle to be the unhindered development of the personality. Those who held the view that future citizens should comply unquestioningly with the uniform social situation as stipulated by the party, contrasted with others who sought to maintain the rights of the individual, and the preservation of a social, intellectual and political plurality. Initially this divergence of views tended to be latent, and was overshadowed by the shared objectives that formed the basis of their ideas about educational policy.

The Reform Programme

In its programme and subsequent implementation, the school reform introduced in the SBZ in 1946 under these terms was one of the most decisive turning points in the history of German education. Notwithstanding the Weimar reforms, the traditionally divided school system was no longer to fulfil a selective role, and no further support was to be given through the school system to the maintenance of previous class distinctions in society as a whole. Consequently one of the distinctive features of school reform and democratisation in the SBZ from the very beginning was the rigorously authoritarian way with which it pursued the break not only with National Socialism, but also with the previous social order and the ruling classes that had arisen with it. From various announcements it was obvious that the intention was to commit the school system, through its structure, curriculum and spirit, to the creation of a new demilitarised Germany where social polarisations would be eliminated. A qualitative distinction in education through various different types of schools was rejected, along with a system in which the next generation was divided socially according to the financial pressures on parents. The concept of streaming according to ability was to be retained from the existing, traditional school structure, leading to specialisation for predetermined future vocations. Irrespective of wealth, beliefs, sex or social origin, each individual should receive a complete education in accordance with social requirements.

This reform programme arose out of the various factors within Germany that had created conflict in educational policy and on a wider social scale, and since the nineteenth century had led to a whole range of unfulfilled early liberal and democratic plans for school reform. The reformers had in mind in particular the planned reforms among elementary-school teachers, the Suevern draft school legislation, the plans linked with the revolutions of 1848 and 1918, the ideas put forward by the elementary teachers' associations, the terms of the Weimar constitution, the proposals by Johannes Tews, Georg Kerschensteiner and Fritz Karsen,[69] and the Austrian reforms of the 1920s.[70] Although they gave their political support to this programme, the Communists had contributed little of their own. Nowhere do we find the idea of polytechnic education as adopted by Marx but largely rejected in practice in Soviet schools.

In its structure, educational objectives and educational planning, schooling in the SBZ contrasted diametrically with that of the National Socialist state. At the insistence of the occupation forces, existing personnel were removed to such an extent that there was a genuine risk of being unable to provide the necessary teaching, and in contrast to the situation under the previous, National Socialist dictatorship, schools became the focus of political interest. Moreover, 'education' reacquired its standing, and a relatively complete overall reform concept was drawn up. The traditional three-way division of German schools that had been retained under National Socialism was abandoned and teaching acquired a far more material bias, especially in those fields of knowledge such as biology, history and German literature, which has been heavily subjected to Nazi ideology.

Despite a contemporary influence, the idea of comprehensive education in the early days of the SBZ did little to negate the traditions of the bourgeois German society. Instead it led to a modern synthesis of what had, intellectually, been widely proposed in the area of education reform in Germany, extending beyond purely conservative concerns about stability. Despite similarities with the comprehensive school models in Scandinavian and Anglo-Saxon countries, the educational programme retained its basic German tradition.[71] Of course there was state control of educational policy, and the system of qualification, using the *Abitur* (school leaving certificate) for the purposes of control and selection, was retained, along with the dual system of vocational training. Standardised education and the importance of a proper awareness of humanity remained familiar features. After sharing eight years of elementary education, pupils' equal education rights were terminated by 'selection according to aptitude'.

A Reversal of the Democratisation of Reformist Discussions

Such a very general linking of the programme with tradition appeared less important to the traditionalists in the Western zones, whose influence in educational policy was on the increase. Furthermore the fact that the reform of the school structure in the SBZ came closest to meeting the Allies' repeated demands in 1947[72] did not improve its low level of political acceptance in the West, or that pedagogues such as Petersen [73] should regard the school legislation of 1946 as the abolition of an already obsolete school organism, and consequently 'the fulfilment of pedagogic demands going back more than two generations'.

Moreover it became apparent that school reform was now motivated hardly at all by social or pedagogic considerations, but was being pursued almost exclusively for political reasons, as Germany became divided and at the same time drawn in to the global East-West confrontation and the uncompromising efforts by both sides to safeguard their own interests. Previous developments had been of a pluralist nature, against a background of a relatively open Soviet policy towards Germany, in response to international developments. It was more in the interests of the USSR to have a neutralised and demilitarised Germany, than the divided nation preferred by the Western Powers and leading politicians in the Western zones. The USSR pursued a dual strategy: on the one hand to achieve an overall German solution, but on the other, making appropriate preparations if this should fail. Consequently, educational policy in the SBZ was designed to be responsive to shifts in consensus as a consequence of developments within and between the various zones of Germany, while at the same time preparations were made to enable the SED to dominate school systems and the educational sciences.

The brief period during which a state system was allowed to evolve on a basis of antifascism and democracy ended in the autumn of 1947. The underlying basis for the objectives of school reform was associated with intellectual challenges, which several representatives of these reforms could have imbued with a considerable potential for both theoretically and historically based reasoning. However, from now on the realities of this reform were determined increasingly by the dictates of rigorous power politics and the intellectual conformity of the initially successful organisers within the SED, which was now well on the way to becoming the party of the state. In a situation characterised by growing international confrontation and the potential for imminent sociopolitical conflict in the SBZ, the SED undertook measures as its second party conference in September 1947 to consolidate and develop its structure, which it was now moulding even more emphatically into that of a Leninist 'party of struggle'.[74] In conjunction with the widespread replacement of personnel at all levels in school administrations, SED members applied their ideology with even greater vigour. Former Social Democrats no longer exerted any significant influence on the formulation of basic guidelines for school policy by the SED, which had previously been notable for a programme of compromise.

The Soviet occupation forces began to step up their campaign of repression against opponents or critics of the sociopolitical line in the SBZ, targeting not only former National Socialist activists but also members of the SED. As Siebert expressed it, a 'second phase' in the implementation of school reform began.[75] In September 1948 Wilhelm Pieck was able to report to the executive committee of the party that 'one could never again write' sentences such as the appeal to the KPD on 11 June 1945 and, given the approval of Marshall Zhukov himself, that there was no intention of 'forcing Germany to adopt the Soviet system'.[76] Wandel stated that the task was now to employ all the power available to the state in order to 'conduct the class struggle with determination', while Ackermann was already on the point of leaving the political scene, questioning whether the need that had arisen for a revolutionary approach still implied 'the eventual recognition of the possibility of a democratic path to socialism'.[77] It was in this way that the decision was finally made to adopt a dictatorial method exercising power.

The Parting of the Ways

As this new direction became apparent, some of the pedagogues no longer saw any future for themselves in the SBZ. Theodor Litt went to Bonn, Peter Petersen applied in vain for a teaching position in the West, Max-Gustav Lange obtained a position at the Free University in West Berlin, while others withdrew from active life. Hans Mieskes,[78] for example, tried to hold out in Jena. However, some of them did comply with the new situation, at least superficially, and in some cases with considerable vigour. A characteristic feature of these pedagogues was that they viewed the introduction of comprehensive schooling as the dismantling of traditional barriers to education, seeing it as a final breakthrough to the realisation of social democracy.[79]

Within the flexibility and differentiation allowed to comprehensive schools[80] they saw the possibility for achieving social equality, and for using the educational system to limit and eventually to abolish a system under which socially advantaged sections of society could perpetuate their privileged position through material possessions, irrespective of the existing political system. It was a fundamental tenet of the new schools that the traditional, popularly based form of education should be abolished and that all children should be given the kind of education that proletarians in the nineteenth century perceived as the privilege of élite social classes.

It was a weakness on the part of these pedagogues that they should be more preoccupied with this idea than with political plurality, or any concepts of pedagogic reform, or even their own original notions of a democratic internal school reform. Their view of the Weimar period included a belief that the overhaul of the traditional educational system by parliamentary means had been an extremely laborious process, and that such achievements were easily lost again. They also saw how this educational system was being successfully reinstated in other vocational fields. Whereas in the Western zones reformers such as Erwin Stein were able quite predictably to frustrate their plans, against the background of the existing political situation, while at the same time strictly respecting parliamentary democracy, another choice was open to pedagogues in the SBZ. Provoked initially by the policy imposed upon them by all the occupation forces, they decided in favour of a contradictory combination of egalitarian reform of the social structure, supported by authoritative political domination by an élite, and in the run-up to the establishment of the GDR they rejected social democracy in favour of social dictatorship. They considered such domination to be a merely temporary exercise of power and, as such, perhaps acceptable, if it could result in the abolition of economic domination that had repeatedly subjected sections of society to starvation, poverty and ignorance. Seen in this light, was not democracy itself a relative concept? Was political freedom only possible at that point where general social accomplishments had become reality? And would dictatorship itself not cease to exist once everyone was living under conditions of social equality and security?

As far as the science of education was concerned, these pedagogues were not prepared to acknowledge its claims for a special position in society. This area of the social sciences had done little to alert educationalists to the dangers of National Socialism. This aristocratic and autonomous professional group with its roots in German intellectualism had produced little in the way of an intellectual defence of democracy, eventually yielding with expectant detachment to the subsequent system. Thus tolerance and autonomy were inadequate guarantees for the survival of democratic pedagogics. And were those who had allowed themselves to be deprived of democracy through parliamentary means to be entrusted with it once again? What kind of historical awareness could they claim, if the evolution of this new society reduced the active opponents of national socialism to a politically meaningless minority? Was everything to be left to the opinion of the majority? After all that they had allowed to happen, were the German majority to be allowed to continue to make the decisions? Could the previous set of conditions, including those of the school system, be overthrown by words alone?

In the historical context such questions are understandable. Their answer in terms of power politics was, however, obvious. An élitist effort to communicate democracy and dictatorship, intellect and power, society and education was attempted anew, in vain, despairing of enlightenment. Science, including that of education, gives its affirmation of politics. Later it became evident that the entire system would have to be overthrown if the freedoms renounced in this way were to be regained.

Those pedagogues who witnessed the new beginning in 1945 encountered conflicts during the process, causing many of them to become disillusioned.[81] At the beginning of the 1960s Deiters confirmed privately in his notes[82] that Communism, and the dictatorship for which he himself felt partly responsible (32/2), would inevitably collapse (31/1). As a pedagogue he had failed to 'formulate the thesis of the interrelationship between politics and pedagogy in such a way as to prevent the possibility of the one being subservient to the other'(6). He had not examined the ground that he himself trod in 1945 in his belief in the probity of politics (3), had 'falsely assessed the internal possibilities of the SED' (26), and failed to realise that the antifascist-democratic system aimed at combating National Socialism 'could produce a different form of dictatorship' (30/1). Based on his basic democratic principles, and despite that fact that it was less efficient, he regarded a command in a republic as being morally superior to the 'dominance of monopolistic financial institutes and industrial associations', but admitted that, without some sort of counterbalance, such an economy would become despotic (317). He had become 'cured' of his 'trust in the creative powers of force' (17/1). In addition, his 'experience with the unbridled power of the state in matters of education' had led him 'back to pluralism' (39). The final, still illusory hope expressed by this emeritus was of an intellectualised and ethical socialism, intent on a conquest of the moral ground in a Germany reunited through a policy of détente.

One need not add anything to this lifetime's summing up of the subject of democracy and dictatorship.

Notes

1. Cf. 'Grundsätze und Ziel der Sozialistischen Einheitspartei Deutschlands vom 21. April 1946,' in: G. Uhlig and K.-H. Günther (eds), *Dokumente zur Geschichte des Schulwesens der Deutschen Demokratischen Republik,* Part I: 1945-1955 (Berlin-East, 1970), p. 207.

2. Anton Ackermann (1905-1973), textile worker, from 1926 member of the KPD, functionary and party theoretician, attended Moscow's Lenin School in 1930/31; underground work in Berlin from 1933 to 1935, followed by work in the KPD leadership in Moscow, played a leading role in formulating the KPD's programme and cultural policies, from April 1946 member and, temporarily, candidate of the Central Secretariat of the SED, member of the Politbureau of the SED Central Committee from July 1950 to April 1954.

3. Cf. Stiftung Archiv der Parteien und Massenorganisationen der DDR im Bundesarchiv (hereafter: SAPMO-BA), IV/2/01/10, Minutes of the 6th Meeting of the Party Executive, 24/25 October 1946, fol. 143: Speech by Ackermann. The discussion stood under the impression of the SED's electoral defeat in Berlin. Although tactical and propagandistic motives also emerged in the discussion, they pinpointed in my view basic theoretical and political differences of opinion. See also H.-J. Krusch, 'Neuansatz und widersprüchliches Erbe. Zur KPD 1945/46,' in: *Beiträge zur Geschichte der Arbeiterbewegung,* vol. 33, no. 5 (1991), p. 622, note 24, with a reference to W. Leonhardt's verdict; G. Dietrich, 'Ein Mitbürger der Vergangenheit, Gegenwart und Zukunft. Anton Ackermann,' in: ibid., no. 1, pp. 109ff.

4. See SAPMO-BA (note 3 above), fol. 141.

5. Ibid., fol. 140.

6. The original programmatic statement of the KPD of 11 June 1945 had proclaimed that 'it would be wrong to force the Soviet system upon Germany, as this path does not correspond to the current conditions of Germany's development.' Quoted in: *Dokumente zur Geschichte der SED,* vol. 2: 1945-1971 (Berlin-East, 1986), p. 12.

7. Cf. SAPMO-BA (note 3 above), fol. 171.

8. Ibid., fol. 186.

9. Richard Weimann (1890-?), commercial employee, member of the SPD, until 1933 director of the Educational and Cultural Department within the SPD Party Executive, underground work after 1933, member of the SED Party Executive from April 1946 to July 1950, from January 1949 in economic management.

10. SAPMO-BA (note 3 above), fol. 168.

11. Paul Wandel (1905-1995), machinist, member of the KPD from 1926, completed course at Moscow's Lenin School in 1931, Comintern functionary and political secretary of Wilhelm Pieck thereafter, from 1942 lecturer at the Comintern (Lenin) School, from 1944 member of a KPD Politbureau commission charged with drawing up an 'action programme' for the period after Hitler's fall, president of the Deutsche Zentralverwaltung für Volksbildung (DZfV) from August 1945, from 1949 to 1952 GDR Minister for People's Education.

12. SAPMO-BA (note 3 above), fol. 163.

13. Ibid., fol. 160.

14. Ibid., fol. 163.

15. This question has been raised again recently in a review by Benno Scholdt.

16. Hans Ahrbeck (1890-1981), studied in Leipzig, Giessen, and Göttingen, from 1929 a teacher at a private school for girls in Magdeburg, received his PhD. from Göttingen in 1925, Studienrat in 1926, Dozent in 1929, from 1930 professor at the Breslau Pedagogical Academy, in 1932 professor at the Halle Pedagogical Acad-

emy, from 1933 Studienrat in Magdeburg, in 1937 at the Studienseminar, denied Nazi Party membership, supported ministers of the anti-Nazi Protestant Bekennende Kirche as well as Jews and Communists, from 1945 work in the school administration, appointed Oberschulrat, from April 1946 professor of education at Halle-Wittenberg University, nominated by the provincial government as caretaker dean of the Pedagogical Faculty there, from March 1950 to autumn 1955 Dean of the Pedagogical Faculty, following its dissolution in August 1955, director of the Institute of Education until August 1957, made emeritus in January 1958 against the vote of the Philosophy Faculty.

17. Heinrich Deiters (1887-1966), Studienrat in Berlin, from 1919 member of the Bund Entschiedener Schulreformer, from 1920 member of the SPD, from 1924 director of a gymnasium in Höchst, from 1927 Oberschulrat in Kassel, forcibly retired in 1933, continued to teach in private schools and from 1942 worked for an unofficial press bureau, from September 1945 in charge of the Teacher Training Department in the DZfV, from October 1946 appointed professor of education at Berlin University, from 1949 Dean of the Pedagogical Faculty, member of many scholarly and cultural-political committees.

18. Robert Alt (1905-1978), studied science and philosophy at Breslau and Berlin from 1924 to 1927, became a member of the SPD in 1924, continued his studies from 1927 to 1929 at the Frankfurt Pedagogical Academy, after 1929 primary school teacher at the Karl-Marx School in Berlin-Neukölln, from 1933 to 1941 teacher at Jewish primary schools in Berlin and lecturer at the Jewish Seminary for Kindergarten Teachers, internment in various concentration camps between 1941 and 1945, from January 1946 work in teacher training in Berlin, professor at the Berlin Pedagogical University after August 1946, also lecturer at the Berlin University Faculty of Education, member of the SED School Commission.

19. Ernst Marquardt (1890-1951), awarded the Abitur certificate in 1908, studied History and Philosophy, from 1921 member of the SPD, taught at the Karl-Marx School in Berlin-Neukölln from 1922, dismissed in 1933, First Vice President of the DZfV, from 1949 responsible for the central library services of the GDR.

20. Ernst Hadermann (1896-1968), awarded the Abitur certificate in 1914, military officer, in 1918 member of a Workers' and Soldiers' Council, studied at Frankfurt, Heidelberg and Marburg, in 1939 military service as captain of an artillery unit, a Soviet POW from June 1941, worked with the Nationalkomitee 'Freies Deutschland' from June 1943, until July 1945 work with the education commission of the Nationalkomitee, from August 1945 director of this commission, appointed to a professorship for German Literature at the Brandenburgische Landeshochschule in autumn 1948.

21. Fritz Rücker (1892-1974), awarded Abitur certificate in 1911, studied philology, from 1921 high school teacher in Berlin-Reinickendorf and member of the SPD, dismissal in 1933 as Oberstudienrat, re-employed in 1934, from 1942 Soviet POW, founding member of the Nationalkomitee 'Freies Deutschland', served as a member of the education commission of the Nationalkomitee, from 1945 Third Vice President of the Brandenburg provincial administration in charge of education, science and the arts, thereafter senior editor with the 'Volk und Wissen' publishing house.

22. Max Kreuziger (1880-1953), from 1902 primary school teacher, member of the SPD from the end of 1917, in 1918 member of the Memel Soldiers' Council, from 1922 principal of an experimental school in Berlin-Wedding, from 1931 employed by the Prussian ministry for Culture under Adolf Grimme, dismissed in 1933, various occupations thereafter, from 1938 manager of a bookstore, arrested in August 1944, interned at Sachsenhausen concentration camp until the end of September 1944, deputy mayor of an urban district in Berlin from the summer of 1945, member of the Central Educational Commission of the SPD, spoke on democratic

school reform at the joint KPD-SPD rally at the Admiral's Palace in Berlin in November 1945, member of the SED Schools Commission, from October 1946 SED local councillor in Berlin, from November 1946 deputy director of the DZfV Schools Department, Stadtrat for Education in East Berlin from November 1948, retired in 1951.

23. Richard Schallock (1896-1956), primary school teacher, chairman of the East Pomerian SPD district, in 1925 co-founder and first president of the Allgemeine Freie Lehrergewerkschaft Deutschlands, from 1928 deputy in the Prussian Diet, dismissed in 1933, temporarily imprisoned, insurance salesman, from April 1945 mayor of Köslin, from August 1945 work with the DZfV and election as secretary general of the Teachers Union in the East German FDGB, between 1947 and 1948 deputy director of the personnel department of the DZfV, after 1948 executive president of the Teachers Union, from 1949 Minister for People's Education in Saxony-Anhalt.

24. Ernst Wildangel (1891-1951), from 1918 member of the Catholic Centre Party, from 1924 member of the SPD and of the KPD from 1930, Studienrat at the Karl-Marx School in Berlin-Neukölln, emigrated to France in 1933, from September 1945 director of the Schools Department for Greater Berlin.

25. Hans Siebert (1910-1979), from 1931 member of the KPD, emigrated to Britain in 1936, inter alia work as secretary of the Free German University, returned to Germany in 1947, from October 1947 director for Schools and Education in the Department for Party Schooling, Culture and Education, from November 1948 director of the Schools Department at the DZfV, founding director of the German Pedagogical Central Institute (DPZI) in Berlin.

26. Walter Wolf (1907-1977), active in communist organisations since 1925, awarded the Abitur certificate by the Gotha Aufbauschule in 1928, studied at Jena University until 1931, primary school teacher at Kulm (Thuringia) between 1931 and 1937, arrested in 1937, interned at Buchenwald from 1938 to 1945, member of the illegal camp committee, participated in the drafting of plans for a future school reform, in July 1945 charged with the formation of a Thuringian administration, nominated Thuringian director for people's education in July 1945, in October 1946 founding director of the Institute for Dialectical Materialism in the Faculty of Social Pedagogics at Jena University.

27. Wilhelm Schneller (1894-1979), teacher, from 1922 member of the KPD, Leipzig town councillor between 1924 and 1933, after his dismissal in 1933 toiletries salesman, from 1939 employed by the Sammelgut-Verkehr-GmbH in Leipzig, between September 1945 and December 1950 director of the education department in the Saxon Ministry for Domestic Affairs and People's Education, in 1950 president of the Berlin Pedagogical University, from 1951 to 1952 Schulrat in East Berlin.

28. Cf. C. Klessmann, *Die doppelte Staatsgründung* (Göttingen, 1991), p. 81.

29. See the Ahlen Programme of the CDU of the British Zone in: R. Steininger, *Deutsche Geschichte, 1945-1961,* Vol. I (Frankfurt, 1990), p. 117.

30. The assessment of the 1918 Revolution remained controversial among the SED leadership. This assessment was also dependent on one's evaluation of political and socio-economic change in the Soviet Zone after 1945. Following the tradition of the KPD, Wandel believed that it was the goal of this revolution to ruthlessly liquidate 'the monopoly industrialists.' See SAPMO-BA (note 3 above), fol. 163. Ackermann, by contrast, rejected this 'criticism of the 1918 Revolution.' Ibid., fol. 207. He added: 'I am probably not misinterpreting the position of the Secretariat [i.e., the SED party leadership] that we do not see the mistakes of the 1918 Revolution in the first place in the fact that the 1918 Revolution did not really effect the democratic transformation of Germany. (Acclaim) Rather [the Revolution] did not secure democracy and peace in Germany.'

31. Cf. J. Wehner, *Kulturpolitik und Volksfront,* 2 vols. (Frankfurt, 1992).

32. Cf. W. Weidenfeld and R. Korte (eds), *Handbuch zur deutschen Einheit* (Frankfurt, 1992), pp. 162ff.

33. Max-Gustav Lange (1899-1963), middle school teacher in Altdamm in 1920, from 1921 member of the USPD, then of the SPD, studied History, Education, Economics, Sociology and Philosophy in Berlin between 1921 and 1927, freelance journalist for socialist papers, lecturer at various SPD and trade union schools, from 1927 teacher at various Neukölln schools, not dismissed in 1933, military service from 1940, in 1944 lecturer at the Zakopane Teacher Training Institute, later at the Neisse Teacher Training Institute, in June 1945 in Brandenburg's teacher training programme, member of the KPD, awarded PhD. in 1946, editor of 'Pädagogik' from March 1946, member of the SED Schools Commission, from March 1947 associate professor of sociology at Halle University, full professor there from November 1947 and director of the Institute of Sociology in the Social Science Faculty, from December 1948 Dean of the Pedagogical Faculty, from 1949 also guest professor at Potsdam University, left his positions in 1950 and began new life in West Berlin.

34. The drafts were part of the preparation of a 'Proclamation of the KPD Central Committee and of the SPD Zentralausschuss for Democratic School Reform' of the SPD Central Cultural Committee of December 1945. See SAPMO-BA, Unterricht und Erziehung, FDGB, 324, Weimann to Schallock, 27 September 1945.

35. Ibid., Volksbildung, IV 2/905/70, fol. 18.

36. Ibid., fol. 22: 'Hauptpunkte unseres Erziehungsprogramms' (Heinrich Deiters).

37. Cf. ibid., 'Richtlinien zur Schulreform. Beschlossen vom Zentralkulturausschuss im Dezember 1945,' fol. 40.

38. Karl Sothmann (1895-1993), teacher at a vocational school, from 1920 member of the KPD, from 1921 contributor to the journal *Das proletarische Kind* and work for the Young Spartacist League, member of the executive of the communist Youth League between 1927 and 1929, from 1929 editor of *Die Rote Fahne,* from 1933 to 1936 teacher at the school of the Soviet embassy in Berlin, thereafter employed in his wife's business, director of the Berlin Schools Department between May and August 1945, subsequently personal assistant to Wandel at DZfV, founder and editor of the journal *Die neue Schule.*

39. See Deutsches Institut für Internationale Pädagogische Forschung. Archiv der Bibliothek für Bildungsgeschichtliche Forschung (hereafter: DIPF-BBF/Arch), K. Sothmann, 35, 'Zur Schulreform. Die demokratische Erneuerung der Erziehung' (draft), 18 September 1945, p. 1.

40. See G. Geißler, 'Zur Schulreform und den Erziehungszielen in der Sowjetischen Besatzungszone, 1945-1947,' in: *Pädagogik und Schulalltag,* vol. 46, no.4 (1991), pp. 410-22.

41. The proclamation spoke of educating people to 'think and act independently, uprightly, freely, and progressively.' See G. Uhlig and K.-H. Günther (eds), *Dokumente* (note 1 above), p. 207.

42. Ibid., p. 208, with the demand to educate 'youth in the spirit of progressive democracy, of friendship among the nations and of true humanity.'

43. The Law prescribed to educate youth to become 'independently thinking and responsibly acting human beings ... who are capable and willing to commit themselves fully to the service for the people.' Ibid., p. 209. Text also repr. in: B. Michael and H.-H. Schepp (eds), *Die Schule in Staat und Gesellschaft* (Göttingen, 1993), pp. 341-45.

44. On 11 June 1946 a 'Schule und Erziehung' committee of experts was established with the SED Central Secretariat. Apart from educational functionaries of the central party apparatus and the Berlin apparatus other SED members were

brought in who occupied leading positions in the DZfV, the Berlin government, the Main and District Schools Offices of Greater Berlin, of the Teachers' Union, of the Free German Youth organisation (FDJ) and in education research. Over time the committee became known as the 'Schulkommission.'

45. Cf. SAPMO-BA, VI/905/3, 5th Meeting of the 'Schule und Erziehung' committee of experts, 16 January 1947, fol. 17/8. However, due to the subsequent shift in educational policy, the programme was never ratified.

46. From the start, prominent educationalists kept their distance from the more radical reformist currents that were initially relatively strong among teachers and those involved in teacher training. See, for example, the sharply criticial statement by Alt 'Die Unterrichtsmethodik in der demokratischen Schule,' 30 July 1947, pp. 24f., in: DIPF-BBF/Arch., H. Deiters, 'Protokoll-Zusammenstellung für den Kursus der verantwortlichen Mitarbeiter der Deutschen Verwaltung für Volksbildung und den Volksbildungsministerien in den Ländern der sowjetischen Besatzungszone.'

47. By contrast, the Teachers Union strictly demanded the Einheitsschule which, they argued, was not the old-fashioned Lernschule, but a school that stressed community and work (Gemeinschafts- und Arbeitsschule): 'What is decisive is not the principle of the teaching material, but the development of [the students'] powers and the method of carrying on. Werkunterricht -Werkstättenunterricht.' Thus the resolution of the union's executive at its meeting on 13 November 1945 in: SAPMO-BA, Gewerkschaft Unterricht und Erziehung, 18/368/119, 'Forderungen des Verbandes der Lehrer und Erzieher zur Schulfrage und Lehrerbildung.'

48. Ibid., Volksbildung, IV, 2/905/70, 'Die neue deutsche Schule. Programm' (draft), fol. 137-40. See also: *Allen Kindern das gleiche Recht auf Bildung. Dokumente und Materialien zur demokratischen Schulreform* (Berlin, 1981), pp. 147-53.

49. For example at Halle University the Dean of the Philosophy Faculty refused the appointment of Max Gustav Lange, a highly regarded pedagogue and sociologist who was generally regarded as a protagonist of the new approach. As the Dean put it, Lange did not qualify for a professorship in sociology on the basis of his scholarship so far; instead he should 'apply to obtain the venia legendi [qualification] in sociology in the prescribed way.' See the Dean's letter of 27 January 1947 in: Universitätsarchiv Halle, Rep. PA, No. 9851. In the eyes of the administration, the Faculty of Education in particular was a centre of resistance 'to staff who did not have a PhD.' In 1948 there was also the widespread view 'that the struggle of the philologists against the primary school teacher has been unleashed on a broad front.' See SAPMO-BA, Gewerkschaft Unterricht und Erziehung, 141, 'Protokoll der Sitzung des erweiterten Ausschusses für Hochschulfragen des Zentralvorstandes der Gewerkschaft der Lehrer und Erzieher,' 11 June 1948, quoting remarks by Dahlmann and Heilmann.

50. See G. Geißler, 'Zur bildungspolitischen Tendenzwende in der SBZ, 1947-1949,' in: *Pädagogik und Schulalltag*, vol. 46, no. 5 (1991), pp. 529ff.

51. The only education representatives of the Gelehrten-Rat in the DZfV at this time were Theodor Litt and Robert Alt. See SAPMO-BA, Gewerkschaft Unterricht und Erziehung, 141, membership list of the Gelehrten-Rat, 3 March 1947.

52. As late as November 1948 Mieskes was able to submit in a speech to the sub-committee for University Questions of the Teachers Union a number of proposals which were unanimously adopted by those present (Reißmann, Leipzig University; Grimmer, Leipzig University; Mehlhose, Technical University Dresden; Fuchs, Halle University; Wolfram, Jena University; Schubbert, Rostock University; Dahlmann, Berlin University). This was the time when 'incriminating material' had already been collected against Mielkes in Jena. See ibid., H. Brumme to Central Executive, 4 November 1948, received on 12 November 1948. The proposals were as follows: '1) establishment of a journal that publishes genuinely free

scholarly ideas for an open scholarly exchange of views. 2) creation of an institution that brings all those interested in pedagogical research together at least once a year; introduction of a pedagogical convention at which only scholarly papers are presented and nothing on educational politics. 3) formation of a committee for educational research attached to the Central Executive or in informal co-operation within the faculty. This committee is to be created by the teachers themselves, who are capable of rendering expert opinions; no more decisions by an administrator. 4) the central authorities should plan soberly and seriously in what ways pedagogical research can be set in motion on a broad basis.' Ibid., Minutes of the Sub-committee Meeting, 12 November 1948.

53. D. Benner and H. Sladek, 'Vergessene erziehungstheoretische, bildungstheoretische und bildungspolitische Kontroversen in der Pädagogik der SBZ und DDR,' MS, 1993, p. 31.

54. H. Merkens (ed. under the auspices of the Bayerisches Staatsministerium für Unterricht und Kultus), *Dokumente zur Schulreform in Bayern* (Munich, 1952), pp. 277-81.

55. The postulate of 'solid learning' was raised as early as November 1945 by a memorandum that argued decidedly against reformist views. See SAPMO-BA, Gewerkschaft Unterricht und Erziehung, 325, 'Denkschrift der Universität Berlin und der Berliner Akademie der Wissenschaften zur Neugestaltung unseres Schulwesens' (with five appendices), November 1945, fol. 4ff.

56. E. Cloer, 'Ausgewählte Aspekte der Entwicklung des pädagogischen Denkens in der SBZ und DDR,' in: *Die Deutsche Schule,* no. 1 (1988), pp. 19-32; C. Kersting, 'Konstituierungsprozeß der Pädagogischen Fakultäten in der SBZ/DDR, 1945-1955,' MS, 1993. The majority of those who taught at these faculties came from primary school background and had received their PhD. only in exceptional cases. See SAPMO-BA, Gewerkschaft Unterricht und Erziehung, 141, lists from Jena and Leipzig Universities, April 1948. The bulk of the 'Dozenten' held appointments as adjuncts (Lehrbeauftragte).

57. The DZfV (from 1946, Deutsche Verwaltung für Volksbildung) had been established by Order No. 17 of the Soviet Military Administration (SMA), dated 27 July 1945. The DZfV aided the SMA in drawing up its orders and was given certain rights to co-ordinate the work of the Länder administrations. Legislative authority rested with the Länder and provinces of the Soviet Zone. However, the guidelines that the DZfV produced on the basis of SMA orders were largely binding. From the end of 1947 the central administration assumed further rights to issue directives.

58. According to Clause 6c of the Schools Act, the conference of teachers was the advisory council to the school's principal. This body was to be 'heard in all essential decisions concerning the school's external and internal affairs'. The DZfV's executive regulations relating to the Act mention as school organs the principal, the teaching staff, and the parents' committee. Thus staff had to be 'heard in an expert capacity prior to all essential decisions concerning the school's internal and external affairs.' Opinion formation at the level of the school, of grades, forms, or special conferences was occur 'in all matters ... by clarifying discussion and subsequent vote.' See SAPMO-BA, Gewerkschaft Unterricht und Erziehung, 325, 'Richtlinien zur Durchführung des Gesetzes zur Demokratisierung der deutschen Schule (nur für den Gebrauch innerhalb des Hauses),' 20 June 1946. The Teachers Union claimed the right of the school conference to participate in the election of the principal. The latter's powers were described by it as follows: 'The principal is primus inter pares among his co-workers. He is not the superior of the teachers employed by the school. He represents the school toward the outside; as chair of the school conference he bears with the latter the responsibility for life in the school as a whole; he looks after the execution of directives from the authori-

ties and of decisions by the conference, and seeks to promote in every possible way the work of the school by providing ideas and by responding understandingly to the rest of the teaching staff.' See Der Volkslehrer. Mitteilungsblatt für die Funktionäre der Gewerkschaft der Lehrer und Erzieher im FDGB, No. 7 (1947), p. 3: 'Beschlüsse des Zentralvorstandes. Antrag des Zonenausschusses für Schulrecht und Schulverwaltung.' The executive regulations relating to the Act that the Conference of Ministers ratified on 3 December 1947 contained the following clauses: … 4) Every teacher is co-responsible for the spirit and the overall work of the school. The teaching staff comes together at conferences to fulfil the common educational tasks and to participate in the administration of the school. 5) Following clarification in free democratic discussion opinion formation takes place through a vote on the agenda items. Conference transactions are subject to confidentiality. 6) If the principal refuses to implement a conference decision, the teachers have the right to appeal to the superior authority for a decision.' See SAPMO-BA, Gewerkschaft Unterricht und Erziehung, 331, 'Ausführungsbestimmungen zum Gesetz zur Demokratisierung der deutschen Schule in der auf der Ministerkonferenz am 3.12.1947 beschlossenen Fassung.' As late as the mid-1950s, attempts continued to be made at some schools to preserve a type of collegial leadership.

59. The Teachers Union had emerged from local and regional committees and had been founded at Zonal level on 13/14 June 1946. It continued to adhere to distinctly Social Democrat trade union traditions and reformist educational ideas; but from the end of 1947 it came increasingly under pressure from the SED as well as from the higher administration. At the same time the Central Executive upheld the position not to have 'the right taken away' from it to 'comment critically on questions relating to schools and teachers.' See SAPMO-BA, Gewerkschaft Unterricht und Erziehung, 68, 'Protokoll der Sitzung des Geschäftsführenden Zentralvorstandes,' 3/4 September 1948, without pagination. Thus the Union tried to secure for itself the right to give advice (Mitspracherecht) at least in the selection of new teachers. As the Central Executive put it (ibid.), what was decisive was not that the person belonged 'to a certain party', but had the 'attitude of an upright democrat.' The 'Teachers Union, and not a particular political party had the right' to choose 'in the first instance.' It was only in February 1954 that the regime succeeded in fully integrating the Union into the system, when it dismissed almost the entire leadership and its chairman Karl Ellrich who was charged with having abetted the activities of foreign agents.

60. Working Groups of Socialist Teachers (ASL): Association of SED Teachers; organized at Zonal level on the basis of the SED Party Executive Guidelines relating to the Formation of Working Groups of Cultural Producers and Workers of the Brain, dated 24 January 1947. See 'Allen Kindern das gleiche Recht,' pp. 143-46. Clear attempts on the part of the teachers to use the working groups for the discussion of pedagogical problems were banned with a directive from the SED Central Secretariat of 18 November 1947 (ibid., pp. 167-74); however, in practice they were not particularly effectively suppressed. The Working Groups were finally dissolved in 1951.

61. Freundeskreise der 'neuen Schule:' these were groups of interested parents that had emerged from support actions in 1945/46 and that the DZfV had promoted. A central 'Initiativkomitee Freunde demokratischer Erziehung' was formed in Berlin on 20 February 1947, from which emerged in November of that year the Arbeitsgemeinschaft 'Freunde der neuen Schule' which was supported by almost all mass organizations and by various offices (Education, Health, sections of the Wirtschaftskommission). Arbeitsgemeinschaften were established at the level of the Länder in 1948. On 28 June 1948, the SED Central Secretariat then passed a resolution decreeing the 'leading role of the SED in the development of the ped-

agogical movement 'Freunde der neuen Schule'.' Ibid., pp. 175-80. Thereafter the main thrust was to struggle 'against the enemies of the new school' and to propagate political aims. See SAPMO-BA, Gewerkschaft Unterricht und Erziehung, 68, 'Beschlüsse der Sitzung des Geschäftsführenden Vorstandes', with minutes on a paper by H. Siebert, 18 October 1948. The dissolution of the organization came in 1951 because it had allegedly not lived up to these new aims.

62. SAPMO-BA, IV/2/1/50, 'Tagung des Parteivorstandes der SED,' 29/30 July 1948, fol. 14.

63. Clara Zetkin (1857-1933), teacher, education expert in the SPD, co-founder of the KPD, from 1920 to 1933 member of the Reichstag.

64. Edwin Hoernle (1883-1952), vicar, from 1910 member of the SPD, co-founder of the KPD, from 1920 director of a regional organisation, in 1921 appointed director of the KPD Education Department, from 1924 to 1933 member of the Reichstag, thereafter emigration to the Soviet Union, after 1945 a leading agricultural policy expert in the KPD/SED.

65. Fritz Ausländer (1885-1943), studied History, German Literature and Geography at Königsberg, received his PhD. in 1908, Studienrat in Berlin, initiated, as a member of the USPD, the founding of the Association of Socialist Teachers in 1919 and the Free Teachers Union of Germany a year later, member of the KPD from 1920, member of the Prussian Diet between 1928 and 1932, interned in a concentration camp from 1933 to 1935 and again in 1939, committed suicide in 1943.

66. Theodor Neubauer (1890-1945), awarded his PhD. from Jena in 1913, in 1919 member of the USPD and of the KPD from 1920, high school teacher in Ruhla, from 1921 to 1923 member of the Diet, thereafter until 1933 member of the Reichstag, imprisoned from 1933 to 1938, arrested again in 1944 and sentenced to death.

67. Ernst Schneller (1890-1944), primary school teacher, in 1919 member of the SPD and of the KPD a year later, from 1921 to 1925 member of the Saxon Diet and of the Reichstag from 1925 to 1933, sentenced to six years of hard labour in 1933 and shot in Oranienburg concentration camp.

68. See SAPMO-BA, Volksbildung, 2/905/77, 'Bericht über die Arbeit der SED auf dem Schulgebiet von September 1945 bis 1948,' 23 June 1948, fol. 75-76. In December 1945 Mecklenburg had 7 Schulräte und 17 teachers who were KPD members, while the SPD counted 14 Schulräte and 24 teachers. In April 1946 some 227 teachers were Communists and 839 were Social Democrats. By November 1946 of 8,026 teachers in Mecklenburg 3,121 were members of the SED.

69. See SAPMO-BA, Gewerkschaft Unterricht und Erziehung, 326, Deutsche Verwaltung für Volksbildung, materials relating to the Einheitsschule question, 4 June 1946.

70. See DIPF-BBF/Arch., H. Deiters, 46, 'Zur geschichtlichen Entwicklung der Einheitsschule,' (October 1946).

71. On this point see H.-E. Tenorth, Bildungsgeschichte der DDR – Teil der deutschen Bildungsgeschichte?, MS, Berlin, 1993.

72. See the Directive No. 54 'Grundsätze für die Demokratisierung des deutschen Bildungswesens,' in: B. Michael and H.-H. Schepp (eds), *Die Schule in Staat und Gesellschaft*, pp. 337-41.

73. See the brochure Gleiches Bildungsrecht für alle. Das Gesetz zur Demokratisierung der Deutschen Schule, solemnly proclaimed in Weimar on 2 June 1946, n.p., n.d., p. 15.

74. G. Geißler, 'Zur bildungspolitischen Tendenzwende in der SBZ, 1947-1949,' in: *Pädagogik und Schulalltag*, vol. 46, no. 5 (1991), pp. 529-43.

75. See DIPF-BBF/Arch., H. Siebert, 74, Hans Siebert's draft 'Leitsätze zur Schulpolitik,' 12 April 1948, p. 4.

76. See SAPMO-BA, IV/2/1, 13, Meeting of the SED Party Executive, 15/16 September 1948, fol. 215.

77. Ibid., fol. 194.
78. Hans Mieskes (1915-), awarded his PhD. at Jena in 1941, completed his habilitation in April 1946, Dozent at Jena University, from 1947 associate professor and director of the Institute for 'Wissenschaftliche Erziehungsberatung und Pädagogische Therapie,' from 1948 member of the sub-committee for University Questions in the Teachers Union, temporary dismissal in January 1949 following procedures to exclude him from the SED, final dismissal in 1956 following his attempt to take the Institute which had traditional ties with church circles out of the Education Faculty when the latter was dissolved and to integrate it into the DPZI, moved to West Germany with five of his collaborators.
79. The democratic ideas of this group of educationalists were not confined to the political constitution, but extended to institutional and social structures. These were to be organised according to the principle of equality within a democratic community. This approach overlapped with the ideas held by the education commissions of the Western Allies. Thus the report of the American commission of September 1946 rejected a limitation of the concept of democracy to the form of government. See the commission's report 'Erziehung in Deutschland,' publ. by Die Neue Zeitung, Munich, 1946, p. 20. In the view of the commission democratization included a structural reform of the school system that established the principle of equality. Ibid., pp. 27ff.
80. For Sothmann Einheitsschule meant: 'Uniform organism, that enables every child to find his or her own way through the school. In other words, no schematism, but lively plurality according to objective considerations. The pupil's capabilities, interests and achievements that exist objectively, can be verified and examined. ... This means: educational reform that is scientifically grounded! No doctrine! No fixed ideas! Above all, no leveling! But also no prejudice (socially conditioned etc.).' See DIPF-BBF/Arch., K. Sothmann, 35, 'Zu den Problemen, die auf dem Pädagogischen Kongress herausgearbeitet werden müssen,' 9 August 1947, fol. 2.
81. The theoretical and intellectual conflicts of this group of educationalists still require differentiated reconstruction which will have to rely primarily on the evaluation of private papers. The texts that were written under the political conditions of the former GDR merely allude to these conflicts.
82. H. Deiters, Reflektionen. Private Aufzeichnungen von 1958 bis 1965, in the possession of Ludwig Deiters. The bracketed references refer to the respective document in Deiters' notes that are largely undated.

Chapter 6

Democratisation and Europeanisation

Challenges to the Spanish Educational System Since 1970

Gabriela Ossenbach-Sauter

Spain has undergone two rapid changes over the last fifty years. On the one hand, it has transformed itself from an agricultural and predominantly rural country to an industrialised one with a large middle class. Spain has, moreover, become a Western democracy, leaving behind almost forty years of Franco dictatorship, to become part of the European Union. But along with these transformations in the economic, social and political fields, there has also been a rapid transformation of the values predominant in society. Spanish society has become secularised surprisingly rapidly, in spite of the pervasive role that the Catholic church has played throughout Spanish history, particularly during the Franco period. It should be pointed out that, as from 1945, the Franco regime identified *Spanishness* with *Catholicness*, dropping other more purely fascist elements and impregnating society with the values of the most traditional form of Catholicism.

The rapid processes of change that have taken place, particularly since the 1960s, have naturally been accompanied by major transformations in the Spanish educational system. The most important of these was undoubtedly the educational reform of 1970. This reform, which took place under the old authoritarian regime, underwent essential alterations during the 1980s as a result of the democratisation of the country's institutions. Nevertheless, the 1970 reform still defines a large part of the structure and organisation of the current educational system and nobody would hesitate to describe it as a fundamental milestone in the history of schooling in Spain, where, for over a century and a half, a nineteenth-century approach to educational policy had survived.

The purpose of this paper, rather than providing a detailed description of the reforms that have been introduced, or of the current structure of the Spanish educational system, is to attempt to make an overall analysis of two-and-a-half decades of educational policy using the two main reference points that make up the greatest challenges to Spanish education today: its contribution to the democratisation and to the 'Europeanisation' of Spanish society. I shall, however, confine myself to primary and secondary schooling and will not enter into an analysis of university policy, as higher education requires in part a different form of analysis. This is particularly true when it comes to analysing the influence of the universities as opposition to the Franco regime, as well as in the process of democratisation that Spain has been undergoing, ever since the 1978 Constitution was declared.

The first of the topics to be discussed here is democratisation. This issue is a complex one to deal with if one refers to educational policy under Franco, i.e., when one looks at the heavy educational reform that took place in 1970. Obviously, the concept of 'democratisation' at that time had to be understood as a massive opening of the educational system to all social levels, as all other aspects of political participation and freedom of expression were conditioned by the dictatorship. But even this was no small achievement if we take into account the low school-attendance rates in Spain in the 1950s and 1960s and the state's lack of involvement in public education. Ever since the end of the Civil War, the state had acted as a mere subsidiary to the Catholic church, particularly in primary education. During its first decade of power, the Franco regime barely dealt with primary education, and in 1951 the school attendance rate for six to thirteen-year-olds was only 50 per cent, almost the same as twenty years previously. In 1966, the school attendance rate was only 87.8 per cent.

The greatest increase between 1956 and 1966 took place in secondary and higher education, which led to a serious structural imbalance in the country's educational pyramid: the base was underdeveloped, while the medium- and higher-level segments were expanding. Moreover, in general terms, the state's contribution at all educational levels was very small, compared to the large number of private institutions that existed (most of which were religious). For example, in 1965, only 21.51 per cent of the population of middle-level schooling attended public institutions. Also, the percentage of the national budget that the state allocated to education was insufficient to set up a public sector in accordance with the educational requirements of a society under transformation, this was just 8.57 per cent in 1960 (Escolano 1992b:293-97).

The 1960s were, in fact, noted for the unusually heavy economic, social and cultural changes that took place, despite continued political immobility: a GNP growth average of over six per cent, rural exodus and emigration both to other parts of the country and abroad, rapid urban development, foreign capital investment and the encouragement of tourism, growth of the middle-class, transition from the extended family to the nuclear family, and the appearance of a consumer society. These were just some of the indicators of the transition from a traditional to an industrial society. In 1968, the year in which the preparations for the educational reform began, the educational system was entirely unsuited to catering for the new requirements of Spanish society, or to the pressure it received from the latter as regards the demand for goods and services, despite the steps that had been taken during the 1960s to increase and improve education.

Besides the low school-attendance figures and the lack of state-school places during the 1960s, the structure of the educational system was clearly discriminatory as regards the transition from primary to secondary school. Entrance examinations for the secondary schools had turned primary education, which at first was compulsory until the age of twelve and was later extended to fourteen, into a watertight compartment inside the educational system, intended for the popular classes.

Given this educational backdrop, the 1970 educational reform was, quite frankly, revolutionary. This fact had been acknowledged by those who promoted it and who at the time spoke of 'a silent and peaceful revolution', that 'would, in the future, involve a thorough reform of society and its old structures' (Minister of Education Villar Palasí). The tool that was used to counteract educational deficiencies and break way from the bi-polar structure of the educational system, was known as General Basic Education (*Educación General Básica*, EGB). This involved a single type of free and compulsory education for all Spanish children from six to fourteen years of age. This meant unifying the entire schooling system as regards institutions, curricula and teaching categories, and a moderate diversification of studies at the higher levels. Although at the end of this basic schooling period, the system led to two channels, Professional Training or *Bachillerato*, the latter was also unified into a single type of institution, rather like a comprehensive school (*Bachillerato Unificado Polivalente*), offering common, optional and technical/professional subjects. Professional Training was still seen as a second-class form of education, not very highly valued and suffering from serious problems as regards quality.

However, because it was the only form of secondary academic education, and due to its comprehensive structure and catering to a majority, the *Bachillerato* – in spite of not being compulsory – also imposed a great unity on the educational system for pupils between six and eighteen years of age. It may be said that, between 1974 and 1988, when middle-level education developed in a spectacular way, roughly one out of every three schoolchildren between fourteen and eighteen years of age went to Professional Training, while two were in *Bachillerato* (Enguita 1992:75-6).

The reform undoubtedly had far-reaching consequences, not only in that it made education available to all Spaniards, but also in that it unified the type of education they received, as we have seen. This was true in spite of the discriminatory features of Professional Training. In 1975, full school attendance was achieved for children between six and fourteen years of age. It may be said that the 1970 reform in primary and secondary education was a result of social change rather than ideological pressure (Puelles 1992b:316).

I shall not try to assess the major defects of the reform as regards teacher training, the quality of professional training, curricular methods and contents, etc. As was discussed at the beginning of this paper, I am more interested in pointing out the positive effect the reform had on the democratisation of education and its social consequences, all of which undoubtedly contributed to the peaceful transition to democracy in Spain. However, I would like to examine one point that deserves special attention, because it gives the Spanish educational system one particular feature. I refer to the great importance that private education still has in this country and the attitude that the state had to adopt as regards this form of education in 1970, in order to guarantee that education was made available to all Spanish citizens. The historical importance of the existence of two parallel educational systems, private and public, since the beginning of the nineteenth century, and the state's lack of participation in education during the first few decades of the Franco regime, meant that making free basic education compulsory until the age of fourteen, brought about a clash between the old Spanish liberal principle of freedom of education – i.e., the freedom to create schools – and the right to free education. This forced the state, whose teaching role was finally recognised, to guarantee the state-school places required by the demand for education. The result of this clash was that a system of grants was set up for private schools. Because there are so many of them, this has meant a duality in the educational system: major differences as regards quality, equipment, prestige, etc., are apparent between state and private schools. This has also contributed to constant clashes and arguments among the state and private schools, parents' associations and the Catholic church.

The rapid growth and consolidation of the educational system after the 1970 reform have undoubtedly been an essential part of the transformation of Spanish society over the last few decades. However, the very rapidity with which changes took place has meant that many qualitative aspects of teaching have been overlooked, and society's attitude towards education still needs to undergo some changes. We must not overlook the fact that the Spanish economic boom during the 1960s took place with an illiteracy rate, even then (1960), of eleven per cent of the total population (Puelles 1991:447). This economic take-off was the work of a group of technocrats who, while still part of the authoritarian regime, were opposed to totalitarianism and national-Catholic exaltation. They wished to bring a new legitimacy to the regime through economic modernisation and liberalisation; opening Spain's doors to the world economy. The social transformations produced by this development had an effect on the need for educational reform, as I have already mentioned, and these created favourable conditions for a peaceful transition to democracy upon the dictator's death. The regime became legitimised by basing itself on economic welfare, although public liberties were still forbidden to society. This was the technocratic policy of rationalisation and planning, efficiency, apoliticality, liberty and economic development and the transfer of techniques of private enterprises to the public administration. This economic development, which was conceived as a panacea to solve every problem, brought about changes that far exceeded those that its initiators had intended, but it always followed the policy that had been in use in Spain since nineteenth-century liberalism, that of starting reforms at the top: a major reform policy, but one that excluded popular or democratic participation.

In the field of pedagogy, this new modernisation policy also brought with it certain 'politically inoffensive' innovations, which were to be seen in the adoption of functional and experimental trends and the carrying out of empirical/statistical surveys, which in the 1960s coexisted with the Catholic educational philosophy typical of the early Franco period (Escolano 1992b:306). Moreover, Spain's gradual emergence from isolation meant that it joined international educational organisations (OCDE, UNESCO), and this provided educational policy with a more technical approach, while at the same time introducing the prevailing educational planning strategies of the 1960s.

However, does this rapid quantitative growth of the educational system, the adoption of technocratic economic development policies and Spain's connection with international organisations mean that it may be said that society underwent a *Europeanisation* process? It has been claimed that the eight-year General Basic Education was based on the model of the Swedish comprehensive school that was being introduced at that time. Moreover, in order to set up the 1970 reform, reports by the OCDE were used, along with the advice of an International Co-operation Committee made up of various European and American figures such as P.H. Coombs, J. Vaizey, H. Becker and A. Bienaymé, along with other experts from developing countries (Díez Hochleitner 1992:272).

Nevertheless, it is fairly significant that the reform measures that were adopted were greatly affected by the planning policies that UNESCO and other international organisations were designing at that time for educational development in Third World countries. Thus, for example, one's attention is drawn to the fact that one of the most important tools for preparing the 1970 educational reform was the econometric model designed by the UNESCO for Asia ('Asian Model', Bangkok, 1967). It is also significant that the main architect of the Spanish reform, the UNESCO official Ricardo Díez Hochleitner, had a great deal of personal experience of educational planning in Latin America. Another interesting event was the foundation, under the same educational reform policy, of the Universidad Nacional de Educación a Distancia (Distance Education University). This was based on the experience of the Correspondence University of Lusaka, Zambia (Díez Hochleitner 1992:267). In my opinion, at the time Spain was so underdeveloped as regards its educational structure that the policies of economic development used for the Third World provided a suitable model for its reform. The liberalisation that the reform involved in general terms, and which also coincided with a liberalisation in the economic field, did not necessarily mean the 'Europeanising' of Spanish education and society, in which very strong archaic elements survived, and which subsequent changes were unable to eliminate entirely.

The above are still challenges for education in Spain and, ever since the transition to a democratic system with the political Constitution of 1978, they continue to be essential objectives of Spanish educational policy. First of all, it is obvious that the initial consequence of democratising Spain was to democratise the management of educational institutions; also, to regulate the educational responsibilities of each autonomous region once the state's autonomous structure had been recognised by the new constitution. Apart from decentralising educational policy, the latter had the fundamental result of officially recognising the use of vernacular languages in teaching, such as Catalan, Basque and Galician. It also recognised autonomy as regards incorporating autonomous regions' culture and current affairs into the school curriculum. This new outlook was extremely significant, given the historical importance of nationalist claims in Spain. In educational legislation these claims had only been catered to for a short period during the Second Republic (1931-39).

Another major step towards democratising the schooling system was the granting and regulating of University autonomy by the 1983 University Reform Law (*Ley de Reforma Universitaria*, LRU), although I shall not discuss this in this paper.

As regards the democratisation of education, I would rather look at the proclamation in 1985 of the Law on the Right to Education (*Ley Orgánica Reguladora del Derecho a la Educación*, LODE). This controversial law regulates the complex relationship between educational liberties and rights as recognised by the Constitution, dealing with the delicate issue of the freedom of schooling, seen as 'the right to create and direct a private school, the right to establish a school's ideology, and the right to choose a school, but also the right to teaching freedom' (Puelles 1991:500). The main point of this law is that it still continues to accept a dual mode of schooling, both public and private, while seeking to integrate public supply and any private supply that voluntarily wishes to help contribute to the provision of free, compulsory public schooling. This means financing private institutions by the state, setting up agreements according to which the owners of private institutions are under certain obligations. The new legislation regulates the participation in teaching of all the elements involved (parents, teachers and pupils), in all institutions financed by public funds. This means the managerial rights of the owner of a state-assisted private institution are somewhat restricted. School councils are also set up in towns, provinces and autonomous communities and all those involved in schooling are also represented in the State Schooling Council (*Consejo Escolar del Estado*), which is the state's advisory body on schooling policy.

This law, of course, produced clashes with the Conservative Party, private teaching organisations and the church concerning state-assisted institutions. But, apart from these ideological conflicts, one of the most highly debated issues of this new law – and one that denoted hesitancy and vagueness as regards the very concept of democratisation of teaching at this time of rapid change – was the one that dealt with school management. The 1985 Law on the Right to Education, as a part of setting up democratic mechanisms for managing schools, established the democratic election of school heads by the school councils, which are composed of teachers, parents and pupils. The head is chosen from among the school teaching staff. At state-assisted private schools, a candidate is chosen who must also be a member of the teaching staff, but who has been proposed by the owner of the school.

This democratic election process has created a large number of conflicts and problems, most of which have been brought about due to power struggles and problems with the relationship between teaching staff and the chosen management team. The result of this policy has been that around fifty per cent of the heads of state schools have been appointed directly by the appropriate authorities, mostly due to the lack of candidates. Moreover, the principle of democratic election of the head of a school has clashed with the issue of his/her professional competence, which legislation and political measures have barely touched upon in the last few years. This is seriously affecting the quality of teaching. Thus, one of the major challenges to the Spanish educational system at the moment is to make school management more skilful, professional and attractive, without losing its present democratic features.

The secular conflict with private education, the recognition of the educational rights of the various nationalities that make up Spain, the democratic internal management of schools and the participation of all those involved in the country's educational policy are not, however, the only steps that have been taken over the last few years in order to democratise education in Spain. A new education law, the 1990 Educational System General Organisation Law (*Ley Orgánica de Ordenación General del Sistema Educativo*, LOGSE), which is gradually being applied, has introduced major reforms that are aimed to improve the quality of teaching, while at the same time, through heavy transformations in the educational system's structure, the law is aimed at democratising schooling. With this in mind, I should first like to point out the priority, as regards both quality and quantity, given to pre-school education in order to increase equal opportunities in education, by compensating for some of the inequalities at this stage of education caused by differences in children's social, cultural and financial backgrounds. This level of education had, since 1970, suffered from low attendance rates and very little pedagogic attention.

More effective, however, was the widespread introduction of compulsory education for all, up until the age of sixteen. This not only intended to increase the level of Spaniards' general education, but also had managed to democratise access to secondary education and to eliminate the discriminatory nature of Professional Training at an early age. Previously, there had been two different types of qualification available at the end of basic compulsory education, providing access to either the *Bachillerato* or Professional Training. Under the new reform, there is only one type of qualification at the age of sixteen, providing access to either secondary academic education or Professional Training. Compulsory secondary education, which, under the new school system, is from twelve to sixteen, is comprehensive, providing the chance to diversify, particularly during the last two years of schooling, and it includes basic professional training.

The basis of this far-reaching reform, which defines unified comprehensive ten-year schooling, is the idea that widespread education is compatible with teaching quality. Educational policy over the last few years has emphasised the need to improve the standard of education, so as to avoid any possible negative influences of the universalisation of this type of schooling (M.E.C. 1994).

The general approach that has been used over the last few years in order to democratise the educational system has been made clear so far. As has been discussed above, democratisation has produced certain problems concerning the standard of teaching, a standard that has mostly been required by Spain's joining Europe. It is quite frustrating to read the official documents on the latest educational reform, as they refer to the 'Europeanisation' of Spain almost entirely in terms of the need to improve Spain's competitiveness with other European countries. In other words, it focuses above all on the school system as a supplier of qualifications, whereas very little is said or done about extending the cultural values of European identity among Spanish society (Marchesi 1992:595, 598).

Thus, the introduction to the 1990 Educational System Organisation Law (LOGSE) explicitly mentions that the 'progressive integration of our society into the community framework places us on a level of *competitiveness, mobility and free movement*, in a training dimension that requires our studies and qualifications to comply with shared references, and that they must now be standardised within the EC, in order not to compromise our citizens' opportunities at present and in the future' (LOGSE, Introduction, p.9; the italics are mine). And while this same law refers to the need for education to contribute to the opening of the individual, political, cultural and productive space of the youth in the European context (ibid., p.8), very little concern to instil such values can be seen in the reform.

The new educational reform does pay far more attention to foreign-language teaching from primary level and it also treats physical, musical and artistic education on the curriculum in an innovative way, that is far more suited to European tradition. In addition, emphasis is being placed on the need to encourage positive attitudes at school towards the environment, sex education, equality between sexes and among races, all of which we feel should be part of the European identity. Nevertheless, the most obvious concerns regarding Spain's introduction into Europe, particularly at a time of heavy economic recession, are undoubtedly professional competitiveness and the need to increase the standard of the population's general education.

It must be acknowledged that Spain still has not solved some of the old problems of identity, and the involvement of education in the autonomic structure process has focused the discussion on the creation of regional and national identities. Vernacular language teaching has played a very important part in this. For this reason, the creation of an European identity has played a secondary role. The intensity of the changes that society has undergone since the 1960s, has also focused attention on other aspects that strongly mark Spanish identity. These are, above all, the secularisation of society and the need to create democratic attitudes.

From an optimistic point of view, let us say that changes have been very rapid, and not enough time has elapsed to consolidate these transformations in a European sense. However, although the crisis of values is affecting the whole of Western society at the moment – and this is to a great extent the responsibility of education – in the Spanish context we are concerned about the fact that democratic transformations in the educational macro-structure and the decision mechanisms I have already described, are causing us to lose sight of the need to teach democratic and European values in the classroom.

On the other hand, the debate on educational values has become heightened over the last fifteen years due to its predominantly political nature. This is mostly due to the clashes that have occurred with Catholic and Conservative pressure groups and, of course, with the church hierarchy. In Spain, there is an agreement between the state and Rome, according to which it is compulsory to teach the Catholic religion in all schools, but it is an optional choice for pupils. This agreement was carefully respected by recent educational legislation, although the rate of attendance in religion classes is very low in state schools. The Catholic church and religious organisations have strongly opposed the fact that state schools have stopped offering ethics as a compulsory alternative to religion. Ethics was imposed after the democratic transition and taught issues related to the new democratic political make-up of Spain and other aspects of coexistence and solidarity among citizens.

The new educational reform under way advocates instead that ethic and moral education should enter into every subject on the curriculum and into the very 'climate' of the school, rather than being confined to one particular subject. Given the degree of immaturity of Spanish democracy in this sense – and this has been seen from some alarming surveys on young people's attitude towards democracy – it would appear insufficient, and in any case fairly difficult, to institutionalise this in schools. Those systems for decision-making and participation in school life, which were introduced by the legislation and have already been described, sometimes seem to be the only things that are done in school to encourage the democratisation of society.

The actual authorities in charge of educational policy (M.E.C. 1994), and other intellectual circles concerned with such problems (see Camps 1993, Lucini 1993), have begun to react to this crisis of values. To my mind, this is a great challenge to state education in Spain at the moment. In a land where private schooling still plays an important role, it turns out that in private schools values appear to be more clearly defined by the very ideology on which the schools were founded. The teaching staff and management team therefore work more coherently and in harmony. In state schools, on the other hand, there is still a great deal of vagueness as regards the values that should be transmitted by teaching, and I would venture to say that the teaching staff in state schools is fairly unclear about the actual meaning of communal and civic values.

When the Ministry of Education, as part of its policy of improving the standard of teaching, attempts to encourage the so-called 'teaching of values' (M.E.C. 1994:22-4, 37-46), these values are understood to be fundamentally civic ones – tolerance, solidarity and participation – that clearly involve the creation of democratic habits. In the official speech of proposal made in 1994 for improving the standard of teaching in schools (M.E.C. 1994), in the section concerning 'teaching of values', there was no mention whatsoever of the terms 'Europe' or 'European', although the speech did refer to international solidarity in general. In this official speech, one misses some reference to the progressive and modernising traditions that, throughout Spanish history, have loudly proclaimed the Europeanisation of Spain as a means to progress and wealth. Ever since the sixteenth-century Counter-Reformation closed Spain's doors to European influences, in a country where such significant European trends as Erasmism had flourished, and in which great thinkers such as Juan Luis Vives felt a strong vocation towards Europe, all subsequent reform and modernisation movements have seen Spain's isolation from Europe as the cause of its backwardness.

This is how it was understood by enlightened thinkers such as Benito Jerónimo Feijóo or by the Regenerationists at the end of the nineteenth century, such as Joaquín Costa and the members of the so called *Institución Libre de Enseñanza*, which had so much influence on Spanish educational policy until 1939. For the philosopher Ortega y Gasset, too, the subject of Europe was one of the most important concerns. All the proposals made by these progressive movements for opening up towards Europe included measures for involving education in the process.

The Franco regime, on the other hand, developed an idea of Spain that emphasised not the aspects that Spain and Europe had in common, but rather the differences. The idea was therefore spread about that the essence of Spain was a result of the glorious Empire period, and the discovery and colonisation of America. Thus, the idea of 'Spanishness' *(Hispanidad),* with its obvious racist connotations, came into being, whereas the subject of Europe survived only in the minds of the political opposition.

Spanish politicians and, above all, teachers must revive this old pro-European tradition. It is one that does not yet seem to have become implanted, with all its consequences, after the democratic transition and Spain's incorporation into the European Union.

References

Bernecker, W. L. (1990) *Sozialgeschichte Spaniens im 19. und 20. – Jahrhundert,* Frankfurt.

Boyd-Barrett, O. (1991), 'State and Church in Spanish Education', *Compare,* Vol. 21, No. 2, 179-97.

Camps, V. (1993), *Los valores de la educación,* Madrid.

Diez Hochleitner, R.(1992), 'La reforma educativa de la Ley General de Educación de 1970. Datos para una crónica', *Revista de Educación, número extraordinario (La Ley General de Educación, veinte años después),* 261-78.

Enguita, M. F. (1992), 'Las enseñanzas medias en el sistema de la Ley General de Educación', *Revista de Educación, número extraordinario (La Ley General de Educación, veinte años después),* 73-87.

Escolano Benito, A. (1992a), *L'educazione in Spagna. Un secolo e mezzo di prospettiva storica,* Milano.

— (1992b), 'Los comienzos de la modernización pedagógica en el franquismo (1951-1964)', *Revista Española de Pedagogía* No. 192, 289-310.

Franzbach, M. (1988), *Die Hinwendung Spaniens zu Europa. Die Generación del 98,* Darmstadt.

Lucini, F. G. (1993), *Temas transversales y educación en valores,* Madrid.

Marchesi, A. (1992), 'Educational Reform in Spain,' *International Review of Education,* Vol. 38, No. 6, 591-607.

M.E.C. (Ministerio de Educación y Ciencia) (1989), *Libro Blanco para la reforma del sistema educativo,* Madrid.

— (1994), *Centros educativos y calidad de la enseñanza. Propuesta de actuación,* Madrid.

Miclescu, M. (1982), *Bildungsreform in Spanien 1970-1980,* Frankfurt.

Ossenbach-Sauter, G. (1992), 'Hauptprobleme in der geschichtlichen Entwicklung des Schulwesens in Spanien seit dem 18. Jahrhundert', in W. Böttcher, E. Lechner and W. Schöler (eds), *Innovationen in der Bildungsgeschichte europäischer Länder,* Frankfurt, 238-57.

Puelles Benítez, M. de (1991), *Educación e ideología en la España contemporánea,* Barcelona.

—- (1992a), 'Tecnocracia y política en la reforma educativa de 1970', *Revista de Educación, número extraordinario (La Ley General de Educación, veinte años después)*, 13-29.

—- (1992b), 'Oscilaciones de la política educativa en los últimos cincuenta años: reflexiones sobre la orientación política de la educación', *Revista Española de Pedagogía* No. 192, 311-19.

Revista de Educación (1992), *Número extraordinario: La Ley General de Educación, veinte años después*, Madrid.

Chapter 7

School Effectiveness:
Its Challenge for the Future

....

Peter Mortimore

Introduction

In almost all societies, attendance at school is considered essential for children between the ages of six and sixteen. Indeed, in some countries, high proportions of students start school earlier and finish later. There is a widespread presumption that schooling *must* have a positive effect (see, for instance, the six ideal types of school recently specified by European educationalists – Husen et al. 1992) even though – for some children and young people – evidence exists that their schooling, in fact, has had a negative impact on their development. This question of the impact of school has also been explored, over the last twenty years or so, by a series of specialist research studies. These have shown that the effects of schooling are differential: some schools promote positive effects; others, negative ones. Furthermore, some researchers have found evidence that the *same* school can impact differentially on groups of students according to their gender, social class or perceived ability.

In this paper, some of the available evidence on variations between schools will be presented. The *mechanisms* that have been identified by researchers as being implicated in the differential impacts of schools will also be discussed and differences between schools in terms of their effectiveness for different groups will also be considered.

A Model of School Effectiveness

Studies of variations between schools exist in both simple and more sophisticated forms. The simpler studies take little or no account of differences in the characteristics of students entering and attending schools. They also tend to focus on only one outcome measure: that of student scholastic achievement. The difficulties of this simple approach, as experienced teachers will recognise, is that schools do not receive uniform intakes of students: some take high proportions of relatively advantaged ones likely to do well in examinations; others (on the whole) receive high proportions of disadvantaged students who, all things considered, are less likely to do well. So to compare the results of scholastic achievement tests or examinations, without taking into account these differences in the students when they enter the school, and to attribute good results to the influence of the school, may be quite misleading.

The more sophisticated form of research endeavours to overcome the problem of differential student intake by using a statistical technique to compensate – as far as possible – for these differences. Ideally, the statistical technique would be replaced by a random allocation of students to schools but, in most countries, this would be considered an unacceptable infringement of parental rights to choose schools. Accordingly various definitions of effectiveness have been formulated. One definition of an 'effective' school that has been used is: 'one in which students progress further than might be expected from consideration of its intake' (Mortimore 1991:9).

It should be noted that this definition does not assume that *all* students from disadvantaged backgrounds are likely to do badly in tests of scholastic attainment. Some individual students from disadvantaged backgrounds will undoubtedly do well; they will buck the trend. What the definition implies is that, all other things being equal, disadvantaged students are less likely to do as well as those from advantaged backgrounds in any kind of assessment that is highly competitive. Accordingly, measures of progress are needed that can take account of the students' initial starting points.

Various methods have been developed by researchers to deal with the problem of intake differences and various statistical methods, ranging from simple standardisation through multiple regression techniques to the latest multi-level modelling, have been employed to compensate for the initial differences. Regardless of the technique used, however, most approaches have been based on an underlying model of school effectiveness.

In this model, a series of outcomes suitable for the type of school needs to be identified. For an elementary school, these might include basic skills of literacy and numeracy, as well as other measures to do with the students' personal and social development. For a secondary school, the outcomes would be likely to be based on achievement but may also include attendance, attitudes and behaviour.

The second stage of the procedure usually followed, is to relate these chosen outcomes to available data on the characteristics of the students as they entered the school. Such characteristics can include earlier reading levels, former attendance rates, behaviour ratings completed by teachers in the previous phase of schooling and any available information on home background, including the occupations of the parents. Using the most sophisticated mathematical techniques available, researchers then attempt to take account of this intake variation, and to adjust the outcome measures accordingly to provide what is increasingly known as a value-added component. In this way an attempt is made to see how the outcomes would look if all schools had received a similar intake. To use the research terminology: like is being compared with like.

Finally, at the third stage, researchers have usually sought to relate the adjusted outcomes to whatever information has been collected about the life and functioning of the school. Researchers sometimes call this 'backward mapping' of *outcomes* to *process* measures. Of course, to avoid a mismatch, these previous measures need to have been collected at the same time as the particular students were passing through the school.

In essence, then, this is the model that school-effectiveness researchers have been refining over the last twenty or so years as they have investigated the differential effects of schools.

Methodological Issues

Like so many other research topics, studies of the effects of schooling vary a great deal in the scope of their designs and in their chosen methodologies. Some of the problems of interpretation of a number of the earlier studies have already been discussed by Rutter (1983) and by Purkey and Smith (1983). More recently, a number of articles in a special edition of the *International Journal of Educational Research* addressed this topic (Scheerens and Creemers 1989; Raudenbush 1989; and Bosker and Scheerens 1989) as does a series of papers in Reynolds and Cuttance (1992). The types of issues that have been raised include:

- the need for clearer conceptualisation and theory development
- the use of more sophisticated statistical techniques (such as multi-level modelling)
- the inadequacy of current sampling techniques
- the choice of appropriate outcome measures
- the methods of relating outcome to process data.

On the whole, the later studies have used more sophisticated methods than the earlier ones. The improvement in methodology, however, has not been matched by similar advances in the development of theory. The need for better theory has now been recognised and a number of research teams working in this area are addressing the issue.

Studies of School Effectiveness

There have been a great number of important studies of effectiveness carried out in the United States, as the register compiled by the Northwest Region Educational Laboratory illustrates (NREL 1995). Here mention will be made, for illustrative purposes, of only a small selection, mainly of the early studies.

The first major American study was carried out in the late 1960s by Weber (1971). In this project Weber studied four inner-city schools, chosen because they appeared to Weber to be *instructionally effective*. The levels of reading achievement in the schools were well above the average for the neighbourhood, which was considerably disadvantaged. The researcher identified leadership and resource distribution as being key factors, as well as the high expectations and relative orderliness of the schools.

The second study followed in 1974 and emanated from the New York Department of Education's Office of Educational Improvement (N.Y. 1974). In this study, two inner-city schools serving poor populations were identified, one which was considered to be high-achieving and the other low-achieving. The researchers identified a number of factors that appeared to discriminate between the two schools. These factors included the administrative role of the principal as well as the school-wide reading strategy used by teachers.

In California, Madden matched twenty-one pairs of elementary schools on the basis of the student intakes (Madden 1976). He found differences between the schools in terms of the attitudes of the principals and the attitudes and actions of the teachers, as well as in the way that time was used within the different schools.

Brookover and Lezotte (1977) carried out a study of effective schools in Michigan. Using data from a standardised testing programme, they studied six schools of which four appeared to be improving and two declining. Using interviewers to visit the schools and elicit responses from both teachers and students, the authors identified differences in the behaviour of staff, in their expectations and in the way the principal carried out his/her job.

Finally, Edmonds and Frederiksen (1979) published a summary of their research, which had focused on the relationship of pupil background and school effectiveness. In this study they included a reanalysis of data from the Coleman Equal Opportunity Survey of 1966 and they identified a number of effective schools that, they argued, had not been found in the original analysis.

The impact of this series of studies was considerable. Spurred on by the rather optimistic outcomes, a number of research agencies endeavoured to institute school-improvement studies based on the methodology of the school-effectiveness research teams. For instance, in New York between 1978 and 1981, Edmonds (who had become special assistant of the Chancellor of the New York school system) inaugurated a school-improvement project. Similar projects were also started in Milwaukee (McCormack-Larkin and Kritek 1982) and in California (Murphy et al. 1982).

According to Lezotte (1986), many of the early school-improvement projects first tried to 'mandate' change, then attempted to pin the blame for the lack of success on the principals of the schools and, finally, resorted to exhortations for both principals and teachers to work harder. In his view none of these techniques was likely to be successful and it is a wonder that the 'effective schools movement' survived this period. In fact, a number of American researchers used the 1980s to take stock of developments (Purkey and Smith 1983; Good and Brophy 1986) and their lessons have generally been well heeded by contemporary researchers (see for example: Springfield and Teddlie 1990).

The switch from studies of effectiveness to programmes of improvement that took place in the United States during the 1980s received a considerable boost by the amendment to federal legislation introduced by the Hawkins/Stafford 1988 Amendment to the 1965 Elementary and Secondary Education Act. This amendment has enabled school districts to spend public money on a range of school-improvement projects.

Work has since continued in a number of different States, much of it co-ordinated by agencies such as the National Center for Effective Schools Research and Development in Michigan or the Center for Effective Schools at the University of Washington, Seattle.

Work on improving schools has also been undertaken in other parts of the world. For instance, Bashi et al. (1990) have reported on developments in effective schools with Palestinian pupils. Creemers (1992) has reported on a number of studies from the Netherlands and Scheerens has provided a very thorough review of this field of work (Scheerens 1992). In Canada, work has been undertaken in Alberta and in a number of school boards in Vancouver. In Ontario work by Stoll and Fink (1989) and by Fullan (1992) is also important in this connection. The methodologies of school effectiveness research have also been reviewed by an Australian researcher (Chapman 1993).

Mention must also be made of the International School Improvement Project (ISIP). This project has been in operation since 1982. It is co-ordinated by the OECD and involves fourteen separate countries in conferences, seminars and workshops. The project has been written up in a number of different books and papers such as Hopkins (1987).

In the United Kingdom, a considerable number of research studies have addressed – directly or indirectly – the question of school effectiveness, but few as yet have systematically been concerned with progress of school improvement. As with the US studies, this selection has been compiled for illustrative purposes. (See for instance, Reynolds (1989) for a more exhaustive account.)

Among the earliest researchers into school effectiveness in the United Kingdom were Power et al. (1967). In this study the researchers attempted to investigate the delinquency rate of students in a number of schools. Having used a crude attempt to control for intelligence, the research team identified stable differences over a six-year period. They showed these differences to be relatively independent of the schools' catchment area. Unfortunately, due to disagreements with one of the teacher unions over the publication of results, the study was never completed. Its chief benefit, therefore, was in the way it opened up the research questions to subsequent researchers.

Brimer et al. (1978), unlike Power, chose to focus on the academic achievement of students. The research team collected information on the prior achievement of a sample of students drawn from forty-four schools. It used measures of parental occupations and educational levels to control for differences in home background. The researchers found differences between schools even when these intake factors had been taken into account.

Both delinquency and academic achievement, together with attendance and student behaviour, were included in the outcomes adopted by the *Fifteen Thousand Hours* study (Rutter et al. 1979). The sample for this study was small (twelve schools) but a wide range of data enabled the question of whether there were differences between schools – once the intake had been taken into account – to be addressed. The controls for intake factors, such as the use of socio-economic background, students' prior scores, attendance records and behaviour questionnaires, were more comprehensive than those used by Power or Brimer.

Working in a totally different environment, Reynolds (1982) examined the impact of schools on attendance, attainment and delinquency in a Welsh mining community over six years. Although this team did not have individual data on students, they were able to collect evidence about the catchments of the schools and to show that schools had received roughly comparable intakes. They identified systematic differences in attainment, delinquency and attendance and, furthermore, in student unemployment rates after leaving school.

Gray et al. (1983) used a sample of Scottish schools to examine the effects of school organisation on student achievement. Drawing on a survey of over twenty-thousand school leavers, they found some evidence of school differences, over and above those influenced by the social class of the students. Another Scottish study (Willms and Cuttance 1985) also used data from the Scottish leavers' survey. Working with a sample of fifteen secondary schools, the researchers used more sophisticated statistical techniques, including multi-level modelling, to examine differences in attainment whilst controlling for intake.

The work of my colleagues and myself on the *School Matters* study switched the focus of British research from secondary to primary schools (Mortimore et al. 1988). We followed a cohort of nearly two-thousand students through four years of schooling from age seven to age eleven. We adopted a series of outcomes including reading, mathematics, writing, attendance, behaviour and attitude to schooling. We were also able to collect data on speaking skills and on students' attitudes towards themselves as learners. With rich measures of the students' backgrounds (including their language and ethnic group, the occupations of their parents, whether they received any welfare benefits, family size, health records and early educational experience) we were also able to gather data on prior attainment in reading, mathematics and writing and to seek a behaviour rating for each student. In our analysis we too sought to use the more sophisticated techniques that had been developing, in particular, multi-level modelling.

We found considerable differences between schools. Interestingly, some schools appeared better able to foster progress in some aspects of student development than in others although, overall, of the forty-nine schools that remained in the sample at the end of the study, fourteen appeared to foster progress across the board.

Tizard et al. (1988) switched focus yet again, this time to infant schools. Tizard and her colleagues focused on the first two years of compulsory schooling with a sample chosen to contain high proportions of students from ethnic minority groups. The researchers paid careful attention to the collection of information on home background. In addition to the more usual measures, they collected data on the educational activities of students' mothers. Some of their other measures included teachers' judgements about students prospects and pupils' views of naughtiness.

In an interesting variation on school effectiveness, Smith and Tomlinson (1989) studied whether schools were effective for students of minority ethnic groups. Their data included information about the ethnic backgrounds of students, their religion and the employment status of their parents, as well as progress in schools. Using a sample of twenty multi-ethnic schools drawn on a national basis, Smith and Tomlinson used a variety of instruments to collect data. In their analysis they made use of methods of variance component analysis, which took account of the multi-level of data. Their conclusion was that school differences were more important than those caused by the ethnic background of students.

Finally, using data collected by the Inner London Education Authority, Nuttall et al. (1989) studied the examination performance of over thirty-thousand students drawn from one hundred and forty schools. Using intake measures including a verbal-reasoning score, ethnic details, sex and a measure of family income, the research team investigated difference between ethnic groups. The team found that school performance varied along several dimensions, with school having powerful effects on some groups of students. Interestingly, they found some variation over time, with some schools being more effective in one year than in others.

This brief account of work in the fields of school effectiveness and school improvement illustrates the range of the activity of educational researchers. By focusing on 'real-world' problems we have left the shelter of the university and the laboratory and sought to chart the complexity of individual, social and institutional influences.

Of course, there are a number of unresolved questions to do with this group of research studies. Do pupils with different levels of ability, or with different gender, class or ethnic characteristics, achieve different outcomes from the *same* school processes? If schools do have different outcomes for different groups of students, is this due to *policy* differences in the way the pupils have been treated, or to differences in the *reactions* that they have elicited from those who work with them. It is not possible to answer these questions with certainty. My own view, however, is that there is overwhelming evidence that, at primary level, effective schools are effective for *all* kinds of students. At secondary level, the evidence is less clear and it is possible that some kinds of schools suit some kinds of pupils better than others. This question forms part of a further study taking place at the Institute of Education.

It is also unclear how much particular pupils elicit from responses from particular schools. It is quite possible that a school, or an individual teacher, may have a policy of treating pupils equitably – in terms of adult time or encouragement – and yet may end up responding to some groups of pupils differentially. In the *School Matters* study, for example, classroom observations showed no evidence of inequitable attention or any obvious signs of bias. Yet the same study produced evidence of lower expectations for certain groups of pupils – in the main those from Caribbean family backgrounds, or those who were chronologically young for the school year. It is not yet possible to *explain* these differences satisfactorily – we do not have sufficiently clear evidence to do so. We can speculate, however, that a mixture of unconscious prejudice (against groups of students from a different cultural background or against students who appeared 'immature') and of successful student strategies involving the elicitation of positive responses by other groups is responsible. Those students with advantaged backgrounds, perhaps, use their advantages to get even more out of their schooling experience.

Characteristics of Effective Schools

The characteristics of those schools that appeared to be more effective with their pupils are:

Strong positive leadership of schools

Although a few studies (notably, Van de Grift 1990) claim that the headteacher (or principal) has little impact or that the leadership of the school can be provided by somebody else, this mechanism was found almost universally to be important.

Different studies have drawn attention to different aspects of head teachers' roles but the American researchers Levine and Lezotte (1990) have provided a clear analysis of how strong leadership can provide mechanisms to aid effectiveness. In their view, this occurs through the rigorous selection and replacement of teachers; 'buffering' the school from unhelpful external agents; frequent personal monitoring of school achievements; high expenditure of time and energy for school-improvement actions; supporting teachers; and acquiring extra resources for their schools.

British studies support this analysis but, perhaps, add a further subtle task: that of understanding when – and when not – to involve other staff in decision-making. The British studies have found evidence that both autocratic and over-democratic styles of leadership are less effective than a balanced style that depends on the crucial judgement of when, and when not, to act as decision-maker. Fullan (1992) has argued that strong leadership, by itself, is not sufficient in a complex, post-modern society. Instead, he argues that heads have to find appropriate leadership roles for teachers.

High expectations: an appropriate challenge for students' thinking

Despite the limitations of the original experimental work by Rosenthal and Jacobson (1968), the concept of expectations and the way that these can affect the behaviour of both teachers and students have been well assimilated. Dorr-Bremme et al. (1990), for instance, draw attention to the differing mind-sets of two groups of teachers from more, and less, effective schools. Members of the less effective group see their work one way: 'We are educators who work hard to take our students' needs into account. This means considering their total life situations and not expecting more of them than they can do.'

In contrast, those in the more effective group saw their similar task in a quite different way: 'We are people who take our students' needs into account as we teach. This means that we challenge our students, make them work hard and do the very best that they can.'

The one group chose a passive role – affected by forces (the students' problems) over which they could have little control. The other group, whilst recognising that problems existed, adopted a more active stance and sought to challenge the difficulties through challenging the students' thinking.

In the *School Matters* research (Mortimore et al. 1988) we looked at ways in which expectations could be transmitted in the classroom. We found that teachers had lower expectations for students who, for instance, were young in their year group (those with summer birthdays) or who came from lower social classes. However, they found that low expectations, as such, were not held in any simple way for either girls or boys *per se*, despite the fact that boys received more critical comments and girls more praise. These data were difficult to interpret and the research team drew on the findings of Dweck and Repucci (1973) to help explain the data. (Dweck and Repucci found that greater praise from male teachers to female students for less adequate work was linked to stereotyped views of female performance.)

Monitoring student progress

Whilst recognising that monitoring, by itself, changes little, the majority of the studies found it to be a vital procedure, both as a prelude to planning instructional tactics, altering pedagogy or increasing/decreasing workloads. They also saw it as a key message to students that the teacher was interested in their progress.

Student responsibilities and involvement in the life of the school

The mechanism – in its various forms – of ensuring that students adopt an active role in the life of the school was also commonly found to be important. By seeking to involve students in school-oriented activities, or by allocating responsibilities so as so elicit a positive response from them, teachers endeavoured to provide a sense of ownership in the school and in the students' own learning.

Whilst examples of talented, but alienated, students can frequently be found in literature, the general rule appears to be that learning is most likely when the students hold a positive view of the school and of their own role within it. The attitudes of students towards themselves as learners was used as a school outcome in *School Matters* (Mortimore et al. 1988). The outcome consisted of a specially designed measure of self-concept. This was the mirror image of the behaviour scale completed by teachers but also completed by students themselves. The measure revealed clear school differences: some schools produced students who – regardless of their actual ability – felt reasonably positive about themselves; others produced students who were negative about themselves even when – in the judgement of the research team and according to their progress – they were performing well.

Rewards and incentives

Unlike punishments, rewards and incentives appear to act as mechanisms for enlisting positive behaviours and, in some cases, for changing students' (and at times teachers') behaviour. Thus, Purkey and Smith note that a key cultural characteristic of effective schools is a 'school-wide recognition of academic success: publicly honouring academic achievement and stressing its importance encourages students to adopt similar norms and values' (Purkey and Smith 1983:183).

Levine and Lezotte (1990) make two further points. First, that the use of rewards extends beyond academic outcomes and applies to other aspects of school life – a point supported by the British research. Second, that school-wide recognition of positive performance may be more important in urban schools – and especially those in inner cities where, because of the correlation with disadvantage, there are low-achieving students.

My colleagues and I (Mortimore et al. 1988) found that rewards could be given in a variety of ways, if the policy of the school was positive. In some schools, the policy was to reward individuals for good work or behaviour, whilst in others it was to focus on sport and social factors. Schools experienced the problem of trying to create a common system of incentives. This was a particular problem for schools where the age range was wide: rewards that appealed to younger pupils sometimes lost their enchantment for older students.

Parental involvement in the life of the school

Parental involvement is possibly one of the most important issues in the current educational debate. The idea is not new and has been pioneered by a number of educational researchers in the United Kingdom and in the United States. There is also a large and rapidly increasing amount of literature on the topic. In the United Kingdom, much of the debate has been about the gains to be made from developing contact between homes and schools with regard to children's learning, as well as about ways to increase the accountability of schools to parents.

The vital role that parents can play in the intellectual development of their children has long been known, but experiments to use this resource more effectively have met with varied success. One pioneering British study (Tizard et al. 1982), however, demonstrated that parental involvement in reading more than compensated for the use of an extra teacher in schools.

The head-start programmes in the United States (Lazar and Darlington 1982) have also provided evidence that the involvement of parents was an important aspect of the programmes' success, and evidence from England shows that the gap between the achievement levels of advantaged and disadvantaged can be reduced (Athey 1990). Mortimore et al. (1988) found that schools varied a great deal in their attitudes towards parents. Some schools kept parents out; other used parents as cheap labour. A few schools involved parents in the school planning and sought to use their talents and abilities in both the classroom and at home. We found, however, that some head teachers appeared to be insufficiently confident in their relationships with parents, especially in more socially advantaged areas. We also found, though, that when the energy and talents of parents were harnessed, the rewards for the school were high. Interestingly, parent-teacher associations were not necessarily positive, in that they could form a 'clique' for particular groups of parents and thus present a barrier to the involvement of others.

The ways in which parents act as a mechanism for effectiveness are not, however, well understood. It is possible to speculate that where both long-term goals and short-term objectives are shared by teachers and parents, where parents are able to offer considerable help through coaching, and where ideas generated in one area of a child's life can be rehearsed and expanded in another, learning will be helped. Interestingly, Stevenson and Shin-Ying's (1990) study of three cities, Taipei (Taiwan), Sendai (Japan) and Minneapolis (USA), illustrates the length to which oriental families will go to involve not just parents, but other relations, in the coaching of children. The authors show that a belief in the supremacy of hard work over natural ability and the willingness to be critical, when combined with high expectations, can provide powerful support for learning. Parental involvement, however, is not without difficulties and those responsible for school programmes need to have clear policies in place *before* embarking on this potentially valuable strategy (Mortimore and Mortimore 1984).

The use of joint planning and consistent approaches towards students

This mechanism has been clearly recognised by many research studies. Levine and Lezotte argue: 'almost by definition, faculty members committed to a school-wide mission focusing on academic improvement for all students tend to exemplify greater cohesiveness and consensus regarding central organisational goals than do faculty at less effective schools' (Levine and Lezotte 1990:12).

Levine and Lezotte argue that cohesion and consensus are especially important to schools (rather than other institutions) because schools set teachers a number of difficult and sometimes conflicting goals. Thus, teachers have to respond to the individual needs of students whilst emphasising the requirements of the whole class. They have to be fair to the group whilst taking account of individual circumstances. These conflicts are sometimes difficult for teachers to resolve to their own – and to their students' – satisfaction. In such circumstances it is easy for what Levine and Lezotte call 'goal clarity' to be reduced and for improvement efforts to be fragmented.

Where students are subject to conflicting expectations and demands and, as a result, become less confident, they often take time to learn the ways of each new teacher. Whilst this exercise may provide a helpful pointer to the ways of adults, it is clearly not a useful mechanism for a school.

The involvement of staff members in joint decisions, of course, relates to the strength of leadership of the institution. There is clear evidence that when teachers and others in authority (including the deputy head) are given a role to play, they – in the best management traditions – will be far more likely 'to feel ownership' of the institution and, as a result, offer greater commitment to it.

Academic press and the emphasis on learning

There has been much research on this mechanism. Some of it has been absorbed in the question of time-on-task (see for instance Sizemore 1987). A number of research studies have also drawn attention to the wastage of time within the school day, particularly at the start of classes, through poor administration and lack of preparation (Blum 1984). Rutter et al. (1979) also found evidence of time wasted at the end of classes. The researchers described the chaotic situation that could develop where a high proportion of classes in the school finished before the scheduled time. The mechanism, therefore, is not simply about time; it is also about the *use* of time. Mortimore et al.

(1988) noted that, whilst some of the schools in their sample programmed extra time (some twenty minutes per day) for classes, a straightforward correlation with effectiveness was not found. The value of time appeared to depend greatly on how it was used.

These were the most commonly cited mechanisms arising from the research literature. Other factors, however, have frequently been studied and may also be of considerable importance for particular schools at particular times. Thus, if schools receive pupils of a certain background, if the community is subject to particular experiences, or if the school authorities invoke a specific series of reforms, other mechanisms for coping with change will come into play. Whilst these should never supplant the prime focus of school – promoting the learning of pupils – they may act as mediating influences and, as a result, distract the attention of teachers and pupils. Moreover, no school – even one that is on all accounts highly effective – can guarantee, without reservation, progress for *all* its students. Over the years most teachers will have encountered pupils with a great deal of talent who lack the motivation to achieve and who fail, despite all the advantages that they bring to their schooling.

Effectiveness and Efficiency

One of the criticisms made of the school effectiveness work is that it has tended to ignore the area of cost-effectiveness. With governing bodies and head teachers in England now responsible for the financial management of the school, this is no longer acceptable. Accordingly, in our book on associate staff (Mortimore et al. 1994) we suggest that:

> 'Cost-effectiveness', 'efficiency' and 'value for money' are words and phrases which often carry meanings, resonances and implications which make them suspect for many education professionals. There will be those who view this language, and its underlying economic calculus, as alien to the endeavour of educationists. Far from harming the quality of educational activity, we suggest that cost-effectiveness analysis can provide a means for enhancing the quality of educational opportunities in schools. Properly applied, cost-effectiveness in schools is concerned with the relationship between the learning of children and the human and physical resources which contribute to that learning. It should not be equated with parsimony or cheapness; the approach is not on financial outlays alone, but on the use of financial and other resources in relation to desired educational processes and outcomes.

> It is an approach which is well-matched to the search for more effective schools. Effective schools are those in which pupils of all abilities achieve to their full potential. Whether that performance is achieved using more rather than less resources is not, strictly, a part of the assessment of effec-

tiveness. On the other hand, the amount of resources is an essential component of the assessment of cost-effectiveness. Thus, if two schools which are comparable in every respect are equally effective in terms of performance, the one that uses the smaller amount of resources is the more cost-effective. A school that uses its resources more cost-effectively, moreover, releases resources which can be used to promote further development. Cost-effectiveness, in this sense of the term, is highly desirable.

We used this approach to carry out a study on the roles of people – other than teachers – who work in schools. The traditional name for such people is non-teaching staff but, for reasons that we explain in our book (Mortimore et al. 1994), we prefer to call them associate staff. In terms of coping with change, we think an approach that looks, radically, at *who does what* in schools and examines the cost-effectiveness of different options, makes a lot of sense. Furthermore, we found that the greater use of associate staff led to the freeing up – for educational tasks – of teachers and, more particularly, deputy head teachers.

Schools of the Future

It is salutary to remind ourselves that the effective schools of the next decades – the first of the new millennium – may look very different from what we consider effective today.

As the recently published National Commission on Education Report (1993) makes clear the availability of cheap and highly capable information technology may lead to:

- *a move away from class-based teaching towards individual learning*
  (students will be able to follow tailor-made programmes of
  study which will make allowances for particular interests.
  Access to specialist expert systems, which permit the students
  to seek information and advice as easily as the computer users
  of today can access a 'helpline' service, is likely to be available)
- *the exploitation of 'smart card' monitoring and record keeping capabilities*
  (students will have access to detailed record systems able to match
  their areas of weakness to future learning tasks and resource banks
  able to provide appropriate assessment)
- *increased contact between learners (and teachers) in different*
  institutions and with outside formal bodies
  (the availability of cheap, efficient communication will permit students to belong to a much wider group of scholars unbounded by
  class, school or age-cohort limitations)
- *the erosion of the school as a geographical entity*
  (freedom to use electronic worlds of scholarship will reduce the
  value of the school as we know it. Traditionally, three of the

principal benefits of schools have been access to information and to knowledge, through the library, textbooks and the teachers. If all of these – or their modern equivalents – are available to an individual student at the time most suited to him- or herself, then much of the argument for the traditional pattern of schools loses its force)

The implications of such changes for those involved in managing, and teaching in, schools would be considerable. Wood (1993), however, doubts whether appropriate software will be available or whether teachers – currently school pupils themselves – will have been sufficiently exposed as students to information technology to have developed the skills (or the motivation) to achieve such revolutionary change.

In my view, schools as we know them are unlikely to disappear altogether. They are too popular – as places of safety where parents can leave children – and as meeting places for students. They are, however, likely to be changed – and in ways which we have not even considered. The challenge for us all will be to try to ensure that their positive aspects be maintained and strengthened, whilst their less positive aspects are reduced. This is a daunting but exceedingly worthwhile task for educators in the new Europe.

References

Athey, C. (1990), *Extending Thought in Young Children*, London.

Bashi, J., Sass, K., Katzir, R. and Margolin, I. (1990), *Effective Schools – From Theory to Practice: An Implementation Model and its Outcomes*, Jerusalem.

Blum, R. (1984), *Onward to Excellence: Making Schools More Effective*, Portland, Oregon.

Bosker, R. and Scheerens, J. (1989), 'Issues and Interpretations of the Results of School Effectiveness Research', *International Journal of Educational Research*, 13, 7, 741-52.

Brimer, A., Madaus, G., Chapman, B., Kellaghan, T. and Wood, D. (1978), *Sources of Difference in School Achievement*, Slough, Buckinghamshire.

Brookover, W. and Lezotte, L. (1977), *Changes in School Characteristics Co-incident with Changes in Student Achievement*, East Lansing, Michigan.

Chapman, J. (1993), Inaugural Lecture, University of Western Australia.

Coleman, J. S. (1966), *Equality of Educational Opportunity*, U.S. Department of Health, Education and Welfare, Washington.

Creemers, B. (1992), 'School Effectiveness, effective instruction and school improvement in the Netherlands', in Reynolds, D. and Cuttance, P. (eds), *School Effectiveness: Research Policy and Practice*, London.

Dorr-Bremme, D. (1990), 'Culture, Practice and Change: School Effectiveness Reconsidered', in Levine, D. and Lezotte, L. (eds), *Unusually Effective Schools: A Review of Research and Practice*, Madison, Wisconsin.

Dweck, C. and Repucci, N. (1973), 'Learned Helplessness and Reinforcement Responsibility in Children', *Journal of Personality and Social Psychology*, 25, 109-16.

Edmonds, R. and Frederiksen, J. (1979), *Search for Effective Schools: The Identification and Analysis of City Schools that are Instructionally Effective for Poor Children*, Eric Document Reproduction Service number ED 179-396, Cambridge MA.

Fullan, M. (1992), 'The Evolution of Change and the New Work of the Educational Leader', Paper presented to the Regional Conference of the Commonwealth Council for Educational Administration, Hong Kong, August.

Good, J. and Brophy, J. (1986), 'Social and Institutional Context of Teaching: School Effects', *Third Handbook of Research on Teaching*, New York.

Gray. J., McPherson, A. and Raffe, D. (1983), *Reconstructions of Secondary Education: Theory, Myth and Practice since the War*, London.

Hopkins, D. (1987), *Improving the Quality of Schooling*, Lewes.

Husen, T., Tuijnman, A. and Halls, W. (1992), *Schooling in Modern European Society*, Oxford.

Lazar, I. and Darlington, R. (1982), 'Lasting Effects of Early Education: a Report from the Consortium for Longitudinal Studies', *Monographs of the Society for Research in Child Development*, serial number 195, 47.

Levine, D. and Lezotte, L. (1990), *Unusually Effective Schools: A Review of Research and Practice*, Madison, Wisconsin.

Lezotte, L. (1986), 'School Effectiveness: Reflections and Future Directions', Paper delivered at the annual meeting of the American Educational Research Association, San Francisco, April.

Madden, J. (1976), cited in Edmonds, R., 'Effective Schools for the Urban Poor', *Educational Leadership*, 37, 1, 15-27.

McCormack-Larkin, M. and Kritek, W. (1982), 'Milwaukee's Project RISE', *Educational Leadership*, 40, 3, 16-21.

Mortimore, J. and Mortimore, P. (1984). Parents and Schools. *Education*, 164, Special Report. 5th October.

Mortimore, P. (1991), 'The Nature and Findings of Research on School Effectiveness in the Primary Sector', in Riddell, S. and Brown, S. (eds), *School Effectiveness Research: Its Messages for School Improvement*, 9-19, Edinburgh.

—— This chapter draws on material from Mortimer, P. (1995), 'The Positive Effects of Schooling', in Ruttes, M. (ed) *Youth in the Year 2000: psycho-social issues and interventions: the positive effects of schooling*, Cambridge.

Mortimore, P., Sammons, P., Stoll, L., Lewis, D. and Ecob, R. (1988), *School Matters*, London.

Mortimore, P., Mortimore, J. with Thomas, H. (1994), *Managing Associate Staff: Innovation in Primary and Secondary Schools*, London.

Murphy, J., Weil, M., Hallinger, P. and Mitman, A. (1982), 'Academic Press: Translating High Expectations into School Policies and Classroom Practices', *Educational Leadership,* 40, 3, 22-6.

New York (1974), cited in Edmonds, R., 'Effective Schools for the Urban Poor', *Educational Leadership.* 37, 1, 15-24.

Northwest Regional Educational Laboratory (NREL) (1995), *Effective Schooling Practices: A Research Synthesis*, Portland, Oregon.

National Commission on Education (1993), *Learning to Succeed*, London.

Nuttall, D., Goldstein, H., Prosser, R. and Rashbash, J. (1989), 'Differential School Effectiveness', *International Journal of Educational Research,* 13,7, 769-76.

Power, M., Alderson, M., Phillipson, C., Schoenberg, E. and Morris, J. (1967), 'Delinquent Schools', *New Society*, 10, 542-43 .

Purkey, S. and Smith, M. (1983), 'Effective Schools: A Review', *Elementary School Journal,* 83,4, 427-52.

Raudenbush, S. (1989), 'The Analysis of Longitudinal Multilevel Data', *International Journal of Educational Research,* 13, 7, 721-40.

Reynolds, D. (1982), 'The search for effective schools', *School Organisation.* 2, 3, 215-37.

Reynolds, D. (1989), 'School Effectiveness and School Improvement: A review of the British Literature', in Reynolds, D., Creemers, B. and Peters, T. (eds), *School Effectiveness and Improvement: Proceedings of the First International Congress: London 1988*, Groningen.

Reynolds, D. and Cuttance, P. (eds) (1992), *School Effectiveness: Research, Policy and Practice*, London.

Rosenthal, R. and Jacobson, L. (1968), *Pygmalion in the Classroom: Teacher Expectations and Pupils' Intellectual Development,* New York.

Rutter, M. (1983), 'School Effects on Pupil Progress: Research Findings and Policy Implications', *Child Development*, 54, 1, 1-29.

Rutter, M., Maughan, B., Mortimore, P. and Ouston, J. (1979), *Fifteen Thousand Hours: Secondary Schools and their Effects on Children,* London.

Scheerens, J. (1992), *Effective Schooling: Research, Theory of Practice*, London.

Scheerens, J. and Creemers, B. (guest editors) (1989), 'Developments in School Effectiveness Research', *International Journal of Educational Research,* 13, 7.

Sizemore, B. (1987), 'The Effective African American Elementary School', in Noblit, G. and Pink, W. (eds), *Schooling in Social Context: Qualitative Studies.*, 175-202. Norwood, New Jersey.

Smith, D. and Tomlinson, S. (1989), *The School Effect*, London.

Springfield, S. and Teddlie, C. (1990), 'School Improvement Efforts', *School Effectiveness and School Improvement*, 1, 2, 139-61.

Stevenson, H. and Shin-Ying, L. (1990), 'Contexts of Achievement: A Study of American, Chinese and Japanese Children', *Monographs of the Society for Research in Child Development*, serial number 221, 55.

Stoll, L. and Fink, D. (1989), 'An Effective Schools Project – The Halton Approach', in Reynolds, D., Creemers, B. and Peters, T. (eds), *School*

Effectiveness and Improvement: Proceedings of the First International Congress: London, 1988, 286-99, Groningen.

Tizard, B., Blatchford, P., Burke, J., Farquhar, C. and Plewis, I. (1988), *Young Children at School in the Inner City,* Hove and London.

Tizard, J., Schofield, W. and Hewison, J. (1982), 'Symposium: Reading-Collaboration Between Teachers and Parents in Assisting Children's Reading', *British Journal of Educational Psychology,* 52,1, 1-15.

Van de Grift, W. (1990), 'Educational Leadership and Academic Achievement in Elementary Education', *School Effectiveness and School Improvement,* 1,1, 26-40.

Weber, G. (1971), *Inner City Children Can be Taught to Read: Four Successful Schools.* Washington DC.

Willms, J. and Cuttance, P. (1985), 'School Effects in Scottish Secondary Schools', *British Journal of Sociology of Education,* 6,3, 287-306.

Wood, D. (1993), 'Like to Join the Class of 2015?', *The Times,* 25 October, p34.

Chapter 8

The New Generational Contract

From Private Education to Social Services

*Thomas Rauschenbach**

'The path from the individual to the society is long. To make it passable, it is necessary to divide it up into stages' (Streeck 1987:471, translated). In his programmatic approach to the role of 'intermediary organizations' in changing environments, the sociologist Wolfgang Streeck uses these words to describe a set of topics that is once more receiving increasing attention from social philosophy and the social sciences: these topics include the consequences of increasing freedom to make decisions, and an increasing lack of commitments; the social 'supports' and interconnections in plural and individualised life states; or the groupings, authorities and aggregates that co-ordinate and clarify human community in a highly complex and universally networked society that can no longer draw on traditional frameworks of lifestyle. This wide-ranging field covering individualisation, solidarity, and milieu erosion (see Beck and Beck-Gernsheim 1994); communitarianism and liberalism (see Brumlik and Brunkhorst 1993; Honneth 1993); or old and new forms of socialisation, is also of fundamental importance to an educational science that is interested in the changed conditions in which today's young generation are growing up.

Most social scientists will probably agree that the family has become the central link and connection between the individual and society in modern times, between single persons and large social groups. And this central role is always assigned to the family from the perspective of parenthood and childrearing, that is, from a pedagogic

Notes for this chapter begin on page 141.
*Translated by *Jonathan Harrow, Bielefeld University*

perspective: the family is accordingly the social location at which education occurs most directly, at which solidarity is most self-evident. The family is the microsocial system that provides the starting point for the generational reproduction of society. It is the temporal and social interface on which the newborn are plugged into the specific world society, and it provides the interaction systems and forms of socialisation that have to ensure an elementary social integration of the young generation into the current society. The family is thus the empirical, biographical and socialisational starting point for the maturation of children in this society; and for this reason alone, it has to be viewed as a central category in any science of education.

This sociopolitical role of the family as a central channel of education is one of the basic insights of modern educational science. For example, Paragraph 1 of the German Child and Youth Welfare Law, follows Article 6 of the German constitution in stating clearly that 'Care and education of children is the natural right of parents and the foremost duty to which they are obliged.' This basic pattern, whose meaning has been embedded in German law since the turn of the century, may be considered to characterise the elementary educational viewpoint of modern times: education is first of all – 'foremost,' in legal German – the right and duty of parents. The family is therefore the centre of education, or at least the focus of private education. In contrast, all other locations and opportunities, all other interaction systems and events – including school – are always defined only as supporting, supplementing or replacing the family. Youth welfare, the central co-ordinating system of social-pedagogic practice, is therefore always understood only as a breakdown service, as a secondary channel and as a special case of educational assistance. Accordingly, the role of youth welfare – referring once more to Paragraph 1 of the German Child and Youth Welfare law – is 'to advice and support parents … in childrearing' and 'to contribute to maintaining or establishing positive living conditions for young persons and their families'. This perspective does not reveal any autonomous educational task for youth welfare.

However, the modern standard version of this microsystem of the family – that is, mother, father, child/children – has clearly been changing, losing stability and gaining in diversity over the last twenty-five years. Functional losses in one direction and an increase in importance in the other, can be seen. The family is becoming more fragile and open to interference. It is becoming temporally limited and even reduced to phases of the life-course, and thus its fundamental nature is becoming eroded. To put it briefly, the family is becoming pluralised and is losing its self-evident character. The 'standard version' is being joined or replaced by the one-parent family, the second family, the successive or patchwork family, the old or new family triads, the bipolar or two-core family, the marriage-like family, the extended family, or the short-term family, to list just some of the labels used (see, for reviews, Lüscher et al. 1988; Markefka and Nave-Herz 1989). Therefore, one possibility that has to be considered is that the standard version of the family – natural parents in a permanent community with their children – no longer seems to be the predictably stable and lasting link between the individual and society, the indissoluble, unavoidable and alternative-free educational community that still seemed self-evident thirty years ago. Franz-Xavier Kaufmann (1988) formulates this as follows:

> It is almost a commonplace that the social phenomena that we label with the word 'family' have changed during the growth of modern society despite almost constant biological trends. ... However, what these changes consist of, how they relate to ... the processes of change in the whole of society in the modern and most recent epochs, and which future perspectives can be derived from the analysis of such relationships has hardly been explained ... up to now. (p. 391, translated)

In this light, educational science needs to pay more attention to the fact that the family has not only multiplied in its configurations, but has also, simultaneously, changed in its role as a social link and as an educational community, or, in more cautious terms, it could change. In many individual sectors, in the subdisciplines and in single publications, this trend is very conspicuous. So far, there is nothing new about this. Nonetheless, it is conspicuous that systematic educational science, in some ways, the 'basic theory department', has – to put it succinctly – hardly or only marginally, applied the insight that family and school may have been joined by other basal locations of socialisation, or, in the terminology introduced above, other intermediary authorities with a fundamental responsibility for the 'symbolic reproduction' of society (see Habermas 1981), that is, for the maturation of children and adolescents and their social reproduction over the life-course.[1]

In the following, I shall investigate the changes that can be observed in educationally relevant intermediary organisations and modalities.[2] My ideas are oriented toward two assumptions: the first refers more to the 'internal' educational relevance of the intermediary channel of the family, that is, the intersubjective level; whereas the second is directed 'outward' and refers to the changed status of private channels of education within a societal context, and is thus directed toward the intermediary level. If the former refers to relations with persons, the latter focuses on relations with educational organisations.

According to the first assumption, it is less the configural multiplication in family or family-like life forms that is the dominant feature from an educational perspective, but rather the epochal changes that this elicits in the educational co-ordinates embedded within the family. If the family as an educational channel is 'broken down' into its component parts, at least three basic elements can be identified: (a) the family as a (private) constant generational structure, (b) the family as a lasting reciprocal interaction system, and (c) the family as an everyday living, welfare and household community. While, at least in the ideal case, all three elements are woven together in a functional 'standard family', this assumption postulates that the change in the structure of the family has led to a disengagement, segmentation and shift away from the family on these three levels.

The second assumption sees modern society engaged in a trend toward fundamental changes in its generational and social reproduction, that is, in the organisation of growing up into society (including the accompanying everyday lifestyle and the balancing out of social needs). These changes are from private to public, from natural to planned, from informal to stage-managed communities, from the family to social services, from an intergenerational to an intragenerational balancing of needs.

When discussing the first assumption, I shall concentrate on one aspect that seems to have been neglected most in educational science: the relations between the generations.[3] In discussing the second assumption, I shall look at the process of the changes that can be seen in education from the perspective of the increasing differentiation of social services and public education.[4]

Generational Relationships and Generational Conditions

Relations between the generations are a neglected topic of scientific analysis. This conclusion is found repeatedly in work on 'generations' (see, e.g., Walter 1993). However:

> Whenever the acceleration of historical processes and sociocultural change is perceived, whenever the problems of continuity and discontinuity in these processes of acceleration and change are discussed, whenever 'generational contracts' seem to be becoming questionable or fragile, then the problems of 'generational relationships' enter the public discussion. (Herrmann 1987:364, translated)

As Kurt Lüscher has rightly noted (1993:17ff.), this does not change the fact that the generational concept is ambiguous. In other words, it does not yet exist as a theoretical and systematic category, and, for this reason, we are still unable to see a unified and unequivocal use of the concept.[5] At least three different implications can be ascertained (see Figure 1).

Figure 1

The Perspectives of the Generation Category

	Microperspective		Macroperspective		
	Participant perspective	Observer perspective	Participant perspective	Observer perspective	
Synchronic perspective	(1a) 'my sister my friends'	(1b) siblings peers	(2a) 'my generation'	(2b) 'wartime generation, the 1960s protest generation'	= Intra-generational level
Diachronic perspective	(3a) 'my father/ mother, my son/daughter	(3b) grandparents parents children, etc.	(4a) Our grandparents' generation	(4b) Change across generations, epochs	= Inter-generational level
	= Generational relationships		*= Generational conditions*		

Level 1: *Synchronic versus diachronic.* If, in one case, the generation debate is concerned with the description of sameness, that is, with objectively or subjectively shared identity-forming features of one generation, the accent in the other case lies on the description of difference, that is, the features that distinguish between members of different generations. While the former emphasises a synchronic perspective within an intragenerational reference system, the latter stresses a diachronic perspective within an intergenerational frame of reference (see Herrmann 1987; Mannheim 1964).

Level 2: *Macro versus micro.* Generations can also be differentiated according to whether attention is focused on a global perspective of 'abstract' membership, that is, the macroperspective of classification to an anonymously networked group (e.g., the 'wartime generation') or on membership in a microperspective of simple social systems in close social space. F. X. Kaufmann (1993:97) has suggested that the macroperspective can be labelled generational conditions in order to differentiate it from the microperspective of generational relationships.

Level 3: *Participant versus observer.* Finally, and this brings us back to educational science, generational connections can be described from either a participant perspective or an observer perspective, to some extent, as a difference between self- and other positions.[6]

If we now wish to consider the scientific utility of this concept of 'generation', there is some support for the idea that, particularly in the case of the combination of a microperspective and a participant perspective (Fields 1a + 3a), probably no discipline is affected so directly by the existence and importance of generational relationships as educational science: mothers and fathers, daughters and sons, grandchildren and great-grandchildren, grandmothers and grandfathers, as ascending or descending 'family lines', form stable, intergenerational longitudinal supports. The family tree or the family chronology is, in some ways, the only permanent set of relationships in which the interactive positions of old and young, of parents and children, are fixed irreversibly. And the difference in position within the family of origin – the parent-child relationship – is simultaneously the *only* stable configuration of interactions that is coupled with a stable and irreversible temporal difference.[7] Mothers do not just remain the mothers of their sons and daughters throughout their lives, this relationship always retains a stable and unchangeable, that is, an intergenerational time interval.[8] In this light, it is somewhat surprising that educational science has made little theoretical and categorical use of these simultaneously banal and basal insights in any systematic way. For example, Hornstein assumes 'that there is no *systematic* reflection on the generation problem from an educational perspective at the present time' (1983:73, translated), although potential links have always been available.[9] Schleiermacher (1983) has already emphasised the intergenerational interface, that is, the concept of generation as a basic element of education, when he states that:

> The human race consists of individual beings who pass through a certain cycle of being on this earth and then disappear again from the same, and they do this in such a way that those who are simultaneously members of a cycle can always be differentiated into the older and the younger generation. ... Much of the activity of the older generation extends to the younger one, and it [the activity] is more incomplete the less is known about what one does and why one does it. Therefore, there must be a theory that, proceeding from the relationships of the older generation to the younger generation, poses the question: what does the older generation actually want with the younger generation? ... On this basis of the *relationship of the older to the younger generation,* we formulate everything that falls within the domain of this theory. (Schleiermacher 1983:9, translated)

Hence, can we join Schleiermacher in regarding the reference to generations as the basic categorical concept of a science of education? Could the intergenerational interface focus attention on something that has previously been neglected, or even excluded in the basic theories of psychology or sociology; something that, nonetheless, could be an elementary building block in educational theory? Have the social sciences in general – and in their wake, also educational science – overemphasised the horizontal-synchronic perspective of a society of adults? As a consequence, although the temporally preceding strata have been viewed as the autonomous age phases of 'childhood and adolescence', the constitutive interfaces in the 'time lines of life age' (Böhnisch and Blanc 1989:7) in the sense of a vertical-diachronic perspective, that is, the interdependencies between the older and the younger as intergenerational interactions, have been more or less blended out. Can the recent discussion on the life-course and biography (see, e.g., Kohli 1985, 1986) as well as Erikson's (1966:18) concept of 'continuity across time' in personal identity be viewed as a latent expression and confirmation – although only a step in this direction – of the increasing importance of this ninety-degree turn in a scientific perspective? Does this not make it necessary to turn educational science upside down, or, better, place it on its feet and make not only the 'educational reference' as a no longer clearly recognisable generation-induced interaction relationship, but also the intergenerational and intragenerational relationships – such as the parent-child relationship or the peer relationship over the life-course – the starting point of analysis? Should not the somewhat monadic perspective on individual or collective biographies be supplemented by an interactionist generational reference in the temporal chronology of the life-course?[10]

Such a shift in emphasis would make it possible to extend the co-ordinates of educational science into two areas with which it continues to have difficulties even today:

First, it would enable an extension toward a – so to speak – '*life-long* interlinking of the generations', an extension that focuses just as much attention on the generational relationships of women in the 'generation in the middle' to their own children as the relationship to their own parents (see, e.g., Schütze 1993; Trommsdorf 1993). This would increase the general focus of educational science with all its subsidiary areas on generational, social, cognitive, and educational differences, and remove the principal problems in differentiating it from adult education, personnel training, rehabilitation of adults and handicapped persons, or from the clients of social work (see, e.g., Winkler 1988:112ff.).[11]

Second, it would allow an extension of the focus of educational science beyond the merely person-related, interaction-centred levels of the generational relationship by including all the activities that one generation applies to the next in order to shape social living conditions (see, also, Hornstein 1983; Kaufmann 1993; Rauschenbach and Trede 1988). From this perspective, the field of educational science would cover social policy for children, family policy, educational policy or youth-welfare policy just as naturally as it covers topics like teaching skills, didactics or the role of the teacher. Siegfried Bernfeld (1973) has clearly seen this extended frame of reference:

> Childhood passing into an adult society, that is the precondition for education. … It [society] has some kinds of institution that exist only because of the fact of development. … Childhood is taken into account in some way in the construction of society. The society has in some way reacted to the fact of development. I propose that the totality of these

reactions of society should be called education. Education is accordingly the sum of the reactions of a society to the fact of development. (Bernfeld 1973:51, translated)

In essence, this formulates an idea of education based on the difference between generations. Nonetheless, it is an idea that shifts the focus to the '*totality* of these reactions of society', as Bernfeld puts it, rather than just the personal, intersubjective level.

Such considerations on generational differences and the accompanying extensions of the theoretical and systemic horizon embedded in the 'parent-child relationship' or the 'mother-child dyad' have triggered comparatively little debate in educational science. Up to now, as far as I can see, they have not led to any autonomous theoretical discourse and the development of specific scientific hypotheses and perspectives, and, in no way, to an independent systematic approach in educational science (see also Herrmann 1987). In contrast, although the theoretical guidelines of the social sciences have been followed to develop interactionist, holistic, or also systemic, perspectives on the 'childrearer-child relationship' or the 'teacher-student interaction', hardly any use has been made of a consequent intergenerational approach. As Hornstein (1983) has remarked: 'You can understand education in any way you like: There is no way to avoid the fact that it is practically always an activity between members of different generations' (p. 59, translated); or, put another way: that education is interaction is the one aspect; that it is simultaneously also an interaction that is specifically related to the difference or sameness of generational memberships, that is, something like an 'inter- or intragenerationally shaped interaction', is another, a second aspect.[12] This topic has both a sociopolitical and an educational side. I shall briefly consider both.

As to the sociopolitical dimension, it is conspicuous that, up to the present, hardly any light has been cast on the societal organisation of this side of the generation contract, that is, the one with the following generation. Instead, it has always been viewed as an unvoiced norm demand directed toward the 'generation in the middle' – above all, the mothers (see also Kaufmann 1993; Schultheis 1993): young persons of marriageable age are expected to have children, and they are expected to rear them as their own responsibility and with their own resources. At any rate, this is how the 'rights' and 'duties' cited above in Paragraph 1 of the German Child and Youth Welfare Law can be construed.

However, this relates directly to the fact that not only the right and the duty to rear children, but also the ability, seems to be simply taken for granted. However, it is necessary to ask whether parents actually possess the necessary economic, social, temporal and psychological resources as well as the corresponding abilities and skills (see, e.g., Pitrou 1993:92). Indeed, one unmistakable indication of the 'loss' or, better, the increasing problems involved in this intergenerational self-evident truth may well be that men are attributed no genuine ability to raise their children and to 'be there for others' (see Beck-Gernsheim 1983).[13]

It may well be that the tacit linking together of the normative assumption that parents are responsible for rearing their children (including the consequences for family policy and taxation law, see Kaufmann 1993; Schultheis 1993; Walter 1993) with the assumption that it is naturally self-evident that they can also cope with the associated demands, is the reason why there is as yet only a small, innerfamilial 'generation contract' with the young generation.

In contrast, discussion about a 'generation contract' in the ascending sequence of generations, that is, between adult children and their aging retired parents, has been common for a long time. Since Bismarck's social welfare laws and the beginning of a state-run welfare system, there has been at least a *sociopolitical* concept of a generation contract with pensioners. However, this is, as is becoming increasingly clearer, a generation contract with a twofold constraint.

Firstly, it forms a one-sided, vertical intergenerational association between old and young in only an ascending line of employed children, to no longer employed parents that is focused on the end of life (and not on its beginnings).

Secondly, it presents a limited focus on intergenerational guarantees of a material and monetary kind (e.g., pensions, health insurance) and not on person-related services like care; in short, a restriction to material care without sufficient attention to nonmaterial care.

The current confusion about whether German pensions are actually secure is a typical example of this constraint, just like the discussion on the need to finance care for the elderly. Hardly any attention is given to the actual problem, the care performance, that is, the quality of the services, the number and qualifications of the necessary personnel, and the competencies required for appropriate personal and professional care, despite the fact that the question of personal care is at least as important as material care. This concerns the other side of the generation contract.

At the same time, recent political efforts to develop a new fiscal policy to support the family and a sociopolitical child policy seem to indicate a historical change designed to lengthen the generation contract in the other direction as well, and also transform the care of the young generation into a state-supported task. However, up to now, insufficient light has been cast upon this social policy for the young generation in either political or scientific terms (for exceptions, see, e.g., Kaufmann 1988; Liegle 1987; Lüscher 1984).

Both considerations can be used to develop a formal framework based on the concept of person-related services proposed by Badura and Gross (1976) in the mid-1970s. This framework summarises these dimensions as social tasks of the 'generation in the middle' (see Figure 2).[14]

Figure 2

Task fields of a 'three-generation contract' (from the perspective of the 'generation in the middle')

	Child Generation	Parent Generation	Medium
Direct person-related social services	Public education (e.g., all-day kindergartens)	Assistance for the aged	Interaction
Indirect person-related social services	Child allowance education allowance	Pensions	Law, money

As regards the educational dimension, the end-result of my first hypothesis postulates a disengagement of the following functions that were previously bound to the family and the household: a constant generational structure, a permanent reciprocal interaction system and an everyday living community. While in the normal family, the young grow up within an inseparable intertwining of generational relationship, interaction system and living community, it has to be assumed that these three levels no longer simply lock together, under the conditions imposed by a trend toward increasing instability of the household family. For example, although a continuous interaction continues with one parent and one child, this does not necessarily have to take place within an everyday life and care community. Extrafamilial peer relationships and institutions of public education may adopt a more important role as stable interaction references without simultaneously being a life and care community. In short, family-linked generational relationships might become more important without being linked in the same way to a shared household, an intensive interaction system, or even a life and care community (see, e.g., Bien 1994; Vaskovics 1993). Accordingly, without being linked to a shared everyday community, the household- and location-independent intergenerational bond between children and at least one parent, still proves to be the most stable pattern of relationships to be observed in the individualised modern world. As a consequence, the changes caused by modernisation seem to be making generation-related efforts to establish permanent interaction systems and everyday life and care communities increasingly more differentiated and disengaged.

What this means for education, childrearing and the maturation of children and adolescents first needs to be spelled out systematically (see the ideas in Hornstein 1983). In discussing my second assumption, I shall point out that this nonetheless leads to a growth in the importance of social services and public education.

From Private Education to Social Services

There are hardly any signs that modern societies will be able to cope any more efficiently with the social issues and problems that they create than they do at present. There are also currently few indications that the individual and informal resources of life-world linked self-regulation will increase to such an extent during the transformation of modern society, that the direct and compound social costs of modernisation can be met permanently and effectively by individual performance. In contrast, it is precisely the traditional forms of 'being there for others', the private balancing of social needs and social assistance in the family, neighbourhood and social proximity enmeshed in the first phase of modernisation that are beginning to show a more than temporary loss of their powers for personal performance, self-regulation and reciprocal help that were long considered to be self-evident, inexhaustible and effective.

Perhaps my impression is false; but it seems as though a systematic educational science founded on basic theories has not given sufficient recognition to the impact of this trend on the locations and modalities of maturation, the intermediary organisations, social prevention and social welfare. For example, it seems as though educational science has not yet realised that this trend has led to a shift in the balance between private and public education in favor of public education. In the centres of theory formulation in educational science, the extension of publicly organised social services and public education continues to be discussed, if at all, as though it concerned only a small or temporary supplement to the informal networks of private education.[15] More to calm themselves or as a preventive appeasement of otherwise distressed feelings, verbal confirmation is given – despite all the contradictory trends – to the dominant importance of internal family education, care and welfare. Nonetheless, there are plausible indications that, in the future, private family education will form only one of the three pillars of the maturation of children and adolescents and the social reproduction of society. On the one hand, the interaction system and life community of the family is subject to internal encroachments through the omnipotent presence of the mass media, almost like the Trojan horse. On the other hand, there are increasingly strong and self-evident trends indicating that the family is being externally supplemented or even increasingly replaced by public education. I shall briefly address the latter point.

The prototype for the evident changes in the external organisation of the maturation of the young is the preschool institution, particularly the kindergarten.[16] The trends in this area could serve as examples for the entire nonschool social, training and educational system. I shall give three empirical examples to support this.

The growth of kindergartens.

All-day preschools are becoming a self-evident and fixed biographical feature for an increasingly large number of children. Empirical findings clearly support this conclusion: At the beginning of this century, a maximum of 10 per cent of an age cohort attended a kindergarten. In the former Federal Republic of Germany, this proportion rose to a national average of approximately 30 per cent in the 1950s and 1960s. Even in 1970, kindergarten places were available for only about 33 per cent of children in this part of Germany. Within the next 5 years, this rose to almost 60 per cent, and, over the following ten years up to 1985, it rose to over 66 per cent (see Tietze 1993; Tietze and Roßbach 1991:556ff.).

Since then, the German parliament has decreed that, from 1 January 1996, every child will have the right to a place at kindergarten from the age of three up to school enrolment (Paragraph 24 of the German Child and Youth Welfare Law). This creates the potential for 100 per cent coverage (which, by the way, already existed in the end-phase of the German Democratic Republic). However, even if this legal right is achieved for only 90 to 95 per cent of each age cohort, or will have to be delayed in some German states, the increase in coverage still clearly indicates a fundamental change in the conditions in which children grow up in this century: The childhood institution of kindergarten is becoming a fundamental and self-evident component of childhood socialisation. This trend shows growth on three dimensions:

1. the increasing number of hours per day (i.e., the increase in all-day kindergartens and all-day elementary schools);
2. the increasing proportion of the years of childhood spent in public education institutions (from the cradle to kindergarten to all-day elementary school);
3. universal participation, that is, not just a few children, but a trend toward all children.[17]

This trend can be viewed as a clear indication of the growing importance of public education: alongside the family and the school, kindergarten institutions from the cradle to elementary school are becoming a general channel of socialisation. The educational and social services of youth welfare are becoming a self-evident and indispensable component of the basic care in society; they are becoming a regular public educational service for children and young adolescents in modern society.

Female employment

This changing situation is reflected in the childrearers, that is, above all, the women and mothers of the 'generation in the middle' (see also Rabe-Kleberg 1993). Clear trends can also be seen here: Between 1960 and 1992, not only has the number of female employees aged between 25 and 50 increased from approximately 4.5 million to over 8 million, but the proportion of this age group among all employed women has also increased from approximately 45 per cent to 62 per cent. In other words, approximately three out of every four 25- to 50-year-old women were employed in the unified Federal Republic of Germany in 1992 (for detailed figures, see Bundesministerium für Bildung und Wissenschaft 1993, pp. 289ff.). Employment has become normal for women during the middle years of life, while rearing a child at home, in contrast, has become a key problem.[18]

The social welfare professions.

As a trend, this development is also reflected in an increase in personnel in the social, educational and care professions, that is, the professional groups in which the majority of employees are women and in which the social and care services that compensate for the decline in household resources are organised. In the social welfare professions alone, the number of employees has risen from about 30,000 persons in the 1920s to well over 850,000 employees at the end of 1993 in the unified Federal Republic of Germany. This field has witnessed the greatest increase in employees on the German labour market in this century, and it has not yet levelled out. Just since the founding of the Federal Republic of Germany (more precisely: between 1950 and 1991), the number has multiplied seven times over (see Table 1).

As 85 per cent of these employees are women, this means that about 700,000 women are currently employed in social welfare professions. This constitutes at least 5 per cent of all employed women. Extended to all educational, social welfare, and health-related professions,[19] that is, roughly to the total group of person-related social welfare professions, it becomes evident that *almost one out of five employed women now work in social, educational, or health professions.*

Table 1

Percentage Increase in Selected Occupational Groups in the Former
FRG (Index 1950 = 100)

Year	Total number of employees		Employees in health social and educational professions '85-89'		Employees in social welfare professions '86'	
	Total	1950 = 100	Total	1950 = 100	Total	1950 = 100
1950	22,074,000	100	867,264	100	67,000	100
1961	26,527,000	120.217	919,000	105.96	96,000	143.28
1970	24,607,000	111.547	1,300,500	149.95	155,000	231.34
1982	26,744,000	121.216	2,305,000	265.78	314,000	468.66
1991	29,684,000	134.547	3,067,000	353.64	540,000	805.97

Note: Taken from census and microcensus data from various age cohorts

Taken together, such findings seem to indicate nothing less than
that women of the generation in the middle are, first, much more frequently employed than they were at the beginning of the 1970s for
example, while, at the same time, they are conspicuously frequently
employed in those sectors that were previously managed by women
privately within their own families, without an independent income,
and without public recognition: in the 'rearing, care, protection and
welfare of others', in some ways, in the feminine triad of caring
mother, wife, and daughter (see also Schütze 1993). With the 'migration' of women from the familial, informal and private 'being there
for others', and their increased entry into vocational training and
employment, two new phases in the education system begin to
acquire greater importance: the phase: motherhood and childrearing
as a profession (see Giesecke 1987; Rabe-Kleberg 1993; Sachße
1986) and the phase: childhood in public education.

However, one can currently gain the impression that this trend,
which, in some ways, is a response to the generational changes in the
family confirmed above, is of comparatively secondary importance
to educational science. For, up to now, there has been hardly any
systematic discussion, at least not in the fundamental theoretical
debate in educational science, on what is probably the decisive difference for the organisation of maturation in the modern world: the
continually increasing transformation from private to public education, from natural familial to professionally organised and planned
education. I consider that this contains the decisive difference that is
currently emerging as a feature of a new generational contract during the second phase of modernisation, a publically organised contract with the younger generation.

There is insufficient space to go into this trend and its intended and
unintended consequences in detail. However, the ambivalences of
modern life will also leave their traces in this formation and reforma-
tion of the organisation of maturation and social reproduction. It

nonetheless would seem that publicly organised forms of education and educationally planned locations of maturation will increasingly become the new standardised sites of lifestyle and of social integration that, as intermediary organisations and constructed milieus of social stability, will probably take over where the susceptible informal networks of private education no longer function as a matter of course, where natural regulation simply becomes too risky (see Schülein 1984:24). Thus, one could speculate that this second phase of professional education – after and alongside the school – is now irrevocably on the agenda of educational science as a new generational contract.

Notes

1. Naturally, this does not imply that other locations and forms of socialisation have not been considered (see, e.g., the debate on kibbutz education that was particularly strong in the 1970s; Liegle 1971, 1987), or that there has not been a permanent discussion on a third channel of socialisation (e.g., employment, youth work). Nonetheless, I consider that the changed modes of youth socialisation beyond family and school have received insufficient attention from systematic educational science (see also Hornstein, 1983).

2. The family is used only as a contrast in the following considerations. This is not the place for a discussion of the family as a channel of socialisation (see, e.g., Karsten and Otto, 1987; Mollenhauer, Brumlik, and Wudtke, 1975).

3. In comparison, the other two elements seem to be less unexplored (on the family as an interaction system, see, e.g., Mollenhauer et al. 1975). But even when looking at these two elements, there is a need for a more detailed discussion on how the structural properties of the 'reciprocal interaction system of the family' influence education (see, e.g., Luhmann 1988; Schultheis 1993), and on the features of the family as an 'everyday life, care, and education community' in an extension of the debates on the everyday/life-world, the milieu and community, and the household family in social policy. In both areas, educational science could probably make important contributions to a communicatively based theory of the social and society.

4. At this point, it is necessary to emphasise one of the aims of this article: the broad framework can explicate only the dominant theme and not the detailed lines of reasoning. As a result, numerous topics will be mentioned only in passing without discussing them in detail.

5. For a discussion on the benefits of a scientific generation category, see Mannheim (1964). For a discussion on its relevance to educational science, see, for example, Hornstein (1983), Schmied (1984), and Herrmann (1987), in which a different use of the category is also to be found.

6. The continuous debate since Mannheim (1964) on the difference between a purely temporal-chronological sequence of generations, that is, a mere summarisation of some age groups in the sense of empirical age cohorts compared to a sociologically founded membership of a generational unit in the sense of shared beliefs, identical habitus and a similar processing of shared events, is of secondary

importance in this context (see Herrmann, 1987, who criticises the 'fixation on cohorts' in Schmied, 1984), because these are to some extent circumvented by educationally relevant statements such as 'those are my parents' or 'those are my children' in the sense of a subjectively relevant membership of a generation. The educational discussion seems to have underestimated this participant-oriented microperspective on generational relationships (see, e.g., Winkler 1988:354).

7. This also implies that a constant difference across time between parents and children is eclipsed by an initial cognitive and social inequality that may undergo lasting changes.

8. In this context, it is continuously pointed out that despite the increasing instability of partner and marriage relationships, it is, above all, parent-child relationships – and here, in particular, mother-child relationships – that still prove to be the only stable interaction relationships (see, e.g., Beck-Gernsheim 1990; Schultheis 1993; Schütze 1993).

9. Although the generation concept has been used repeatedly in educational science (see, e.g., Herrmann 1987; Hornstein 1983; Mollenhauer 1964), it still cannot be viewed as one of the key concepts in the discipline (unlike education, learning, school or teaching).

10. It is easy to find examples of this in individual life phases: for early mother-child dyads, see, for example, Lorenzer (1972, 1976) or, in general, the psychoanalytically oriented discussion; for the conflict between the generations in adolescence, see recently, for example, Böhnisch and Blanc (1989) or Hornstein (1983), as well as the discussions in the 1950s and 1960s related to the work of Eisenstadt and Schelsky; for intergenerational problems in the 'sandwich generation', see, for example, the papers in Lüscher and Schultheis (1993), Borchers and Miera (1993), and Bien (1994). However, all these discussions have generally been restricted to a specific life phase and have not led to a general treatment at the centre of educational science. Therefore, it is not surprising that a complete analysis of the course and change of intergenerationally linked parent-child relationships across the life-course from a micro- and macroperspective is still not available from a systematic educational science perspective.

11. Klaus Mollenhauer (1964) argues in a similar direction when he states that 'the relation between the generations is a general problem in educational science [that] has become particularly important for the field of social pedagogics' (p. 30, translated).

12. The criticism that these inter- and intragenerational interactional interfaces lose their importance through the modernisation process, that is, age becomes relative (e.g., Böhnisch and Blanc 1989) or that intergenerational differences in the parent-child relationship are being replaced by a more partner-like and friendly parent-child relationship may well be true. However, such statements can only be meaningful when they are contrasted with intergenerational relationships, that is, when they are linked back to diachronic differences. Apart from this, contradictory findings could also be interpreted as a strengthening of the intergenerational relationships: 'While the bonds of the married form of partnership seem to be declining, "avowed parenthood" seems to be becoming more and more of a strict commitment' (Kaufmann 1993:106, translated; see also Schütze 1993; Vaskovics 1993).

13. Two comments on this: first, in order to avoid unnecessary misunderstandings, it must be stressed that, even if parents did lack resources and abilities, this would in no way imply that education should be transferred completely to professionals and thus completely removed from the private sphere. This can be illustrated with an analogy: in a society that can no longer function without motorisation, the ability to speed up travel can be assigned to experts, and, as a private person, one can let oneself be driven in cabs, buses, or taxis, that is, travel with the help of experts. Or,

on the other hand, one can oneself also learn to drive (which also has to be planned, initiated and carried out in a publicly responsible manner).

Second, this is naturally in no way a claim that we are dealing with an objective 'loss' that can be diagnosed as such. Instead, it is suggested that the increasingly more complex framing conditions contribute to making 'spontaneous, carefree education' more difficult, just like the increased potential for reflection leads to a greater sensitivity that also results in higher expectations regarding 'educational competence'.

14. With reference to Badura and Gross (1976), it is possible to discriminate four task fields of a 'three-generation contract': (a) direct, person-related social services (e.g., all-day kindergartens) compared to (b) indirect, person-related social services for the young generation (e.g., child allowance, education allowance, etc.) on the one side; and (c) direct, person-related social services (e.g., assistance for the aged) compared to (d) indirect, person-related social services for the older generation (e.g., pensions and health care) on the other. This makes it possible to differentiate the direct and indirect forms following Kaufmann (1982) as 'sociopolitical' and 'educational' forms of intervention.

15. Admittedly, this criticism does not apply to educational science informed by the social sciences or to debates from the perspective of feminist policy (see, e.g., Rabe-Kleberg, 1993, who also provides detailed further references).

16. For a discussion on the kindergarten and its changed role, see, for example, Erning et al. (1987); Großmann (1994); or Rabe-Kleberg et al. (1986).

17. For a discussion of this trend and its theoretical explanation, see Barabas et al. (1975, 1977) and Blanke and Sachße (1978).

18. This problem has been pointed out repeatedly by women and in feminist research (see, e.g., Beck-Gernsheim, 1980; Krüger, 1992; Krüger et al., 1987; Rabe-Kleberg, 1993).

19. These figures also increase enormously when data are based on the broader professional category of social and educational professions that also includes teachers. In the former Federal Republic of Germany, the number of employees almost doubled from approximately 815,000 in 1973 to 1.58 million in 1991 (FRG in total: 2.145 million). If the category of person-related social services is extended to include the health professions, the most recent findings from the 1991 microcensus indicate that more than 3 million (FRG in total: ca. 4 million), and thus more than 10 % of all employees in the former Federal Republic of Germany, work in social, educational and health professions (compared to under 6 % in 1973 and 3 % to 4 % in 1950). Projections for 1993 and the entire Federal Republic of Germany indicate that this figure has now reached about 4.5 million, 70 % of whom are women. Assuming that approximately 16 million women were employed in the entire Federal Republic of Germany at this time, this means that almost 20 % of employed women work in an educational, social or care profession.

References

Badura, B. and Gross, P. (1976), *Sozialpolitische Perspektiven. Eine Einführung in Grundlagen und Probleme sozialer Dienstleistungen*, Munich.

Barabas, E. et al. (eds) (1975), *Jahrbuch der Sozialarbeit 1976*, Reinbek.

Barabas, E. et al. (eds) (1977), *Jahrbuch der Sozialarbeit 1978*, Reinbek.

Beck, U. and Beck-Gernsheim, E. (eds) 1994, *Riskante Freiheiten – Zur Individualisierung von Lebensformen in der Moderne*, Frankfurt.

Beck-Gernsheim, E. (1980), *Das halbierte Leben. Männerwelt Beruf – Frauenwelt Familie*, Frankfurt.

Beck-Gernsheim, E. (1983), 'Vom "Dasein für andere" zum Anspruch auf ein Stück "eigenes Leben". Individualisierungsprozesse im weiblichen Lebenszusammenhang', in *Soziale Welt* 34, 307-40.

Beck-Gernsheim, E. (1990), 'Alles aus Liebe zum Kind', in U. Beck and E. Beck-Gernsheim, *Das ganz normale Chaos der Liebe*, Frankfurt, 135-83.

Bernfeld, S. (1973), *Sisyphos oder die Grenzen der Erziehung*, reprint of 1925 edn, Frankfurt.

Bien, W. (ed.) (1994), *Eigeninteresse oder Solidarität. Beziehungen in modernen Mehrgenerationenfamilien*, Opladen.

Blanke, T. and Sachße, C. (1978), 'Theorie der Sozialarbeit', in A. Gärtner and T. Sachße (eds), *Politische Produktivität in der Sozialarbeit*, Frankfurt/New York, 15-56.

Böhnisch, L. and Blanc, K. (1989), *Die Generationenfalle. Von der Relativierung der Lebensalter*, Frankfurt.

Borchers, A. and Miera, S. (1993), *Zwischen Enkelbetreuung und Altenpflege. Die mittlere Generation im Spiegel der Netzwerkforschung*, Frankfurt/New York.

Bronfenbrenner, U. (1993), 'Generationenbeziehungen in der Ökologie menschlicher Entwicklung', in Lüscher and Schultheis (1993), 51-73.

Brumlik, M. and Brunkhorst, H. (eds) (1993), *Gemeinschaft und Gerechtigkeit*, Frankfurt.

Bundesministerium für Bildung und Wissenschaft (1993), *Grund- und Strukturdaten – Ausgabe 1993/94*, Bonn.

Erikson, E.H. (1966), *Identität und Lebenszyklus*, Frankfurt.

Erning, G., Neumann, K. and Reyer, J. (1987), *Geschichte des Kindergartens*, vols I and II, Freiburg.

Giesecke, H. (1987), *Pädagogik als Beruf. Grundformen pädagogischen Handelns*, Weinheim/Munich.

Grossman, W. (1994), *Kindergarten. Eine historisch-systematische Einführung in seine Entwicklung und Pädagogik*, 2nd edn, Weinheim/Basel.

Habermas, J. (1981), *Theorie des kommunikativen Handelns*, 2 Bände, Frankfurt.

Herrmann, U. (1987), 'Das Konzept der Generation', in *Neue Sammlung*, 27, 364-77.

Honneth, A. (ed.) (1993), *Kommunitarismus. Eine Debatte über die moralischen Grundlagen moderner Gesellschaften*, Frankfurt.

Hornstein, W. (1983), 'Die Erziehung und das Verhältnis der Generationen heute', in *Zeitschrift für Pädagogik*, Supplement 18, 59-79.

Karsten, M.-E. and Otto, H.-U. (eds) (1987), *Die sozialpädagogische Ordnung der Familie. Wandlungen familialer Lebensformen und sozialpädagogische Interventionen*, Weinheim/Munich.

Kaufmann, F.-X. (1982), 'Elemente einer soziologischen Theorie sozial-politischer Intervention', in F.-X. Kaufmann (ed.), *Staatliche Sozialpolitik und Familien*, Munich/Vienna, 49-86.

Kaufmann, F.-X. (1988), 'Familie und Modernität', in Lüscher et al. (1988), 391-415.

Kaufmann, F.-X. (1993), 'Generationsbeziehungen und Generationenver-hältnisse im Wohlfahrtsstaat', in Lüscher and Schultheis (1993), 95-108.

Kohli, M. (1985), 'Die Institutionalisierung des Lebenslaufs', in *Kölner Zeitschrift für Soziologie und Sozialpsychologie* 37, 1-29.

Kohli, M. (1986), 'Gesellschaftszeit und Lebenszeit. Der Lebenslauf im Strukturwandel der Moderne', in J. Berger (ed.), *Die Moderne – Kontinuitäten und Zäsuren* (special edn 4 of *Soziale Welt*), Göttingen, 183-208.

Krüger, H. (ed.) (1992), *Frauen und Bildung*, Bielefeld.

Krüger, H. et al. (1987), *Privatsache Kind – Privatsache Beruf: Zur Lebenssituation von Frauen mit kleinen Kindern in unserer Gesellschaft*, Opladen.

Liegle, L. (1971), *Familie und Kollektiv im Kibbutz*, Weinheim.

Liegle, L. (1987), Welten der Kindheit und Familie. Beiträge zu einer pädagogischen und kulturvergleichenden Sozialisationsforschung, Weinheim.

Lorenzer, A. (1972), *Zur Begründung einer materialistischen Sozialisationstheorie*, Frankfurt .

Lorenzer, A. (1976), 'Zur Dialektik von Individuum und Gesellschaft', in Th. Leithäuser and W. R. Heinz (eds), *Produktion, Arbeit, Sozialisation*, Frankfurt, 13-47.

Lüscher, K. (ed.) (1984), *Sozialpolitik für das Kind*, Frankfurt et al.

Lüscher, K. (1993), 'Generationenbeziehungen. Neue Zugänge zu einem alten Thema', in Lüscher and Schultheis (1993), 17-47.

Lüscher, K., Schultheis, F. and Wehrspaun, M. (eds) (1988), *Die 'postmoderne' Familie. Familiale Strategien und Familienpolitik in einer Übergangszeit* (*Konstanzer Beiträge zur sozialwissenschaftlichen Forschung*, Band 3), Konstanz.

Lüscher, K. and Schultheis, F. (eds) (1993), *Generationenbeziehungen in 'postmodernen' Gesellschaften. Analysen zum Verhältnis von Individuum, Familie, Staat und Gesellschaft* (*Konstanzer Beiträge zur sozialwissenschaftlichen Forschung*, Band 7), Konstanz.

Luhmann, N. (1988), 'Sozialsystem Familie', in *System Familie* 1, 75-91.

Mannheim, K. (1964), 'Das Problem der Generationen', 1928 reprinted in K. Mannheim, *Wissenssoziologie. Auswahl aus dem Werk* (edited and with an introduction by K.H. Wolff), Berlin/Neuwied, 509-65.

Markefka, M. and Nave-Herz, R. (eds) (1989), *Handbuch der Familien- und Jugendforschung*, Band 1: *Familienforschung*, Neuwied/Frankfurt.

Mollenhauer, K. (1964), *Einführung in die Sozialpädagogik. Probleme und Begriffe*, Weinheim.

Mollenhauer, K., Brumlik, M. and Wudtke, H. (1975), *Die Familienerziehung*, Munich.

Pitrou, A. (1993), 'Generationenbeziehungen und familiale Strategien', in Lüscher and Schultheis (1993), 75-93.

Rabe-Kleberg, U. (1993), *Verantwortlichkeit und Macht. Ein Beitrag zum Verhältnis von Geschlecht und Beruf angesichts der Krise traditioneller Frauenberufe*, Bielefeld.

Rabe-Kleberg, U., Krüger, H. and Derschau, D. v. (eds) (1986), *Qualifikationen für Erzieherarbeit*, Band 3: *Beruf oder Privatsache – eine falsche Alternative*, Munich.

Rauschenbach, Th. (1992), 'Soziale Arbeit und soziales Risiko', in Th. Rauschenbach and H. Gängler (eds), *Soziale Arbeit und Erziehung in der Risikogesellschaft*, Neuwied et al., 25-60.

Rauschenbach, Th. (1992), 'Sind nur Lehrer Pädagogen? Disziplinäre Selbstvergewisserungen im Horizont des Wandels von Sozial- und Erziehungsberufen', in *Zeitschrift für Pädagogik* 38, 385-417.

Rauschenbach, Th. and Trede, W. (1988), 'Arbeit und Erziehung. Ein Beitrag zur soziologischen Debatte um Arbeit in pädagogischer Absicht', in *Neue Praxis* 18, 12-31.

Sachße, Chr. (1986) *Mütterlichkeit als Beruf. Sozialreform und Frauenbewegung 1871-1929*, Frankfurt.

Schmied, G. (1984), 'Der soziologische Generationsbegriff', in *Neue Sammlung* 24, 231-44.

Schleiermacher, F. (1983), *Pädagogische Schriften I. Die Vorlesungen aus dem Jahre 1826* (edited by E. Weniger), Frankfurt et al.

Schülien, J.A. (1983), 'Gesellschaftliche Entwicklung und Prävention', in Wambach, M.-M. (ed), *Der Mensch als Risiko*, Frankfurt, 13-28.

Schultheis, F. (1993), 'Genealogie und Moral: Familie und Staat als Faktoren der Generationenbeziehungen', in Lüscher and Schultheis (1993), 415-33.

Schütze, Y. (1993), 'Generationenbeziehungen im Lebensverlauf – eine Sache der Frauen?', in Lüscher and Schultheis (1993), 287-98.

Streeck, W. (1987), 'Vielfalt und Interdifferenz. Überlegungen zur Rolle von intermediären Organisationen in sich ändernden Umwelten', in *Kölner Zeitschrift für Soziologie und Sozialpsychologie* 39, 471-95.

Tietze, W. (1993), 'Institutionelle Erfahrungsfelder für Kinder im Vorschulalter. Zur Entwicklung vorschulischer Erziehung in Deutschland', in Tietze and Roßbach (1993), 98-125.

Tietze, W. and Roßbach, H.-G. (1991), 'Die Betreuung von Kindern im vorschulischen Alter', in *Zeitschrift für Pädagogik* 37, 555-79.

Tietze, W. and Roßbach, H.-G. (eds) (1993), *Erfahrungsfelder in der frühen Kindheit. Bestandsaufnahme, Perspektiven*, Freiburg.

Trommsdorff, G. (1993), 'Geschlechtsdifferenzen von Generationsbeziehungen im interkulturellen Vergleich. Eine sozial- und entwicklungspsychologische Analyse', in Lüscher and Schultheis (1993), 265-85.

Vaskovics, L. (1993), 'Elterliche Solidarleistungen für junge Erwachsene', in Lüscher and Schultheis (1993), 185-202.

Walter, W. (1993), 'Unterstützungsnetzwerke und Generationenbeziehungen im Wohlfahrtsstaat', in Lüscher and Schultheis (1993), 331-54.

Winkler, M. (1988), *Eine Theorie der Sozialpädagogik*, Stuttgart.

Chapter 9

Tendencies towards Pluralisation in Society and the Pedagogical Control of Risk

Frieda Heyting

Introduction

'Pedagogical scientists are abandoning their social mission' (Winter 1993) – this statement could be read in the headlines of a national morning paper. It was a reaction to a long article entitled 'Schools talk, pedagogues keep silent' (Schöttelndreier 1993), which had been published some days previously. It was rather remarkable that the content of this article was derived from a series of statements by a number of pedagogical scientists, all of them theoreticians, with respect to the pedagogical questions of the day. Apparently, the editors of the newspaper could interpret their opinions, which covered half a page, only as silence.

On closer consideration, it appeared to be rather easy to summarise the almost identical core of those theoreticians' views in a single sentence: all we can do is learn to accept the uncertainty generated by the fact that different people have different opinions on proper behaviour and life values. The failure that was imputed to the scientists was even more strongly emphasised in the sharp antithesis the writer of this article made with the behaviour of Dutch pedagogical scientists in the 1950s. In those days pedagogues, confronted with the demoralisation of youngsters apparently brought about by the war, had advocated a new communal spirit emphasising personal development and responsibility. Compared to this spirit, the reticence shown by contemporary pedagogues cuts a sorry figure.

'So it seems that nowadays pedagogical issues must be solved without any guidance', is the rather despondent conclusion of the writer.

That much is clear: diversity and uncertainty appear to be the problem and its acceptance is not regarded as a possible solution. I will pay some attention to this theme, mainly because it implies an obvious appeal to us, pedagogical scientists. Based on some examples of Dutch educational policy I will examine which forms of diversity are considered problematic and relevant for education, and in what way policy deals with them. Subsequently I will discuss some characteristic aspects of the concepts of child development, of social development and, in line with these, of education, which are implied by Dutch educational policy. These concepts of development and education appear, though, to be less alien to pedagogical science than one might surmise after becoming aware of the gap just mentioned between theory and educational policy in the Netherlands; fortunately, in fact, because in this case theory will also profit from this analysis. In the end, the most important gap does not separate theory and educational policy, but current social analyses and scientific activities, on the one hand, and the dominant educational concepts in theory as well as practice, on the other. The conclusions for our educational conceptions of recent views from the social sciences and the philosophy of science are far from being entirely drawn.

Before proceeding to the actual analysis I will discuss my own point of departure. This perspective will be further developed in the course of the analysis.

Unity and Diversity

Although the pedagogical problematic mentioned has been related to pluralisation processes, it is not difficult to indicate processes of universalisation that are just as typical of our modern society. The development towards a world economy, for instance, is accompanied by worldwide communication structures, partly stimulated by migration, partly by improved means of communication. In the wake of this development a number of standardisation processes are taking place. In this connection Beck (1986:210) mentions areas such as finance, law, mobility and education. These universalising developments are also noticeable in the daily life of children. Almost all West European children go to school and follow curricula that, in various countries, are becoming more and more alike. Religious education, as well as other forms of specifically (sub)cultural education do still exist, but nowadays they are often made optional, made universal by constructing new perspectives (such as 'knowledge of world religions') or left open to personal initiative. In these processes of universalisation the ideas of time and space are also changing. Communication and experience are less and less restricted by limits of time or space. The media plays a very important role in this 'intrusion of distant events into everyday consciousness' (Giddens 1991:27).

Individualisation processes that also score very highly as characteristics of our current society are, at first sight, an illustration of pluralisation processes. In this connection Giddens (1991) points out that personal integration, the development of one's identity, has currently become an individual task, the responsibility for which can no longer be ascribed to anybody else, not even to the family. According to Bauman (1987), moreover, this task must be carried out under the aggravating conditions created by the fragmentation of authority. Universalisation aspects, however, are also noticeable in these processes of individualisation. Giddens, for instance, states that worldwide structures of production and consumption have become an important medium for the expression of the required reflexive individuality: 'Modernity opens the project of the self, but under conditions strongly influenced by standardising effects of commodity capitalism' (1991:196). Beck speaks of individualism as a 'neuen Modus der Vergesellschaftung' ('new mode of socialisation') (1986:5). He indicates that establishing one's course of life is more and more prestructured and restricted by institutions that use fixed standard biographies.

By this last remark I do not want to pretend that diversity, which appears to cause such a great deal of anxiety among Dutch educational policymakers, has turned out to be less troublesome than was expected. Rather I would like to emphasise that, depending on the perspective taken, one will notice either unity or diversity. For this reason it is important to analyse further the pedagogical perspective of our educational policy. At first sight one aspect is already obvious: the solution to the problem is expected not from coincidence or fortune, but from us. This kind of approach to our problems is the core of what is currently called our modern 'risk society' (Beck 1986, Giddens 1990, Luhmann 1991). What one could generally express as balancing the makable with the given has a central position in such a society. Both our individual biographical future and our social future is considered to be dependent upon our own decisions, which are to be based on rational risk calculation.

Risk calculation offers no certainty with regard to goal achievement, but it does provide a balance of probabilities. Even in the case of an unlikely outcome one can still maintain that the right thing was done (Luhmann 1992:144). Nor is it possible to give an objective and univocal assessment of the content of risk. What can be regarded as risk in a given situation depends on the conceptual perspectives underlying the calculation. The bases for risk calculation are the formulated problem (regarded as the makable) in combination with the relevant circumstances and the required knowledge (regarded as the given). Consequently risk assessment is also dependent on what is judged as reliable knowledge. According to Giddens the concept of risk is inextricably connected to the concept of trust, which becomes apparent when one has to appeal to the rightness of abstract principles that one cannot entirely understand. In our modern technological society this happens more and more. We cannot imagine this society without experts and expert systems to appeal to (Giddens 1990:88ff.).

In view of the above our problem now is the reconstruction of the perspective from which educational policymakers regard risk in pedagogical issues. The significance and the pedagogical concern for diversity must be seen as part of this. With regard to educational policy this implies questions such as: what does the combination of the stated problem, the considered circumstances and the required knowledge look like? Can the reasons for the extent of the undermining of the trust once vested in theoretical pedagogy as an expert system be understood? And is it possible to do something about this situation?

Cultural Diversity and Learning Deficits

The first example of pedagogical policy to be discussed here concerns the improvement of the educational chances of children with non-Dutch linguistic and cultural backgrounds. The so-called family intervention programmes occupy a major place in this policy. The Minister of Welfare, Health and Cultural Affairs, d'Ancona, describes the specific aim of these programmes as follows: 'the introduction of language, reading and play activities, particularly in migrant families with children. This should be done by helping parents to stimulate the learning process of their children by means of so-called informal instruction' (1992:6). The target group is further restricted to children from 'ethnic minorities'. This term is used for 'groups with foreign cultural origins and objectively a low social position' (Meijnen 1992:21).

According to the minister these children lack elementary conceptual and language skills that are important in order to keep pace with school education. Conceptual development in their own language also shows obvious deficits (1992:4). D'Ancona points out that the social and cultural climate in both family and neighbourhood are important for conceptual development in children. Because, as she states, those children who belong to minority groups often experience 'discrepancies between (pedagogical) norms, values, and habits' (1992, 4) in family, schools, and neighbourhood, and it should be obvious that family and neighbourhood are to be recognised as relevant contexts for intervention. In order to achieve a good contact with the families, one should get members of their own ethnic group to teach parents how to deal with the available educational materials of the programme. All in all, a strictly structured approach is defended, which is also recommended by various policy-supporting researchers. Such an approach is expected to stimulate general learning and thinking skills, which are important for transfer and generalisation (Leseman 1992:43).

In the sensitive field of minority policy one can always expect criticism, and of course this case is no exception. Family intervention programmes do not operate in a totally orthodox way, 'by the book', and they also take into account the original culture of the migrant groups, by seeking a connection with the children's families. All the same many critics launched more or less direct accusations of cultural hegemony against these programmes. The differences between home and school situations, pointed out by Minister d'Ancona, are endorsed by these critics. They are opposed, however, to the opinion that the consequential differences in thinking and conceptual development should be interpreted as *deficits* (see also Pels 1991). A gap between the children's conceptual and language skills and the presuppositions of the Dutch educational system should, according to these critics, not simply be seen as an objective deficit.

Many critics also point to parallels with the compensatory programmes that were developed in the 1960s and 1970s, for children from lower socio-economic classes (Singer 1991). Something similar was expressed then. The policy at the time was also based on a deficiency hypothesis as opposed to the critics' differential hypothesis (Velgersdijk 1991). Furthermore, one has not forgotten that these compensation programmes scored quite poorly (Slavin et al. 1989).

Finally, the structured approach of the intervention programmes is criticised, because they do not leave enough room for the active role of children in their own development (Kloosterman 1991, Hermanns 1992). Such an approach would result not in the stimulation of general and transferable thinking and conceptual skills (cf. Leseman 1992) but rather in a limited training.

No matter what one might think of these criticisms they highlight the kind of risk calculation underlying the policy. As is mentioned above, I would express this calculation in terms of the stated problem, the kinds of circumstances considered relevant, and the resulting need for knowledge. The general problem underlying the family-oriented intervention programmes for children in disadvantaged circumstances, concerns the deviation of migrant children from the starting point as assumed by the educational system. The diversity that, from a pedagogical point of view, is regarded as problematic is thus related to this deviation. The cultures of family and neighbourhood are considered the relevant circumstances in this context; the basis for educational capital is, or should be, founded there. The knowledge required in order to solve the problem, finally, is a method of influencing the interaction with the children concerned in such a way that they will still meet the starting requirements of school education.

I will return to this type of pedagogical risk calculation when I discuss further the concepts of development and education implied in this policy are discussed here. But first I will give another example of Dutch educational policy in which diversity plays a role and in which comparable modes of thinking are used.

Delinquency and the Decay of Moral Principles

The social mission that, according to the newspaper article mentioned at the beginning of this essay (Schöttelndreier 1993), has been abandoned by the theoreticians was related only indirectly to the above-discussed problem of educational deficits. Of primary concern was an issue, which even called for a new word in Dutch: *normvervaging* (decay of moral principles). As a result of the growing delinquency in the Netherlands in recent decades, newspapers and periodicals have published vehement discussions of its possible causes. Headlines such as 'Holland deprived of moral principles' ('Normloos Nederland'; NRC, see Ende 1993) provide a good indication as regards to the present line of thought.

Via memoranda and interviews, Minister of Justice Hirsch Ballin made a strong plea to schools, churches, and families to restore morality (Ende 1993; Nouwen 1993). During a symposium, Prime Minister Lubbers stated that the concept of 'citizenship' should be reinstated: civilians in co-operation with policemen, educators and clergymen should create a type of morality that is strong enough to harmoniously unite Dutch society.

Although these statements might create the impression that Lubbers and Hirsch Ballin believe that morality in the Netherlands has vanished, this is not what they mean to say. They do not wish to restore the straitjacket of the past (Hirsch Ballin, see Ende 1993) or (re)create narrow, homogeneous morals (Lubbers, see Ende 1993). In some respects they even observe moral progress. Hirsch Ballin, for example, finds that people these days attach more value to honesty and equality of sexes, races, religions and philosophies of life (see Nouwen 1993). Such considerations induced Assistant Secretary Kosto, from the Ministry of Justice, to use the concept of 'fragmentation' rather than that of decay or vanishing morals. All of the above-mentioned government members do agree, however, that the individualistic perspective, the orientation towards one's own situation and interests, is too dominant. As a result current moral codes lack unifying power.

There is also a second point on which they all agree: the solution must be found in education. Hirsch Ballin holds that education should provide a basic package of norms and values. He directs this appeal to parents, schools and churches, all of which he regards as traditional guards of virtuousness. His Assistant Secretary, Kosto, also sides with this increased concern for moral education (Ende 1993). Prime Minister Lubbers, finally, pleads for more order and discipline in education and for a firmer line with delinquent youths by sending them to 'encampments' where they should be put to work.

In this climate the Minister of Education and Science, Ritzen, obviously does not want to be left out. On the contrary, he further elaborates its pedagogical aspects. Although, in his opinion, parents are primarily the ones who should set a good example, he makes a special appeal to school education (Ritzen 1992:88). He refers explicitly to the current situation in Europe, which, apparently, must account for the increased moral diversity in our present society. Against this background he asks schools to take their pedagogical task more seriously, by paying particular attention to the transfer of norms and values. As Ritzen states: 'the vanishing of traditional normative standards enormously increases the importance of the old pedagogical role of schools' (Ritzen 1992:85). Although Ritzen, just like his colleagues, is not pleading for the introduction of homogeneous guidelines, it is still his opinion that the concept of 'community' deserves revaluation in this transfer of norms and values in order to establish and secure the limits of personal freedom. The same goes, in this context, for the concept of 'order'.

This educational policy on norms and values, of course, also inspired the critics. One even spoke of state pedagogy (N.L. Dodde, quoted by Ende 1993), perhaps one of the strongest possible expressions of disapproval in the Netherlands. Here religious dissensions have so long been regulated by means of *verzuiling* (literally: pillarisation, meaning something like denominational segregation), the organisational principle that was also applied to the education system. Would such a country now wish to transfer a national morality – no matter how reflectively conceived – via school education? The situation must look grave if one calls upon this kind of pedagogy. This kind of appeal to pedagogy seems all the more remarkable if we realise that juvenile delinquency has not increased since 1980 – on the contrary, it has diminished – and, moreover, that violent offences occur chiefly between youngsters themselves (Soetenhorst 1993). The efficiency of the transfer of norms and values as well as the quest for more order and discipline, of course, have also been questioned (Soetenhorst 1993). Values have never been established by a simple transfer and, in this context, one of the participants in the discussion complained that the government seems to seek a different kind of people, i.e. the kind that lived here twenty years ago (Knapen 1993).

The most fundamental opponents, however, were the theoreticians mentioned in the introduction, who were asked to comment on Ritzen's policy proposals. According to them the context in which the solution was sought did not allow these proposals at all. Speaking about '*the* pedagogical task of education' means an inadmissible simplification of the problem because in the school situation there are, by definition, *certain kinds* of values at stake, which cannot compensate for education in other contexts. According to these pedagogues, diversity should be approached by means of discussion in the very context in which it appears (cf. Haaften 1992 and Spiecker 1992). They see diversity as a characteristic of our modern society, which cannot be outlawed by means of education (Imelman, in Schöttelndreier 1993).

It is obvious that these pedagogical scientists, unlike their colleagues in the 1950s, cannot meet the expectations that result from the risk models implied in the authorities' educational policy. The risk calculation in this policy starts from the stated problem of increased delinquency. With respect to this problem the decay of unifying moral standards and of community-oriented values is considered the most relevant circumstance. In this context the concept of individualism, interpreted as selfishness, has been mentioned repeatedly, by among others our Vice Prime Minister Kok (quoted by Malen and Versteegh, 1993). As was the case in the previous example (sub)cultural diversity has been assigned an important role with regards to this process of moral decay or fragmentation (Ritzen 1992). In spite of decreased juvenile delinquency the solution to the problem of increased delinquency, finally, seems to be sought by all policymakers in education. The necessary groundwork to a solution of this problem is expected to consist of a pedagogical method designed to create a new basis of unifying communal norms and values that will keep diversity within limits. The solution of the delinquency problem, it is expected, will follow as a matter of course.

When we compare the two risk models, certain similarities come to light. In both cases diversity is regarded as problematic: the diversity of children's cultural capital when they enter school, as well as the diversity and the related self-orientation of norms and values in our society. In both cases education is expected to reduce this diversity either by finding ways of transferring the required skills to children before they enter school or by finding ways of transferring via school education those community-oriented values that, apparently, no longer exist elsewhere.

A series of presuppositions are incorporated in the Dutch authorities' expectations of pedagogy. Those presuppositions contain the concept of upbringing and education as handled by the authorities. I cannot discuss all aspects and details of this concept. I will focus on a few elements that I consider to be of great importance, that is to say: ideas concerning child development, the development of society, and the way in which we can take into account some idea of the future in the education of children. I will first discuss the concept of social development and the related representations of the future.

Pedagogical Representations of the Future

Risk calculations in a social context always imply a prognosis of the future. As they are constructed in the present, however, they are part of our present culture. Consequently elements of risk calculation as characteristics of our modern society will contribute to our contemporary prognoses of the future. In other words: we no longer attribute the development of social reality to fate but to man's works and decisions (cf. Giddens 1990; Luhmann 1992). Apart from prognostic elements, which already imply a large dose of uncertainty, pedagogical representations of the future also include important idealistic elements. Each pedagogically inspired view of the future contains, implicitly or explicitly, an answer to questions about the sort of society we wish our children to live in (cf. Heyting 1992).

With respect to this desirable future our policymakers seem to be relatively explicit. There is a noticeable tendency towards a community-oriented 'closure' of our culture. They have a society in mind in which the individual's behavioural regulation must find its limits in the community, rather than a society that limits the development of the community in accordance with individual rights. Formulated in this way the antithesis shows its affinity to the philosophical controversy between ethical communitarians and liberals. I do not intend to discuss this controversy here. Although I now have arrived at a point where it will be difficult to discriminate between forecasting and idealistic elements, I will try to extract some descriptive aspects from this picture of the desired future. For instance, what is the foundation of the expectation that we can realise a community-oriented society in the future? Or, what is the foundation of the idea that such a society will enable a higher degree of mutual consideration? The answer to these questions will reveal the major characteristics of the concept of social development we are looking for.

It should not be regarded as self-evident that Dutch people see a connection between the concept of community and that of consideration for their fellow human beings. Kossmann (1987:45ff.), a historian, sketched a picture of Holland in the seventeenth and eighteenth centuries in which there seemed to be little coherence either in politics or in the composition of the population. As a result of the flood of Flemings, Walloons, Germans, French, English and Jews, more than half the population of the larger cities consisted of foreigners (Deursen 1991:44ff.). Language and habits were much less fixed than today and there were no central authorities who could establish these matters. Thus, the Dutch would have had access to rather limited means if they had wished to pursue a policy of intolerance. Although, at that time, tolerance was perhaps not very fundamental, the various groups within this plural society could easily maintain their positions.

The variegated Dutch society of the Golden Age shows that the community-oriented society is perhaps not the only system that involves the much-desired mutual consideration. But this example also brings me to the next point: are we able to realise a community-oriented society by our own agency? Our ministers leave this point unmentioned; the philosophers who put forward and defend the ethical community ideal, however, do mention it. In this respect they repeatedly refer to the past, when communal societies appear to have actually existed. By projecting this past into the future, a kind of representation of the future is created, which seems to serve as a guideline for our policymakers.

Phillips, a sociologist, provides a further analysis of the three historical societies that are most often mentioned as examples of the community model. The results seem almost obvious. Neither in medieval households, villages and towns, in the pioneering days of American society, nor in ancient Athens, could he find the stability, public spirit and collective values that are considered so specific to community-oriented societies. Phillips's findings should of course not be interpreted as a negative answer to the question of whether we can still wish and hope for such a community-oriented society; as an ideal, this thought has not been undermined by the foregoing. Phillips's results indicate, however, that our reconstructions of the past are dependent on our perspectives.

This shows not merely that our historical reconstructions are relative, but furthermore that extrapolation into the future is problematic. This is not changed by the realisation that extrapolation cannot take place without annotations and corrections. As an image of the future that guides our actions, this picture also suggests that we can create our future at will. A complete model of society is considered to be realisable by planned human action. In this retrospective sort of representation of the future we tend to overlook the uncertainties involved in every decision in the context of risk calculation. Because of these uncertainties we will continue to be confronted by unexpected situations. From this point of view all sorts of stable, unchanging images of future societies must be seen as unrealistic guidelines for action. In the opinion of Luhmann (1992:140): each prognosis of the future is only provisional and its value lies not in the certainty, but in the possibility of a fast and specific adaptation to a reality, which turns out to be different from that which was expected.

If the extrapolation of a historically constructed view of society into the future is found to be problematic, this refers not only to the idea of community, but to each teleological view of the future (Luhmann 1992:138). Intentions and purposes are instruments constructed for the present moment in order to deal with the circumstances as we see them; they are unsuited to control the development of a complete society.

Concepts of Child Development

As with the concept of social development, the concept of child development included in the government's policy can be regarded as retrospective. The retrospectivity in the latter case refers not to society's past, but to a predetermined final situation in the child's development. From this situation development is examined in a more or less backward direction and pedagogical thinking is geared to this process. In the first example mentioned, that of family-oriented stimulation of disadvantaged children, this final situation was defined by the starting requirements of school education. In the field of educational deficits one has learned from the experiences of the 1960s, for instance, that one should not confine oneself to specific cognitive and conceptual skills (Leseman 1992), or that cognitive development should not be regarded separately from other developmental dimensions (Ancona 1992). In these respects current social-priority programmes have undoubtedly been improved. But still unchanged is the fact that, these days no less than in the 1960s, the final goal (which has to be achieved) is entirely determined in advance, thus defining pedagogical action.

Something similar can be shown in the second example. No matter how strongly Minister of Education Ritzen emphasises the importance of reflectivity in moral education and no matter how hard Minister of Justice Hirsch Ballin and Prime Minister Lubbers reject the idea of returning to the rigidity of former norms and values, ultimately they all share the view that education should bring into being a communitarian morality in children and in the end in society as well.

This view of child development and education leading to situations that can be determined in advance seems very natural. This conceptualisation of child development, moreover, fits very well in our modern society, which lays such a strong emphasis on our own possibilities of manipulation. Thinking in terms of risk almost requires a prognosis, a basis from which we can examine the consequences of our actions. I have already noted this in the above-mentioned representations of our social future. Still, in that connection, the importance of flexibility instead of fixity has also been revealed. A retrospective concept of child development could be even more problematic.

The problem is not merely that in these fixed educational goals the idea of predictable child development presents itself in a new shape. Pedagogical scientists have already fulminated enough against this view. Nor is the fact that such a concept of development does not leave enough scope for the idea of 'transaction', i.e. of a constitutive reciprocity between children and their environment, the only problem. Piaget's critics have not failed to draw attention to this problem (see, for instance, Bruner and Haste 1990). The critics of the social-priority programmes have called attention to a related issue, namely, the impossibility of allowing for the active participation of children in their own development. The consequences of this criticism are quite dramatic. They imply, for instance, that morality, and not only morality, is formed via communicative negotiation and not via transfer (see Knapen 1993). Still, there are more problems with this retrospective concept of child development than just the predictability, and the assumed passivity of children that are implied in it.

The fundamental limitations of a retrospective view of child development have been clearly uncovered in a recently published study by Breeuwsma (1993) about the foundations of psychology. I will follow his line of thought. When we describe child development as starting from the perspective of a developmental stage that will be reached at a certain point in time (e.g. formal thinking in the case of Piaget), we construct an image that allows only for specific routes. The properties that can be discerned at earlier stages are, after all, restricted to the scale that can be regarded as a preamble to the final stage. This implies a special kind of selectivity that also creates the impression that there is little variation and diversity between individuals and between cultures (Breeuwsma 1993:17, 18). The stages in cognitive and moral development, as described by Piaget and Kohlberg, provide a clear example of this. A child can reach a lower or a higher stage in its development, but it cannot develop differently.

In life-course psychology one is less inclined toward this backward-looking view in which human development is constructed from the perspective of predetermined future situations. Life-course psychology deals mainly with adults, and in this context it seems more natural to take the initial situation as the point of departure in the description. Consequently it is not surprising that from this approach a much wider variety of developmental routes emerge. This prospective, rather than retrospective, approach to development hinders prediction, not so much because of an indeterminist view of development but rather because each initial situation appears to allow many different subsequent routes. The great flexibility of psychic systems is held responsible for this phenomenon, and in this context various authors point to the 'butterfly effect' as described in chaos theory (Gergen 1991:235; Vroon 1992). Very small changes within one sector could cause major changes within the whole system. In this view the great sensitivity to change determines the enormous adaptability of the system.

Although prospective models allow more variation, this view of development has, undoubtedly, its own selectivity. The selectivity of the retrospective view, however, concerns not only the developmental routes it can describe. In addition, this perspective allows the description only of those domains that can be seen as lying along the route of a linear development towards a predetermined final goal. Domains such as dreams, magical thinking and the artistic do not belong in this category. These so-called 'purposeless structures' (Breeuwsma 1993:258) are systematically disregarded. Apart from those already mentioned a wide range of intuitive and subjective aspects of psychological functioning can be classed among these purposeless structures. These aspects appear to play an important role in adult functioning, to such an extent that some psychologists even saw this phenomenon as a reason to add a post-formal stage to the well-known route of cognitive development (Breeuwsma 1993:120). This last stage, however, cannot be called a stage in the proper sense because the preceding stages do not create necessary conditions for its development. The point under discussion thus remains unsolved. In a retrospective approach, in other words, it is impossible even to 'see' these 'purposeless structures' in psychological functioning.

A Prospective Concept of Education

It may appear that if I have digressed from the pressing problems I was considering to begin with. It could seem, moreover, as if I were depriving our policy makers of their last weapons by stating that education cannot be seen as a process leading to predeterminable ends, no matter whether they are stated in psychological or in social terms. The question follows, then, whether it is actually possible to educate people without a clearcut ultimate goal.

In the practice of family education these things appear not to cause much trouble. Parents seem to be completely aware of the fact that they can make no fixed life plans for their children and they do not appear to aspire to the role of all-knowing model educators (Bois-Reymond 1993:130, 131). Youngsters themselves regard the steps they are presently taking less and less as a preparation for a specific biography in their adult lifes. Perhaps the rather uncertain labour market has been an influence here. There is no longer a direct connection between school and labour; rather one takes roundabout routes, one opts for transitional stages and so on (Fuchs-Heinritz 1990). In this way, as regards parents and youngsters, pedagogical interaction is acquiring more often the character of a two-sided transactional process, in which both sides can and should reconsider their position at every stage. As in all cases of pedagogical interaction, of course, specific pedagogical intentions still play a role, but they are mainly characterised by a large degree of flexibility.

Policy seems to be less able to realise this amount of flexibility. Still, the preceding allows certain concluding suggestions. First, I think that we should not underestimate the significance of so-called purposeless structures in child development. Our modern society asks more from the younger generation than just a good school education. The above-mentioned necessity to develop an individual, reflexive identity is just one of those requirements and one which could cause additional difficulties to children growing up in foreign cultures. From this point of view it does not seem to be wise to deal with pre-school and extracurricular education in too strictly structured a way, a way that could result from a retrospective perspective on education. From a prospective view it seems wiser to adapt school education to children, rather than vice versa. Outside the school one should perhaps try a less structured enrichment of the educational environment.

Regarding the problems of criminality and individualisation I am not so pessimistic. In any case a pedagogical orientation on the virtues of a communal society does not seem to bring a solution. I doubt, moreover, whether the association of individualism in our modern society with selfishness is valid. For Giddens (1991:225), for example, this same individualism plays a crucial role in the 're-moralisation' of our society in an authenticity-oriented direction. Others emphasise individual rights and freedom. This kind of social morality could fit in with the high demands that are made upon the reflexivity of individual identity in our modern society. Our minister of justice also noticed the tendencies towards authenticity, but he appreciated them in a different way. Although the question whether of there is any reason for despair may still be unanswered, we will have to reconcile ourselves to the fact that in the end morality itself is the result of a transactional process, and not of pedagogical transfer.

A concept of education as advocated here does not leave much room for a guiding role for pedagogical science. The traditional pattern of mutual expectations between pedagogical science and the authorities cannot be unproblematically restored. This does not mean that we, the theoreticians, should resign ourselves to doing nothing. Apart from further developing analytical criticism, we could elaborate a prospective concept of education by concentrating on the transformation mechanisms in developmental processes rather than on successive developmental stages (Breeuwsma 1993:139 ff.). In the tradition of psychology some initiatives towards a prospective approach can be found, but until now they have not received much attention. Breeuwsma mentions, for example, Werner's orthogenetic principle, which describes psychic developmental processes as cyclical processes of increasing differentiation and integration. In sociology this kind of view on development can be found in Luhmann's systems theory, which contains an evolutionary perspective on social development, in which later stages cannot be predicted from preceding ones.

From this kind of developmental knowledge we will learn more about dynamics than about desirable content. This might seem quite empty, especially for those pedagogical scientists who would still like to appoint themselves as guides. But even this emptiness could perhaps be accepted if we could subscribe to Bruner's conclusion that the 'language of education is the language of culture creating, not of knowledge consuming or knowledge acquisition alone' (1986:13).

References

Ancona, H. d' (1992), 'Het WVC-beleid met betrekking tot gezinsgerichte stimulering van kinderen in achterstandssituaties', in J. Rispens and B. F. van der Meulen (eds), *Gezinsgerichte stimulering van kinderen in achterstandssituaties*, Amsterdam.

Bauman, Z. (1987), *Legislators and Interpreters*, Cambridge.

Beck, U. (1986), *Risikogesellschaft*, Frankfurt.

Bois-Reymond, M. du (1993), 'Pluraliseringstendensen en onderhandelingsculturen in het gezin', *Amsterdams Sociologisch Tijdschrift*, 19, 113-44.

Breeuwsma, G. (1993), *Alles over ontwikkeling. Over de grondslagen van de ontwikkelingspsychologie*, Amsterdam.

Bruner, J. (1986), *Actual Minds, Possible Worlds*, Cambridge, Mass.

Bruner, J. and Haste, H. (eds) (1990(2)), *Making Sense. The Child's Construction of the World*, London/New York.

Deursen, A. T. H. van (1991), *Mensen van klein vermogen. Het `kopergeld' van de Gouden Eeuw*, Amsterdam.

Ende, D. van den (1993), 'De politieke discussie over normen en waarden', *Staatscourant*, 20, 4.

Fuchs-Heinritz, W. (1990), 'Jeugd als statuspassage of geïndividualiseerde jeugdbiografie?', *Jeugd en samenleving*, 7/8, 451-73.

Gergen, K. J. (1991), *The Saturated Self. Dilemmas of Identity in Contemporary Life*, New York.

Giddens, A. (1990), *The Consequences of Modernity*, Cambridge.

–– (1991), Modernity and Self-Identity, Cambridge.

Haaften, A. W. van (1992), 'Stellingen bij De voordracht van de Minister', *Pedagogisch Tijdschrift*, 17, 91-5.

Hermanns, J. M. A. (1992), *Het sociale kapitaal van jonge kinderen*, SWP, Utrecht.

Heyting, F. (1992), 'Pädagogische Intention und pädagogische Effektivität. Beschreibungsformen und Perspektiven der Pädagogik', in N. Luhmann and K. E. Schorr (eds), *Zwischen Absicht und Person. Fragen an die Pädagogik*, Frankfurt.

Kloosterman, A. (1991), 'Met welke stappen op stap?', *Vernieuwing*, 50, 46-8.

Knapen, B. (1993), 'De ethische basis van de democratie', *NRC-Handelsblad*, 1 May, 8.

Kossmann, E. H. (1987), *Politieke theorie en geschiedenis. Verspreide opstellen en voordrachten*, Amsterdam.

Leseman, P. P. M. (1992). 'Doel en strategie van voorschoolse stimulering-sprogramma's', in J. Rispens and B. F. van der Meulen (eds), *Gezinsgerichte stimulering van kinderen in achterstandssituaties*, Amsterdam.

Luhmann, N. (1991), *Soziologie des Risikos*, Berlin.

–– (1992), Beobachtungen der Moderne, Opladen.

Malen, K. van der and Versteegh, K. (1993), `Vertrouwt u er maar op dat 't denkwerk doorgaat', *NRC-Handelsblad*, 20 January.

Meijnen, W. (1992), 'Schoolloopbanen van allochtone leerlingen: een beschrijving', in J. Rispens and B. F. van der Meulen (eds), *Gezinsgerichte stimulering van kinderen in achterstandssituaties*, Amsterdam.

Nouwen, P. (1993), '"Tijd voor herijking verhouding overheid en samenleving"', *Staatscourant*, 20, 5.

Pels, T. (1991), '"Mag jouw mama misschien ook niet dansen?" Marokkaanse kleuters en de ontwaarding van hun culturele kapitaal op de Nederlandse basisschool', *Vernieuwing*, 50, 21-7.

Phillips, D. L. (1993), *Looking Bacward. A Critical Appraisal of Communitarian Thought*, Princeton.

Ritzen, J. M. M. (1992), 'Onderwijs 1995 en daarna', *Pedagogisch Tijdschrift,* 17, 85-9.

Schöttelndreier, M. (1993), 'De school praat, de pedagogen houden zich stil', *Volkskrant,* 10 November.

Singer, E. (1991), 'Amerikaanse ervaringen', *Vernieuwing,* 50, 10-14.

Slavin, R. E., Karweit, N. L. and Madden, N. A. (1989), *Effective Programs for Students at Risk,* Boston.

Soetenhorst de Savornin Lohman, J. (1993), 'Suggesties voor werkkampen onzinnig opvoedingsmiddel', *NRC-Handelsblad,* 18 naart.

Spiecker, B. (1992), 'Stellingen bij De voordracht van de Minister',. *Pedagogisch Tijdschrift,* 17, 90-1.

Velgersdijk, J. (1991), 'Een pakket dominante normen', *Vernieuwing,* 50, 27-31.

Vroon, P. (1992), 'Chaostheorie en menselijk gedrag', in C. van Dijkum and D. de Tombe (eds), *Gamma Chaos. Onzekerheid en orde in de menswetenschappen,* Bloemendaal.

Winter, M. de (1993), 'Pedagogen laten maatschappelijke missie liggen', *Volkskrant,* 13 November.

Chapter 10

The State of Research into Education Economics
A General Overview and the French Situation

François Orivel

1. Historical Overview

Education economics, as we now understand the discipline, is a field of relatively recent origin. The first works associated with it were published in the United Sates toward the end of the 1950s and early 1960s, notably at the University of Chicago. Although there had been numerous precursors to this discipline in the course of the history of economic thought, they had remained undeveloped intuitions rather than becoming a field of autonomous research with its own theoretical hypotheses and concrete data subject to systematic empirical verification. Over the course of its thirty years of existence, education economics has gone through several distinct phases, each with specific concerns tied to the socio-economic context of the period. Although sharp divisions always have something arbitrary about them, for the purposes of this paper it will be useful to distinguish three periods: the 1960s, a decade of construction; the 1970s, a decade of inquiry, criticism, and theoretical reformulations; and the 1980s to the present, a decade and a half of pragmatic thinking.

1.1. The Founding of Education Economics

During its first decade of existence the theoretical foundations of education economics were gradually laid; parallel to this construction, empirical studies were carried out that for the most part confirmed the theory. The initial emphasis in the discipline was on the economically productive nature of education, on education's role in the professional development of individuals, on its ability to increase the revenues of economic players and to reduce the likelihood of their becoming unemployed. It was also argued that education played an important role in the attainment of equality, since it allowed persons of modest means to attain levels of social status once reserved to those with family wealth. In brief, this was a period when economists tended to emphasise the positive aspects of education. They encouraged policy makers to do more to promote education for all, not only in the area of primary education but especially in secondary and higher education. The political climate could hardly have been more propitious for this kind of thinking, since the launching of the first satellite into outer space by the Soviet Union had convinced the American authorities that a massive effort in favor of education would constitute the most appropriate response to this challenge.

Before the development of education, economists had a tendency to treat work as an homogenous factor, with little differentiation. The introduction of work into the functions of production was considered to occur in a simple, quantitative manner, one worker being equal to another. From this point of view education was considered a form of consumption; its primary aim was not to provide the economy with individuals equipped with necessary skills but rather to satisfy desires for themselves. Education economics completely overturned this idea, viewing education not as a form of consumption but as an investment; an investment embodied in a human person who thus became, by analogy with material investments, 'human capital', an expression that would later give name to a new theory. From this perspective educational outlays were to be seen as investment outlays, and like any investment they would produce a return during the entire life of the capital thus produced. These returns could later be compared with the initial cost of the investment, and if they were superior to it (which was usually the case), a return on investment could be calculated; that is to say, a return on education. The return attributed to education could be calculated empirically, by comparing differences in individual revenues on the basis of educational level. Using this method dozens and dozens of case studies were carried out in different countries. The results, although somewhat variable, nevertheless tended to show that education produced a more than ten percent return on investment, which is generally agreed to be the minimum level for a successful investment of the traditional material kind.

1.2. Criticism and New Approaches

The basic thrust of the second phase, which occurred during the 1970s, was the calling into question of the results of the first phase.

While the 1960s had been dominated by the concerns – and reputations – of the economists in the geographic origin of the discipline's pioneers, the University of Chicago, the intellectual climate of 1970s was marked by a certain challenge to the established order. (It should be recalled here that, from the point of view of economics, the 'Chicago School' is seen as extremely liberal in the sense that its economists champion the free market over the State as the best regulator of the economy. The graduates of this university, sometimes called 'the Chicago Boys', had a reputation for preaching the gospel of this form of extreme *laissez-faire* economic liberalism in the sphere of political economy. Although this was not the case with the pioneers of education economics, they were nevertheless involuntarily associated with this trend by some of their critics.)

Much of the work of this period was devoted to a critique of the initial studies. Some of it was restricted in scope, some of it sweeping. Marxist critics used the theory of 'reproduction' in order to accuse the educational system of doing nothing more than reproducing already existing inequities, since the children of lower social strata had access to much less impressive academic opportunities than did the children of the wealthy. Others, such as Bowles and Gintis, took a somewhat different tack, asserting that the educational system had as its primary function the preparation of individuals for the social division of labour; the purpose of education was therefore to inculcate *attitudes* necessary for the needs of capitalism, such as teaching the value of submission to future workers and employees of the lower ranks who were destined to carry out orders.

A more orthodox approach was represented by the Nobel economics laureate Arrow, who called into question the entire idea of whether education played an important role in inter-individual productivity differences. Such differences, the orthodox critics asserted, were fundamentally innate: the role of school was simply to reveal them, to 'signal' them to potential employers as Spence, one of the representatives of this approach, termed it. As these economists saw it, the role of the educational system was to 'filter' individuals. The result of this process was the emergence of the most capable, competent and productive individuals. It is important, however, to note here that empirical studies on the basis of this theory produced no particularly convincing results.

The more restricted studies focused for the most part on the difficulties in measuring labour productivity and thus the contribution of education to this productivity in particular. Employees' salaries, they argued, are in fact determined in a rather complex manner. Among the multiplicity of factors that enter into it are the sector of economic activity, social history, the negotiating powers of the individual

employee, imperfections in the marketplace, and all the kinds of discrimination, including ethnic, sexual and social. Salaries thus only
very imperfectly reflect the real productivity of work. The theoreticians of orthodox economics had clearly shown that in a universe of
pure and ideal competition the productivity of labour is perfectly
expressed in the equilibrium of salaries. However, it is well known
that all the conditions required for pure and perfect competition are
rarely found, and that there can be significant distortions, difficult to
quantify, between salaries and productivity.

Equally important, the discrepancies in earnings between individuals of differing educational levels can be attributed to causes other than
education. One of these, which coincides with Arrow's critique, is that
the most educated individuals tend themselves to be the most 'capable'
ones, that is, they would most probably have earnings superior to their
less-educated homologues even if they had not received education.
Consequently, only a part of the discrepancy in earnings between educated and uneducated individuals can be attributed to education.

1.3. Changes in the 1980s

The evolution of research in this area over the last ten or more years
has been centered around two main concerns: the role that education can play in economic growth, and how to deal with a relatively
new phenomenon that has grown in importance over the last two
decades: the slowing of the growth of resources available for the
educational system. This slowing, which began sometime around
the mid-1970s, is the result of two factors that complement each
other in an unfortunate way: world economic growth that is slower
than has been the case in the past, and a stabilisation of the per cent
of gross national product allocated to education. We shall now examine in more detail the results of this period of research, first in an
international context, then in the French one.

2. Recent Works on Education Economics Worldwide

2.1.

Since 1962 the scientific literature on economics has been catalogued
as part of a bibliographic data base administered by the American
Economic Association. Currently this data base can be accessed
either through a periodical, *The Journal of Economic Literature*, or its
equivalent on CD-ROM. The materials are divided into as many
sub-headings as necessary; currently there are approximately five
hundred. The rubrics 'Education Economics' and 'Human Capital
Theory' more or less encompass the field of education economics.

During the ten years covering the 1980s *The Journal of Economic Literature* recorded 1,060 articles in these two fields, taken from 183 different economics' journals. On average, therefore, each journal published 5.8 articles on the subject in ten years, or one article every other year. Only two journals devoted exclusively to the subject of education economics exist while the other 181 journals publish articles in a wide variety of sub-topics in economics. The 1,060 documented articles are part of a total body of some 133,000 articles, which demonstrates that education economics occupies a rather modest place in the overall field of economics (less than one per cent of the total in the field). Over the decade of the 1980s the proportion evolved in the following manner:

Table 1

Proportion of articles on education economics in relation to the total number of articles published on economics.

Year	Per Cent
1980	1.0
1981	0.6
1982	1.1
1983	0.5
1984	0.6
1985	0.5
1986	0.7
1987	0.9
1988	0.8
1989	0.8

Although not in any particular decline, it is difficult to detect any significant change in the importance of this study for economists in general. The fact that education economics represents no more than 0.75 per cent of economics' publications can, however, be seen as a sign of the limited interest that the subject holds in general for economics' research, given that education itself mobilises between six and seven per cent of a nation's resources. It also attests to an implicit hierarchy in the study of economics: works of an abstract, formalised and theoretical kind, which concern the economy as a whole, are more highly valued than ones that are empirical and sectoral.

The 1,060 publications are associated with 1,600 authors' signatures, which means that on average each article is signed by 1.5 persons. Since several authors are cited several times, the number of different names in this list of sixteen hundred is in fact only eleven hundred, which means that each author is cited on average 1.45 times, and that each of the authors produced an equivalent of 0.96 articles (1100 / 1060) over the ten year period. Of the total of eleven-hundred authors, 866 of them are mentioned only once, 133 of them two times, and 101 authors are mentioned between three and nine times. Only two – and who therefore participated in the writing of at least one article per year on average – are cited more than ten times. It would thus appear that some eighty per cent of the economists who participated in the production of an article on economics education published in a peer-review journal over the last ten years did so only once, which testifies to a certain weakness in the discipline's ability to retain the interest of researchers.

Part of this weakness is in part attributable to the field's extremely narrow focus: it is hard for a university to justify the creation of a team of researcher-teachers devoted to such a narrow specialty. This is why most of the research is dispersed; why most of the researchers are not part of a permanent and structured team; and why many researchers leave the field to take up the study of other problems. There are hardly more than ten locations in the entire world where there exist real teams working permanently on these issues. They are mostly to be found in the United States, the Netherlands, Britain, and France.

2.2. An Analysis of Works Produced in the 1980s

The contents of works on education economics have been divided into nine categories. They are: 1. theoretical works of a general character, 2. articles that take up the question of costs, 3. financing, 4. internal efficiency, 5. external efficiency, 6. supply and demand in education, 7. the study of certain factors in production, such as teachers and the new media, 8. the politics of education, and 9. the relations between education and research. The interest in these various sub-categories evolved in the following manner in the course of the two halves of the decade of the 1980s:

Table 2

Evolution of Subjects Treated in Education Economics

Subcategory	1979-1984		1984-1989		Total	
	Number	%	Number	%	Number	%
Theory	33	6.1	28	5.4	61	5.8
Costs	23	4.3	25	4.8	48	4.5
Financing	51	9.4	56	10.8	107	10.1
Internal Efficiency	81	15.0	105	20.2	186	17.5
External Efficiency	190	35.2	136	26.2	326	30.8
Supply and Demand	100	18.5	138	26.5	238	22.4
Separate Inputs	41	7.6	22	4.2	63	5.9
Ed. Politics	13	2.4	9	1.7	22	2.1
Ed. and Research	8	1.5	1	0.2	9	0.8
Total	540	100.0	520	100	1060	1060

2.3. Theory, Costs, and Financing

The first three sub-categories, theory, cost, and financing, make up approximately twenty per cent of all articles on education economics. These have been the classic themes of education economics since the discipline's inception and are an area of study in which economists have enjoyed a virtual monopoly. This differs from the remaining topics, in which interdisciplinary approaches have predominated. If one were to characterise the general framework of the studies devoted to problems of financing and cost written in the 1980s, it could be said that they were marked by the realisation that public financing of education was limited in scope; that budgetary constraints would be felt with greater and greater sharpness in the future; and that the future development of the educational system would depend on a more efficient allocation of available resources and the development of alternate forms of financing. This diversification of financing concerned both the public sector (national, state, and local governments) and the private sector (families and businesses). In the earlier period of research there had been a tendency to assume that the necessary democratisation of access to education would entail a more and more important, if not exclusive, role for public financing of education. However, the quasi-monopoly of public financing in education had not produced the expected results as regards equality, and it was even noticed that in some cases the benefits of public financing were appropriated by socially favoured classes.

These studies, often using developing countries as a model, tried to show in what cases and contexts an increase in educational participation could lead to an increase not only in the effectiveness of the educational system but to an increase in inequality. In order to illustrate this apparent paradox in a simple manner, the following situation was often described: a society in which a significant proportion of school-age children lacks access to primary education, while children of the wealthy have access to free universities and are often even provided with stipends. Since higher education in these countries rarely leads to local opportunities, the frequent result of public-financed higher education is emigration. Thus this kind of public investment in education contributes neither to the general economic development of the country nor to the promotion of a higher level of equality.

2.4. Internal Efficiency of Institutions and Systems

The study of the fourth sub-category, the economic analysis of internal efficiency, was the principal beneficiary of the change of interests noticeable in this third period of research into education economics. This change was a direct result of the foregoing recognition, that is, that the period of rapid growth in educational outlays was over:

henceforth decision-makers would have to engage in rigorous analyses of choices in order to determine reasonable compromises. The change was also a result of the often unexpected conclusions drawn from the first studies devoted to the relationship between resources and 'performances' of educational institutions. In general the studies showed that the relationship between resources and results was either weak or even nonexistent. In the earlier period, however, economic resources had been used as a primary measure of differences in 'quality' between schools; that is, schools with larger budgets were considered *a priori* to be of higher quality than schools of more modest means.

These initial findings, troubling in themselves, led to a series of studies that called into question some very established assumptions. It was found, for instance, that classes with small numbers of students were not necessarily better than classes with large numbers; that teachers who received a longer education were not necessarily more competent than those having received a shorter one; that programmes designed to aid low achievers often did more harm than good; and that the professionalisation of studies did not necessarily make students more qualified to enter the workforce. At their heart these studies called into question two frequently encountered attitudes in the educational world: a confusion between the ideas of optimum and maximum, and the assertion of *a priori* defined norms that serve to determine educational policy.

On the first point we encounter a law that is often used by economists in fields other than education: the law of diminishing returns. For example, it has often been observed that when the first books are introduced into primary schools in poor countries there is an immediate improvement in scholastic performance: this initial progress, however, diminishes with the addition of more books and approaches zero as the number of books continues to multiply.

As for the 'norms' that some pedagogues insist must be respected in order to reach fixed goals: they are often found to be more arbitrary than usually assumed. These norms not only disregard the constraints imposed by available resources, but are based more on *a priori* judgments than on empirical observations that can be statistically verified. A particularly widespread example of the disregard for local constraints is when specialists from rich countries seek to transpose to poor ones methods of educational organisation that function well in the country from which they come but which encounter the immediate obstacle of extremely small budgets in many developing countries.

The primary conclusion to be drawn from these studies is that there does not exist a single and unique solution to the problem of the rational management of an educational system. Instead the solutions are multiple, depending on the general aims pursued, the available resources, and the priorities (or preferences) of the local officials in each country. The direct consequence of this is the following: since constraints evolve in step with the overall process of economic development, and the same can be said of needs, then solutions that are relevant at one moment of history may not be relevant at another. An educational system must therefore be able to evolve, reform itself, and assimilate reforms imposed from without.

2.5. External Efficiency of Education

As was mentioned at the outset, the subject of the external effectiveness of education was the one that gave rise to education economics: the concepts of human capital and educational investment were derived directly from it. Although table two demonstrates the continuing importance of this subject of study, (nearly a quarter of all work on education economics was devoted to it), the table also shows a nearly ten per cent decrease in interest in the subject over the second half of the 1980s. To begin with, there was a noticeable decline in studies devoted to the calculation of returns on educational investment. It is a striking fact that, when referring to these kinds of studies, one is quite often obliged to rely on work done in the 1970s. As a result, these data in many cases are no longer reliable since the relative revenues have fundamentally changed since that period.

This decline of works that study the profitability of education in the narrow sense was compensated for by a rediscovery of the subject of the influence of education on general economic growth and development. This rediscovery, however, was not always the doing of specialists in the field of education economics: the theoreticians of growth and specialists in macro-economic models played a leading role as well. Unfortunately, this is a relatively complex subject for non-specialists and would be difficult to summarise within the limits of this paper. Let it suffice to say that the classical models developed by economists to explain economic growth and understand its mechanisms (in order to foster economic policies appropriate to developing countries and for those in recession) failed to account satisfactorily for education-based growth. Traditionally, capital and work have been viewed by economists as the two factors in productivity. More recently, authors like Romer and Lucas have attempted to introduce other factors, such as knowledge (as stock and flux) and ideas, which permit the introduction of more efficient methods of production and new goods. There appears to be an important link between the education of individuals and their ability to be innovative on the one hand, and between education and the diffusion of knowledge on the other. This has led to the creation of two distinct models of economic growth; one which largely depends on the exploitation of knowledge produced by others, which is the model of economic growth prevalent throughout much of South-East Asia, and one which is based on research and development of new products and processes, which is more typical of Europe and North America.

The 1980s also saw theoretical and empirical progress in two other areas of study that concern the external efficacy of education: the role of education in the productivity of farmers in developing countries (Jamison, Lau, Lockheed), and education's role in the assimilation of individuals in the workplace. The interesting thing about the studies in the first category is that they have been able to show a direct relation between education and the quantity of agricultural goods harvested, without having to rely on the very tenuous hypothesis of equalisation of salaries and labour productivity. These studies have therefore confirmed the approach that regards education as a form of human capital, which itself reinforces the idea of the existence of individual productive capacity independent of natural aptitudes. According to this view, the productivity of educated individuals is in part a direct result of the education they have received: it is not merely a matter of their possessing an inherently higher aptitude.

The study of the relationship between education and the labour market changed considerably during the 1980s. During the first two decades of education economics (the 1960s and 1970s) many economists tried to plan educational systems in relation to the future needs of the economy; that is, they tried to produce professionally qualified students in proportion to the projected needs of each profession. These exercises almost always ended in failure, producing virtually systematic errors in prediction. The most important lesson learned from this failure concerned the very organisation of educational systems: educational systems must give up on the idea of producing future employees who are extremely narrowly specialised, unable to adapt to the evolution of labour markets and technologies. Instead the skills of future employees must be fluid, convertible, adaptable; and the employees themselves must be prepared for continuous education, intellectual flexibility, and multiple activities. The very concept of 'profession' or 'occupation' in the narrow sense must be rethought. Ten years ago the skills required for a watchmaker were primarily of the mechanical kind: today's watchmaker must possess skills more closely associated with electronics. Changes of this kind are progressively affecting all the traditional professions, and the central role of the educational system must be to prepare individuals to meet these changes. Although we have yet to draw all the necessary conclusions from this evolution, two observable tendencies give some indication of where educational organisation is heading: the first is a tendency toward a lengthening of courses of study, without yet knowing exactly what the desired amount of time is; the second is a reacknowledgement of the superiority of general knowledge over an overly-narrow technological kind. This is because the rapid obsolescence of technologies makes the ability to understand the world in general and to adapt to its changes more important than ever.

2.6. Supply and Demand in Education

The study of this sub-category was the second most popular among works published in the area of education economics in the 1980s. Its importance increased over time. Along with classical economics articles investigating the question of what determines the demand for education from a personal point of view, and what determines the demand for education considered from an overall economic point of view, the majority of articles took up the interrelations between supply and demand and the problems of discrimination and inequalities engendered by these interrelations. In North America most of the research centered on ethnic and sexual discrimination, while in Europe the studies more often concerned minorities, particularly immigrants, as well as discrimination tied to the socioeconomics of the family environment. Some researchers noted that the great hopes placed in education as a means of eradicating inequality were often disappointed, and that educational handicaps continued to affect certain social groups more than others. Others even speculated on whether education did not increase rather than reduce inequalities. Finally, it was shown that programmes designed to counteract scholastic failure by offering special services to at-risk students, rarely succeeded in alleviating the problem in any statistically significant manner.

3. The French Contribution to Research on Education Economics

The National Institute of Pedagogic Research (INRP) has recently (1993) published its first yearbook of French researchers in the field of the economics and finance of education. Unlike in other countries, such as Germany, in France there is no professional association for education economists. The latter belong either to *l'Association Française d'Economie Sociale* or to *l'Association Française de Sciences Economiques*. This yearbook contains fifty-three names, of which fifteen persons belong to the Research Institute of Economics Education (IREDU). This organisation, headquartered in Dijon on the campus of the University of Bourgogne, derives its membership from both the CNRS (*Centre Nationale de Recherche Scientifique*, which accounts for about sixty per cent of its members) and higher education faculty members (the remaining forty per cent). Although the INRP yearbook probably contains some lacunas, it also lists some persons who have done only a limited amount of research in the area of education economics. The field is therefore a relatively small one, since these fifty-three economists represent less than five per cent of those researchers who have published works in the field of economics over the last ten years. It should also be noted that less than half of these fifty-three names appears in the list of eleven hundred names that comprises The Journal of Economic Literature's authors' list.

Although it is hard to come by precise data on this point, it would appear that the other European countries are no more active than France in this area. The United Kingdom is probably the most active in Europe, with two or three other countries – the Netherlands, Sweden, and perhaps Germany – on the same level as France. All of Europe together is equal to less than half the forces in North America, while North America alone constitutes more than half the entire world's potential in education economics.

Over the past twenty to twenty-five years the volume of work on education economics carried out in France has more or less held its own, although in reality the field as such has more probably declined. For example, at the end of the 1970s the number of active university teams devoted to the field was four or five: today there remain only one or two. A significant portion of the research in education economics is carried out by isolated researchers, who because of their isolation are not unlikely to change fields. This fluidity of interest undoubtedly has a negative effect in terms of the accumulation of knowledge. This problem is not limited to France however; it affects all the other European countries, sometimes even to a greater degree than France. Nevertheless, the social need for works on education economics has shown a tendency to grow, both in response to the need for guidance of educational systems in relation to the needs of the workplace and the economy, and in order to rationalise and make more effective the allocation of the ever more scarce resources in a sector that often gives the impression of being able to absorb and consume them without limit.

One advantage that France, and in particular Paris, has over other European countries is the presence on its territory of two or three international organisations which have small teams specialised in this research field. The first of these is UNESCO. Although it employs only a small number of economists – especially in comparison with other specialised disciplines – it does at least have a minimal presence. The second organisation, which is associated with UNESCO, is called *l'Institut International de Planification de l'Education* (IIPE). Among its tasks is the training of multifunctional specialists who can be of help to developing countries, the planning of international conferences on different aspects of the management of educational systems, medium-term administration of educational budgets, and analysis of costs and financing. The IIPE also carries out research and publishes works on all the subjects just outlined. Finally, it is worth mentioning the OCDE (The Organisation for European Community Development), whose job it is to insure the regular publication of all kinds of national data, including economic data on education, for all twenty-four member countries. The OCDE also evaluates national educational policies. One of the benefits of these evaluations is that they make possible the comparison of one educational system with another, which can help us better to understand the advantages and disadvantages of different modes of organisation. The evaluations also tend to relativise specific national policies that may be regarded as untouchable and absolute within one educational system but which may have secondary importance in another. Finally, since 1987, the OCDE has undertaken the creation of a system of national educational indicators that will make it possible to identify the state of health of various educational systems and to better understand the relationship between the mobilisation of resources and the results ultimately obtained.

As for French research itself, it can be said to be relatively diverse, covering most of the areas mentioned earlier; that is, French research reflects the general interests of researchers in the 1980s. The IREDU is particularly concerned with methodological rigour and the need for empirical verification of theoretical hypotheses. It has carried out studies in a wide variety of geographical locales: not only in France, but throughout Europe, as well as in other developed and developing nations, and among the latter not only in sub-Saharan Africa.

The IREDU has gone through the various stages enumerated in the historical overview. In the third period it has done extensive work in various areas; internal efficiency, cost-efficiency analysis, the evaluation of different levels of educational production (both macro and micro economic). It has also studied national and local educational policy, and students and teachers. This process has been combined with an ongoing effort at multidisciplinarity, specifically trying to achieve ever greater cooperation between sociologists of education and specialists in the science of education.

Researchers who work in greater isolation have a tendency to prefer more narrow topics; topics that do not require the kind of large-scale on-site inquiries carried out by the IREDU or that make use of archival materials and data bases produced by others. This is the case with such varied studies as theoretical inquiries into education and growth, the analysis of historical data as regards educational outlays, and the policies of firms in matters of professional training and continuing education.

Much of the research currently underway is an attempt to respond to the need for adequate information by policy makers who must formulate and administer educational policy. What per centage of the gross national product ought to be devoted to education? What per centage of school-age children should attain to such and such a level of education? What per centage of education should be devoted to general studies, and what part to technical and professional training? How should professional education be organised, and what role should private industry play in its financing and administration? Although these questions are addressed not only to education economists, it is clear that economic analysis can contribute to the finding of adequate answers.

One of the obstacles frequently encountered by education economists is the unreliable and incomplete nature of the available data. This is a problem rarely encountered in other sectors of the economy, where a constant flow of reliable and complete information is available. Most countries know more or less exactly how much a family spends on shoes or underwear, but these same countries have no reliable information on educational outlays. While all countries have recourse to the same methods for calculating national economic accounts, there does not yet exist a common method of calculating accounts for education and training. Two recent initiatives may help overcome this problem in the near future: the first is the project of the OCDE mentioned above in regard to the development of international educational indicators, and the other is a recent report from the UN (dated February, 1994) that recommends the adoption of a form of national accounting that would include a satellite account for education. Such an account would in large measure respond to accounting needs that cannot currently be satisfied. It can only be hoped that these two initiatives will converge and thus allow for new advances in the analysis of education economics.

Notes on Contributors

Dietrich Benner
Professor of Education at the Humboldt Universität Berlin and Dean of the Philosophische Fakultät. The former President of the German Association for Educational Research, he has previously held the position of Professor of Education at Bonn University. His publications include, *Die Pädagogik Herbarts. Eine problemgeschichtliche Einführung in die Systematik neuzeitlicher Pädagogik*, 1993 (2nd edn), *Allgemeine Pädagogik*, 1987, and *Studien zur Theorie der Erziehungswissenschaft. Pädagogik als Wissenschaft, Handlungstheorie und Reformpraxis*, 3 vols, 1994-1995.

Gert Geißler
Since 1992 Senior Fellow at the Deutsches Institut für Internationale Pädagogische Forschung, Frankfurt/Main; previously Senior Fellow at the Akademie der Pädagogischen Wissenschaften of the GDR. In 1981 he received his PhD for a study on the relations in education between Germany and the Soviet Union 1925-1944. He wrote his habilitation on the work of F. A. W. Diesterweg up to the Revolution of 1948. He edited the *Jahrbuch für deutsche Erziehungs- und Schulgeschichte* from 1985 to 1990. Since 1991 he has published numerous studies on the history of the school and education in East Germany since 1945.

Frieda Heyting
Associate Professor of Philosophy of Education at the University of Amsterdam. She is Vice-President of the Department of Educational Sciences Research of the German Society for Educational Sciences and a Member of the Programming Committee INPE'96 (International Network of Philosophers of Education). She is a member of the NWO Research Group 'History and Foundations of the Behavioural Sciences'. Her main areas of research are epistemological questions in

the educational sciences, and systems theory and general theory of education, and her publications include papers written on these topics.

Andrea Kárpàti

Associate Professor in the Department of Education, Eötvös Loránd University and Associate Professor and Deputy Department Head of the Institute for Teacher Training, at the Hungarian Academy of Crafts and Design. She is member of the Didactics Sub-Committee of the Educational Commission of the Hungarian Academy of Sciences and Arts Coordinator for the Final Examination Project of the Dutch Educational Testing Centre, CITO and the Hungarian Ministry of Education. Her publications include, *Implications of Politico-Economic Liberalisation for Higher Education in Hungary*, 1992, *Hungarian Education and Adolescents of the Nineties: A Double Portrait in the Frames of Transition*, 1994 (co-author), *Umwelterziehung in Ungarn: eine Geschichte der kunsterzieherischen Paradigma und Rollenmodelle*, 1994 (co-author) as well as numerous articles on the arts and education.

Dieter Lenzen

Professor of Education at the Institute of General and Comparative Education, Freie Universität Berlin, President of the German Association for Educational Research. He has previously held the position of Professor for Educational Studies at the University of Münster and was Dean of the Faculty of Education, Freie Universität Berlin until 1995. A Founding Member of the Interdisciplinary Centre for Historical Anthropology, Berlin, his many publications include *Didaktik und Kommunikation*, 1973, *Die Struktur der Erziehung und des Unterrichts*, 1975, *Vaterschaft. Vom Patriarchat zur Alimentation*, 1991, *Krankheit als Erfindung*, 1991. Among others, he has edited the *Enzyklopädie Erziehungswissenschaft*, 12 vols, 1983, *Kunst und Pädagogik*, 1990, and *Erziehungswissenschaft. Ein Grundkurs*, 1994.

Hans Merkens

Professor of Empirical Educational Sciences at the Freie Universität Berlin, he studied Educational Sciences, Psychology and Philosophy at the Technische Hochschule Aachen, and received his first Professorship at the University of Trier. His main areas of research are educational problems among ethnic minorities, value systems of youth in Eastern and Central Europe and enculturation processes in corporations. Among his publications are *Unternehmenskulturentwicklung*, 1992, *Strategie, Unternehmenskultur und Organisationsentwicklung im Spannungsfeld zwischen Wissenschaft und Praxis*, (co-ed.) 1990, *Lebenslagen Schuljugendlicher und sozialer Wandel im internationalen*

Vergleich, (co-ed.) 1995, *Social Capital and Controlling Right-Wing Extremism in Berlin Youth* (co-ed.) 1995.

Peter Mortimore

Director of the Institute of Education and Professor of Education at London University. He has worked as a secondary school teacher, an inspector and an educational administrator and for six years held the post of Director of Research and Statistics for the Inner London Education Authority. He was also Director of the School of Education at the University of Lancaster for three years. His publications include, *Fifteen Thousand Hours* and *School Matters* and is currently involved in research projects including studies of *School Improvement,* and *School Development Planning.* Professor Mortimore was awarded the OBE for services to education in 1993.

François Orivel

François Orivel is Professor of Economics of Education at the University of Bourgogne, Dijon, France, and was Director of IREDU (Institut de Recherche sur l'Economie de l'Education), affiliated to the French National Research Agency (CNRS) from 1985 to 1994. He has carried out numerous studies on the costs and finances of education, on the cost effectiveness of new technologies in education, on the evaluation of educational systems at the micro and macro levels. He has conducted empirical studies on these subjects in many countries, both developed and developing, and published several comparative papers, in particular in the field of educational indicators. Among his recent publications are *Evaluating Education and Training: Comparative Approaches,* 1993, *French Speaking Universities in Sub-Saharan Africa: Critical Impasse,* 1993, *Distance Education: Economic Evaluation,* 1993, *Education in a new Europe,* 1992, and *The Development of Cost and Resource Indicators,* 1992.

Gabriela Ossenbach-Sauter

'Profesora Titular' of History of National Educational Systems at the Department for History of Education and Comparative Education of the National University for Distance Education, Madrid. She is the Secretary of the Spanish Society for the History of Education and a member of the International Editorial Board of the journal *Pedagogica Historica.* Her main field of research is the History of Latin-American Educational systems in the late nineteenth and early twentieth centuries. In 1992/3 she was a Visiting Professor at the Department of Comparative Education at the Humboldt Universität, Berlin. Among many contributions to books and journals she has co-edited *Génesis de los sistemas educativos nacionales*, 1988, and *La Revolución Francesa y su influencia en la educación en España*, 1990.

Thomas Rauschenbach

At present the Chair of Social Pedagogy at the University of Dortmund, he is also Dean of the Faculty of Education and Biology. His current interests include the theory of social work, youth work, social work education and volunteers in social work. Amongst his publications are *Handbuch Jugendverbände*, 1991, together with L. Böhnisch and H. Gängler, *Jugendhilfe Ost*, 1994, together with M. Galuske, and *Von der Wertgemeinschaft zum Dienstleistungsunternehmen. Wohlfahrtsverbände und Jugendverbände im Umbruch*, 1995, together with Th. Olk and Ch. Sachße.

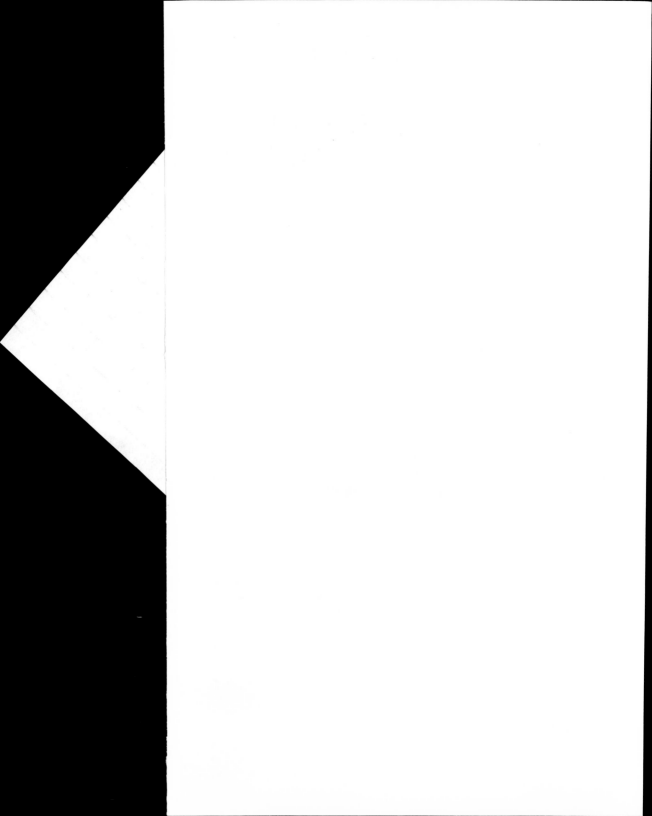

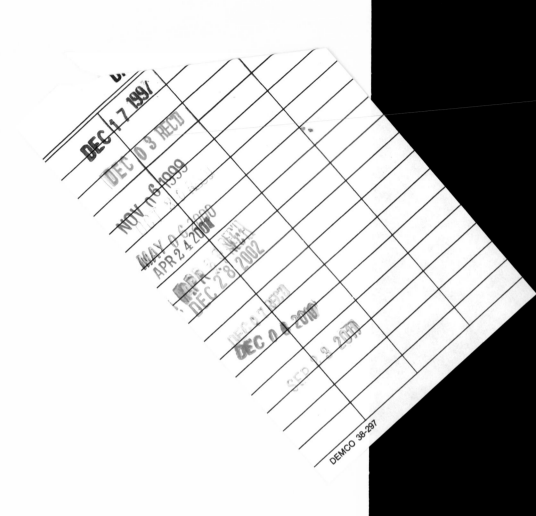